AF323288

SAMUEL PALMER REVISITED

Varied and deliberately diverse, this group of essays provides a reassessment of the life and work of the popular, but critically neglected nineteenth-century artist Samuel Palmer. While scholarly publications have been published recently which reassess Palmer's achievement, those works primarily consider the artist in isolation. This volume examines his work in relation to a wider art world and analyses areas of his life and output that have until now received little attention, reinstating the study of Palmer's work within broader debates about landscape and cultural history. In *Samuel Palmer Revisited*, the contributors provide a fresh perspective on Palmer's work, its context and its influence.

Simon Shaw-Miller is Professor of History of Art and Music, Birkbeck College, University of London and Honorary Research Fellow, Royal Academy of Music, London, UK.

Sam Smiles is Emeritus Professor of Art History at the University of Plymouth, UK.

Samuel Palmer Revisited

Edited by
Simon Shaw-Miller and Sam Smiles

ASHGATE

Published by
Ashgate Publishing Limited
Wey Court East
Union Road
Farnham
Surrey, GU9 7PT
England

Ashgate Publishing Company
Suite 420
101 Cherry Street
Burlington, VT 05401-4405
USA

www.ashgate.com

British Library Cataloguing in Publication Data
Samuel Palmer Revisited.
    1. Palmer, Samuel, 1805-1881–Criticism and interpretation.
    I. Miller, Simon, 1960- II. Smiles, Sam.
    759.2-dc22

Library of Congress Cataloging-in-Publication Data
Samuel Palmer revisited / Simon Shaw-Miller and Sam Smiles [eds].
        p. cm.
    Includes index.
    ISBN 978-0-7546-6747-6 (hardcover : alk. paper)
    1. Palmer, Samuel, 1805-1881–Criticism and interpretation. 2. Landscape in art. 3. Romanticism in art. I. Palmer, Samuel, 1805-1881. II. Shaw-Miller, Simon. III. Smiles, Sam.

    N6797.P237S26 2010
    760.092–dc22

                                                            2009047144
ISBN 9780754667476 (hbk)

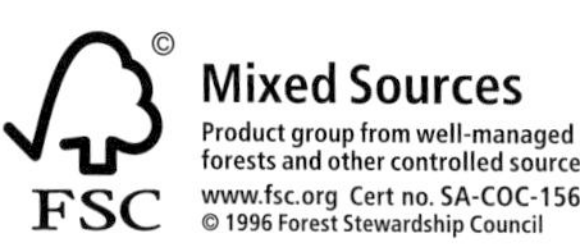

Printed and bound in Great Britain by MPG Books Group Ltd, Bodmin, Cornwall

Contents

List of Illustrations

5.2   Samuel Palmer, 'The Sleeping Shepherd – Early Morning', 1854-57. Etching on chine collé, 3rd state, 12.4 × 10.3 cm. BM 1872-5-11-984. © The Trustees of the British Museum.

5.3   Samuel Palmer, 'The Rising Moon or An English Pastoral', c.1855-57. Etching, proof of 2nd state, 14.5 × 22.4 cm. BM 1872-5-11-977. © The Trustees of the British Museum.

5.4   Samuel Palmer, 'The Lonely Tower', 1879. Etching, 4th state, 18.8 × 25.1 cm. BM 1910-7-16-20. © The Trustees of the British Museum.

6   From the valley of vision to the M25: Samuel Palmer and modern culture

6.1   Frederick Landseer Griggs, 'Sellenger', 1917. Etching, 35.7 × 24.2 cm. BM 1923,0413.1. © The Trustees of the British Museum.

6.2   Graham Sutherland, 'Lammas', 1926. Etching, 11.0 × 16 cm. BM 1949, 0411.489. © The Trustees of the British Museum. © Sutherland estate.

6.3   Paul Drury, 'September', 1928. etching, 10.4 × 13.3 cm. BM 1928, 1110.21. © The Trustees of the British Museum. © Estate of Paul Drury.

6.4   Robin Tanner, 'Martin's Hovel', 1927. Etching, 16.7 × 21.5 cm. Devon Learning Resources collection. © Crafts Study Centre, University for the Creative Arts, Farnham.

7   Palmer and the dark pastoral in English music of the twentieth century

7.1   Leith Hill Tower, Surrey. Constructed 1765. Photograph by Dr Elizabeth Stanway (Astrologist).

7.2   Samuel Palmer, 'The Lonely Tower', 1879. Etching, 18.8 × 25.1 cm. Yale Center for British Art, Paul Mellon Collection, USA/The Bridgeman Art Library.

7.3   *Ralph Vaughan Williams Choral Works*, CD, Hyperion Records, 2008. (Cover: Samuel Palmer 'The Lonely Tower', 1868. Watercolour and bodycolour and gum arabic on London board, Yale Centre for British Art, Paul Mellon Collection, USA/The Bridgeman Art Library).

7.4   Samuel Palmer, 'The Rising of the Skylark'. Oil on board. © National Museum Wales/The Bridgeman Art Library.

List of Music Examples

Ex. 7.1   Opening violin cadenza, Ralph Vaughan Williams, *The Lark Ascending*. © J. Curwen & Sons / Faber Music Ltd, London. Reproduced by kind permission of the publishers.

Ex. 7.2   Accompaniment figure, Ralph Vaughan Williams, *The Lark Ascending*. © J. Curwen & Sons / Faber Music Ltd, London. Reproduced by kind permission of the publishers.

Ex. 7.3   First movement, Ralph Vaughan Williams, *Pastoral Symphony*. © J. Curwen & Sons / Faber Music Ltd, London. Reproduced by kind permission of the publishers.

Ex. 7.4   Second movement, Ralph Vaughan Williams, *Pastoral Symphony*. © J. Curwen & Sons / Faber Music Ltd, London. Reproduced by kind permission of the publishers.

Ex. 7.5   Opening of second movement, Ralph Vaughan Williams, *Pastoral Symphony*. © J. Curwen & Sons / Faber Music Ltd, London. Reproduced by kind permission of the publishers.

Ex. 7.6   Second movement of Ralph Vaughan Williams, *Pastoral Symphony*. © J. Curwen & Sons / Faber Music Ltd, London. Reproduced by kind permission of the publishers.

Ex. 7.7   Third movement of Ralph Vaughan Williams, *Pastoral Symphony*. © J. Curwen & Sons / Faber Music Ltd, London. Reproduced by kind permission of the publishers.

Ex. 7.8   Last movement of Ralph Vaughan Williams, *Pastoral Symphony*. © J. Curwen & Sons / Faber Music Ltd, London. Reproduced by kind permission of the publishers.

Ex. 7.9   Opening of David Matthews, *In the Dark Time*. © J. Curwen & Sons / Faber Music Ltd, London. Reproduced by kind permission of the publishers.

Ex. 7.10   Coda of David Matthews, *In the Dark Time*. © J. Curwen & Sons / Faber Music Ltd, London. Reproduced by kind permission of the publishers.

Contributors

PAUL GOLDMAN is an Associate Fellow at the Institute of English Studies, School of Advanced Study, University of London, and Honorary Professor at the School of English, Communication and Philosophy, Cardiff University. He has published widely on prints and print-making, especially in the Victorian era. His books include *Victorian Illustration: The Pre-Raphaelites, the Idyllic School and the High Victorians* (1996, rev. ed. 2004). He curated the exhibition *Samuel Palmer: Visionary Printmaker* in 1991.

CHRISTIANA PAYNE is Reader in History of Art in the School of Arts and Humanities at Oxford Brookes University. Her publications include *Toil and Plenty: Images of the Agricultural Landscape in England, 1780-1885* (1993), *Rustic Simplicity: Scenes of Cottage Life in Nineteenth-century British Art* (1998) and *Where the Sea meets the Land: Artists on the Coast in Nineteenth-century Britain* (2007). Her monograph, *John Brett, Pre-Raphaelite Landscape Painter*, will be published in 2010.

MARTIN POSTLE is Assistant Director for Academic Activities at The Paul Mellon Centre for Studies in British Art. He was previously curator and Head of British Art to 1900 at Tate. He has published extensively on British art from the eighteenth to the twentieth century. His publications include *Sir Joshua Reynolds: The Subject Pictures* (1995) and *Gainsborough* (2000). He co-curated *Art of the Garden* (Tate Britain, 2004), and *Joshua Reynolds: The Creation of Celebrity* (Tate Britain, 2005). He has recently contributed essays to forthcoming exhibitions on Joshua Reynolds, Paul Sandby, and The Artist's Studio. He is currently working on an exhibition of the works of Johan Zoffany.

SIMON SHAW-MILLER is Professor of History of Art and Music at Birkbeck College, University of London. He is also an Honorary Associate and Research Fellow of the Royal Academy of Music and has a particular interest in the interrelationships between music and the visual arts. His books include

Visible Deeds of Music: Music and Art from Wagner to Cage (2002) and *Eye hEar: Art, Music, Film and the Culture of Synaesthesia* (forthcoming).

SAM SMILES is Emeritus Professor of Art History at the University of Plymouth. His books include *J.M.W. Turner: The Making of a Modern Artist* (2007), *The Turner Book* (2006), *Eye Witness: Artists and Visual Documentation in Britain 1770-1830* (2000) and *The Image of Antiquity: Ancient Britain and the Romantic Imagination* (1994). He is currently completing a book on Turner's last years.

GREG SMITH is an independent art historian specializing in the history of British watercolours. Formerly Assistant Keeper of Art at the Whitworth Art Gallery in Manchester, he has also worked as Head of Exhibitions at the Design Museum in London. He has organized many exhibitions, including *Thomas Girtin: The Art of Watercolour* (2002) and *Thomas Jones (1742-1803): An Artist Rediscovered* (2003), as well as a number of design shows including *1966 And All That, Design and the Consumer, 1960-1969* (1986) and *Walter Crane: Artist, Designer, Socialist* (1989). A particular interest in the social history of watercolours has resulted in *The Emergence of the Professional Watercolourist* (2002) and articles on the Society of Painters in Water Colours and on watercolourists at the Royal Academy (the latter included in *Art on the Line. The Royal Academy Exhibitions at Somerset House 1780-1836* (2001)). Future projects include a second volume on the social history of watercolours which takes the work of J.M.W. Turner as its starting point.

WILLIAM VAUGHAN is Professor Emeritus of the History of Art at Birkbeck College, University of London. He has published widely on Romanticism and British and German Art. In 2005 he organized the bicentenary exhibition of the works of Samuel Palmer (British Museum, London, and Metropolitan Museum of Art, New York). He is currently completing a monograph on Palmer.

Preface

Sam Smiles and Simon Shaw-Miller

The majority of papers assembled in this volume were first delivered on the occasion of the conference 'Samuel Palmer: a British Romantic Artist Reassessed', held at the Paul Mellon Centre in London on 13 January 2006, to complement the exhibition *Samuel Palmer: Vision and Landscape* at the British Museum. To these we have added two contributions by William Vaughan, the leading curator of the exhibition and the organizer of the conference. The purpose of the collection is to bring together a variety of approaches to Samuel Palmer and his legacy: close examination of his technical procedures; information on his life and career; analysis of his aesthetic principles in relation to the nineteenth-century art world; investigations of his rediscovery in the modern era and the lasting value of the pastoral vision associated so strongly with his art.

In combination, what these chapters reveal is that the common perception of Palmer as a maverick artist, whose singular achievement removes him from normal contextual understandings of nineteenth-century art, is much too limiting. Vaughan's Introduction reviews the development of Palmer's modern appreciation and the consequences of this romanticized view of his achievement: his 'outsider' status provoking his omission from recent surveys of British nineteenth-century art. One aspiration of this volume is that it will help to demystify Palmer. A case in point is Vaughan's chapter on Palmer's upbringing, providing new evidence about Palmer's early years in London and documenting more precisely the social and economic conditions of his youth.

It is undeniable that in his Shoreham period Palmer was an idiosyncratic artist, but, as Greg Smith shows, Palmer's artistic standpoint can be seen as engaged in dialogue with the prevalent practical and theoretical aesthetic norms of the early nineteenth century. Thus, although the younger Palmer's position was frequently at odds with the dominant taste of the time, his view of art makes sense as a considered response to the art world he encountered. In his later years Palmer found himself much more in accord with the views of his fellow professionals, whether exploring similar subject matter or supporting developments in the instruction of art students. Martin Postle tracks Palmer's own training and his subsequent interest in art education across his career, showing the extent to which Palmer's inspirational art could be reconciled with academic instruction. Christiana Payne's chapter on Palmer's coastal paintings, and Paul Goldman's on his etchings, concentrate on Palmer's work in the second half of his career and reveal an artist maintaining firm commitments to a particular view of art practice, combining technical proficiency with strong emotional investment. Our revised understanding of the seriousness of intent, and self-consciousness about means and ends, evident in Palmer's formation and development as an artist is important; it helps to overcome the clichéd division of the younger visionary Palmer from the professional Victorian artist of his later years. These chapters show something of the deeper-lying continuities in Palmer's commitment to the practice of art, a commitment which sustained him throughout his career, irrespective of the radical differences in appearance between his earlier and later works.

Palmer's legacy is the subject of the chapter by Sam Smiles, concentrating on the enthusiasm for his art in the 1920s and 1930s, especially the response made by contemporary print-makers to his work, and the difficulties inherent in any desire to prolong a pastoral vision into the machine age. Simon Shaw-Miller's chapter extends the concerns of this collection by examining the impact of pastoral on music. The development by modern British composers of a 'dark' pastoral may be understood as working with Palmer's concerns but refurbishing them in a manner more suited to modern consciousness.

The Palmer that emerges from these several enquiries is less mysterious than the Palmer of popular imagination, but he is not thereby diminished. His artistic character remains distinctive; the sincerity of his endeavour is enhanced the more his circumstances are understood.

Acknowledgements

The editors would particularly like to thank Erika Gaffney, Meredith Norwich, Emily Ruskell, Anthea Lockley and Tom Norton at Ashgate for their help and support. The editors would also like to express their profound thanks to Lindsey Shaw-Miller for all her attentive care.

William Vaughan is grateful to The Master and Fellows of Pembroke College, Cambridge for permission to publish extracts from the diary of Benjamin Wrigglesworth Beatson.

Introduction:
The perception and study of Palmer's work in the later twentieth and early twenty-first centuries

William Vaughan

Samuel Palmer is one of the most original and distinctive of British artists. In his youth he produced vivid images of enfolded rustic scenery that are unforgettable. Although these fit broadly within the tradition of lyrical pastoral landscapes, they are unlike any that were produced before him in their boldness and intensity. While little known in the artist's own lifetime, they have subsequently attracted a large following and have had a definitive effect on the development of British landscape painting, particularly in the mid-twentieth century. Critics and artists at that time were struck by the extent to which these bold oils, watercolours and sepias seemed to foreshadow later developments, particularly that of the Post-Impressionists. It was contemplation of such daring and ecstatic works as 'In a Shoreham Garden' that caused many at the time to label Palmer 'The English Van Gogh'.[1] However inappropriate such a designation may be, it does draw attention to that combination of vigorous painterly exploration and mystical devotion to the forces of nature that both these artists do indeed share. Within a British context, Palmer seemed in the twentieth century to provide a way to combine modern experimentation with an indigenous tradition – what Paul Nash described at the time as 'going modern and being British'.[2]

The impact of Palmer's early work – essentially that produced when he was resident in the Kent village of Shoreham c.1826-35 – was all the more striking because of the suddenness of its emergence. This occurred principally through the major retrospective of his work held at the Victoria and Albert Museum in 1926.[3] Up to that time Palmer had been known largely (outside connoisseurial circles at least) as a Victorian painter of elaborate and somewhat melancholic watercolours and etchings. Knowledge of his life and work largely depended on the monumental study by his son, A.H. Palmer.[4] In this comprehensive study – still a valuable source book – both early and late works by Palmer were covered. However, it was the Victorian career that commanded most attention. Now it was seen that there was quite a different side to his work, one that seemed much more in tune with the modern spirit. However, while the great reputation that Palmer achieved at this point some fifty years after his death raised the appreciation of his work to a new level, catapulting him into the category of 'all time greats' (at least within a British context), it also created problems – ones that have marked the shape of Palmer scholarship over the subsequent decades.

In the first place the adulation of modernizing British artists in the mid-twentieth century has brought about the almost inevitable reaction. Already in 1949, in his magisterial *Landscape into Art*, Kenneth Clark remarked that Palmer had become 'almost too influential' in recent years.[5] His particular brand of British pastoralism seemed to become inextricably entwined with the Neo-romanticism then in vogue. As that movement declined, so Palmer was to some extent diminished with it. He seemed to have far less to say to the urbanized American-orientated artists, the abstractionists and pop-artists of the sixties. Furthermore, Palmer began to fall foul of those critics and historians who read artistic production in terms of political ideologies. This situation was exacerbated by a study that had emerged out of the Palmer cult of the mid-twentieth century. Geoffrey Grigson's *Samuel Palmer; The Visionary Years* of 1947 is the most brilliant study of the artist ever to have been produced. Focusing entirely on that moment early in Palmer's career when he had produced his most experimental work, it provided a rich and convincing image of the social and intellectual world in which the artist operated at that time. It had always been known that Palmer had been inspired by Blake at this period and that he himself had regarded the influence of this visionary painter and poet as the single most important event in his life. But Grigson went far beyond this to contextualize Palmer's extraordinary art with a context of cultural and political revivalism that was a distinctive feature of late Romanticism throughout Europe. Amongst other things, this contextualization brought into high relief Palmer's own political affiliations which were – as he put it himself – 'old high Tory'. Nothing could be further from the radicalism of Blake – and indeed of his other mentor of the period, the landscapist John Linnell – than Palmer's impassioned defence of traditional values, his adulation of the squirearchy and High Church Anglicanism, his near-hysterical opposition to the Reform Bill of 1832. Grigson proposed an interesting association between the decline of visionary fervour in Palmer's art with his disillusion at the destructive effects of the modern world on the rural community in the 1830s.

Viewed with this context in mind, certain critics shifted their gaze from Palmer's visual experimentation to focus on the 'unreal' evocation of what seemed to be a cosy traditionalist community in his 'visionary' art. In his review of the Council of Europe *Romantic Art* exhibition, held at the Tate and elsewhere in London in 1959, the Marxist critic John Berger listed 'among my personal *bêtes noires*, Samuel Palmer with his landscapes like furnished wombs'.[6] Berger wished to defuse the impact of Palmer's vivid art by suggesting that a stifling escapist enclosure lay at the heart of his vision. He contrasted this with what he saw as the bold, outward-looking naturalism of Palmer's older contemporary, John Constable. The latter could be fitted more comfortably into a narrative that saw all strivings towards pictorial realism in the nineteenth century as symptomatic of that progressive spirit that also energized the rise of socialism.

It is somewhat ironic that Berger's hero of the 'real' countryside, Constable, was every bit as much a high Tory traditionalist in his politics as Palmer. The uncomfortable relation between Constable's supposed authentic record of the countryside and the actualities of rural misery at the time were yet to be uncovered in 1959. This occurred 21 years later in John Barrell's *The Dark Side of the Landscape* of 1980. In the meantime Palmer had been fading from the mainstream artistic and critical interest; so much so in fact, that Barrell did not think it was even worth mentioning him in his exposé of the ideological structure of British landscape painting in the early nineteenth century.

But while no longer of interest to mainstream modernists and the academic avant-garde, Palmer did not disappear. Instead he became something of a 'niche' interest amongst a new generation of traditionalists, such as the Brotherhood of Ruralists. Palmer has remained a guru for such groups to the present day. This has been made clear in Jerrold Northrop Moore's recent *The Green Fuse*, in which a genealogy of rural traditionalists is constructed, from Palmer through the nineteenth and twentieth centuries to the present day.[7] Informative though such a lineage is, it must be remembered that, like the genealogies of families, it tends to be selective and limiting. In the age of postmodernism, land art and eco-warriors, engagement with Palmer has been more wide-ranging and complex. This is an area that remains largely to be explored, though a number of chapters in the present collection do much to open up wider issues relating to Palmer's impact.

Scholarly interest in Palmer also continued to flourish. The discovery of further Palmer material still preserved in his family led to new archival information becoming available, and to the publication of one of the most attractive of all Palmer books – that of his 1824 sketchbook.[8] This was the only surviving sketchbook from Palmer's 'visionary period' and contains many of his most remarkable images, as well as evidence of strong poetic interests. This work certainly enhanced respect for Palmer's brilliant draughtsmanship and imaginative power. It was followed a decade or so later by an event, however, that threw some of his work into doubt. This was the uncovering of the paintings of the forger Tom Keating, who had successfully launched on the art market what he called his 'Sexton Blake's' – faked Palmers.[9] There were many red faces in the dealer and museum world, since a number of Keating's productions had been celebrated as masterpieces of the Shoreham period. This also raised a sense of unease about many other works, some of which did not have satisfactory provenances. Although this crisis is now over and there are perhaps no more than a handful of works about which there might remain doubts, the incident did dent confidence. For some, indeed, this led to a lack of confidence in 'Shoreham' Palmer altogether. For if a forger as manifestly incompetent as Keating could fool the art world, then it might be the case that early Palmer pictures were not that special after all, and that the fuss about them was simply because they looked a bit like more recent modern work. This was far from being a majority view. But it cast a shadow of doubt over some of the claims that had been made about early Palmer.

While interest in Palmer's early 'Shoreham' work began to level off after 1970, other factors were in play to foreground quite different dimensions in his art. Consideration of Palmer's later career had largely disappeared after the rediscovery of his early work in the 1920s. In the 1960s, however, the revival of interest in Victorian society and art prompted reconsideration. It is no coincidence that the 'official' life of Palmer – that published by his son in 1892 – was reissued in 1972.[10] Although this book had given coverage of Palmer's Shoreham period and paid due attention to the influence of William Blake, it was, as has already been mentioned, far more concerned with the artist's later career as a watercolourist and etcher. Interest in the later Palmer had already been aroused by Edward Malins' *Samuel Palmer's Honeymoon*, in which the story of his post-Shoreham visit to Italy was told.[11] Malins' account drew on the largely unpublished correspondence still in the possession of the descendants of Palmer and his friends. This was soon to be followed by the extensive documentary publications of Raymond Lister. For a generation Lister was the dominating figure in Palmer scholarship. With amazing energy he produced no fewer than eleven separate books on Palmer, including a full scale biography, a two-volume edition of his letters and a complete oeuvre catalogue.[12] The latter remains a touchstone of Palmer scholarship. It makes clear – apart from anything else – how tiny the amount of material remains that belongs to the experimental early period of Palmer's career. It effectively counts for about one tenth of what is now known of the artist's total production.

Lister's publications made clear how much there remained to be discovered about Palmer's later career. It is not surprising to find that this aspect has stimulated the largest amount of research in recent years. This has tended to take place as much if not more in museums and galleries as in academic institutions. Amongst the most memorable achievements are the publication of Palmer's Milton series, in connection with the exhibition devoted to these at the Victoria and Albert Museum in 1978, and Paul Goldman's exhibition of Palmer's prints for the British Museum in 1991. It is striking that leading scholars in Palmer studies today, such as David Blayney Brown (cataloguer of the most important collection of Palmers – that in the Ashmolean Museum, Oxford),[13] Colin Harrison and Timothy Wilcox[14] – tend to come from a museum background.

It is also worth pointing out that, despite the growing interest in 'Victorian' Palmer, there are few who would actually suggest that this part of his oeuvre was more interesting than his early productions, either aesthetically or historically. Actions speak louder than words in this case, and it is surely significant in this context that – despite the Keating scandal of the 1970s – the current market valuation of a 'Shoreham' Palmer is typically at least ten times that of an equivalent Palmer from the later period.

While studies of aspects of Palmer's work continue, it is somewhat disappointing to see that he appears to have fallen out of the frame of wider academic discourse on landscape. The last thematic exploration that gave a significant place to Palmer was Robert Rosenblum's *Modern Painting and the Northern Romantic Tradition* (1975), where he is assigned a key role in the development of a line of spiritually inspired painting that Rosenblum traces from Friedrich to Rothko. He is strikingly absent (or only minimally represented) in the more recent studies that have looked at landscape from a socio-political perspective. He has no place, for example, in W.J.T. Mitchell's *Landscape and Power* (1994) nor – perhaps more surprisingly – in Simon Schama's *Landscape and Memory* (1995). This contrasts with Turner and Constable who remain prominent in such studies. Perhaps the sheer historical ambiguity of the Shoreham work acts as a disincentive. After all, most of this work was all but unknown to his contemporaries and had no impact outside a tiny circle of sympathizers. It is, however, as David Bindman has shown in an important essay, richly relevant for the discussion of contemporary political movements.[15]

Academic obsessions change and none of the books mentioned above make any claim to comprehensive coverage. One can hardly take issue with them, then, for the omission of one particular artist or another. It is a different matter when a book does claim comprehensiveness. It is therefore particularly regrettable to see no entry on Palmer amongst the artists treated in the reference section of the much praised recent *Oxford Companion to the Romantic Age*; a work that advertises itself as including 'all the significant figures' of the period.[16] Such an omission is the equivalent in artistic terms of excluding Keats or Shelley from the list of relevant poets.[17]

The relative lack of interest in Palmer in the academic community contrasts strongly with the wider cultural interest in Palmer. Palmer's scenery remains an important touchstone in both literary and artistic creative fields, and a leading cultural symbol for a certain kind of intense engagement with nature. This can be seen, for example, in its treatment by Iain Sinclair in his record of his epic journey around the M25, in which he pays tribute to Palmer's pivotal role in creating a form of 'visionary tourism'.[18]

The recent Palmer exhibition at the British Museum provided an occasion for gauging the artist's current standing amongst critics and the public.[19] The critical reception suggested that respect for the artist was as high as ever. None of those reviewers who wrote having seen the exhibition had any doubt about Palmer's status as a major artist. All seemed to accept the enduring power and interest of the Shoreham period. The only point of dispute was whether Palmer's later work merited attention as well as the early work. Some – like Luke Herrmann and Andrew Wilton – felt that it did.[20] Most considered the later work was at least interesting and deserving of respect. A few still clung to the dismissive position adopted back in 1947 by Geoffrey Grigson. The most condemnatory was Andrew Graham-Dixon, who censured the exhibition for what he called its 'foredoomed ambition to kindle interest in the artist's later work'.[21] Graham-Dixon's interest may not have been kindled, but there was no doubt that public enthusiasm for the show – which was strong – spread beyond Shoreham to much of the later work, particularly such fine etchings as 'The Bellman'. It was clear from the comments of visitors, too, that Palmer was one of those artists still held in great affection by a significant section of the public. The exhibition also provided the opportunity for the bringing together in the catalogue of a group of essays by scholars currently active in Palmer studies, ranging through various aspects of the artist's life and career, helping to resituate the study of Palmer within broader debates about landscape. This present collection further adds to the compendium of recent research and ranges beyond Palmer's life and works to consider as well his art in wider social and artistic contexts – several addressing precisely those areas that have been absent in recent studies on landscape.

Notes

1.   Notably Graham Sutherland. See Andrew Lambirth, 'Force of Nature', *The Spectator*, 17 September 2008.

2.   Paul Nash '"Going modern" and "being British"', *Week-End Review*, vol. 5, no. 109, 9 April 1932, pp. 443-4.

3.   Martin Hardie and James Laver, with notes and introduction by A.H. Palmer, *Catalogue of an Exhibition of Drawings, Etchings and Woodcuts by Samuel Palmer and other Disciples of William Blake*, London: Victoria and Albert Museum, 1926.

4.   A.H. Palmer, *The Life and Letters of Samuel Palmer, Painter and Etcher*, London: Seeley, 1892.

5.   Kenneth Clark, *Landscape into Art*, London: John Murray, 1949, pp. 71-2.

6.   Quoted by Tom Lubbock in his review of the Samuel Palmer exhibition at the British Museum 2005; 'Heaven and Earth Show', *The Independent*, 31 October 2005, p. 46.

7.   Jerrold Northrop Moore, *The Green Fuse: Pastoral Vision in English Art, 1820 – 2000*, Antique Collectors' Club, 2006.

8.   Martin Butlin, *Samuel Palmer. The Sketchbook of 1824*, Clairvaux: Trianon Press, 1962. Reissued by Thames and Hudson, 2005.

9.   Tom Keating, Geraldine Norman and Frank Norman, *The Fake's Progress: The Tom Keating Story*, London: Hutchinson and Co., 1977.

10.   A.H. Palmer, *Life and Letters*; facsimile reprint with an introductory essay by Raymond Lister and a preface by Kathleen Raine, London, Eric and Joan Stevens, 1972.

11.   Edward Malins, *Samuel Palmer's Italian Honeymoon*, London: Oxford University Press, 1968.

12.   R. Lister (ed.), *The Letters of Samuel Palmer*, 2 vols, Oxford: Clarendon Press, 1974; R. Lister, *Samuel Palmer: A Biography*, London: Faber and Faber, 1974; R. Lister, *A Catalogue Raisonné of the Works of Samuel Palmer*, Cambridge: Cambridge University Press, 1988.

13.   David Blayney Brown, *Samuel Palmer 1805-81: Catalogue Raisonné of the Paintings and Drawings, and a Selection of Prints in the Ashmolean Museum*, Oxford: Ashmolean Museum, 1983.

14.   Colin Harrison, *Samuel Palmer*, Oxford: Ashmolean Museum, 1997. Timothy Wilcox, *Samuel Palmer*, London: Tate Publishing, 2005.

15.   David Bindman, 'The Politics of Vision: Palmer's *Address to the Electors of West Kent*', in William Vaughan, Elizabeth E. Barker, Colin Harrison et al., *Samuel Palmer (1805-1881): Vision and Landscape*, London: British Museum Press, 2005, pp. 29-32.

16.   Iain McCalman (ed.), *An Oxford Companion to the Romantic Age: British Culture 1776 – 1832*, Oxford: Oxford University Press, 1999; see back cover.

17.   The reference section does have a brief piece on the group that centred on Palmer, The Ancients. They are referred to here (unusually and inaccurately) as the 'Shoreham Ancients'. The piece is so casually written that the author manages to describe the group, founded in 1824, as 'Early Victorian'. He ignores their art utterly and appears only to have chosen to mention them in order to castigate them for 'canonizing Blake by muffling his eighteenth-century artisan origins' (pp. 704-5).

18.   Iain Sinclair, *London Orbital. A Walk Around the M25*, London: Granta Books, 2002. See especially pp. 418-22.

19.   Vaughan, Barker, Harrison et al., *Vision and Landscape*.

20.   Andrew Wilton, in *Apollo*, 1 January 2006, pp. 76-8.

21.   Andrew Graham-Dixon, 'Samuel Palmer', *The Sunday Telegraph*, 13 November 2005, p. 45.

1

Samuel Palmer's Houndsditch days

William Vaughan

This chapter explores the earliest stage of Palmer's artistic career, from the time when he first took steps to develop as a serious painter, around 1817, to the moment when he began to have work accepted for exhibition and started to attract professional interest in his work, around 1820.

On the face of it this might not seem such an interesting period. It preceded by a year or so his fateful meeting with John Linnell, the 'good angel from Heaven' who was sent, as Palmer put it 'to pluck me from the pit of modern art'.[1] There was no hint as yet in his work of the extraordinary visionary fervour that developed under Linnell's tutelage, which was further inflamed by his meetings with William Blake. Yet while, on the surface, Palmer might have seemed to be no more than a precociously talented yet conventional landscape watercolourist, below the surface it was a different matter. The mind that responded with such excitement to Linnell and Blake's spiritual approach to art was one already in turmoil, one that had, as Palmer himself recalls, been deeply stirred by religion and literature from an early age. It was his father, as Palmer recalls in the autobiographical sketch that he provided for *The Portfolio* in 1871,

... who, by little and little, made me learn by heart much of the Holy Scriptures. He carried in his waistcoat pocket little manuscript books with vellum covers, transcribing in them the essence of whatever he had lately read, so that in our many walks together, there was always some topic of interest when the route was weary or unattractive.[2]

It is perhaps not surprising that Palmer's first ambition was to go into the Church. The decision to become a painter instead seems to have been made more at the instigation of Palmer's parents than himself. This is certainly the implication given in his autobiographical letter where he states: 'It was thought right that I should attempt painting as a profession.'[3]

The period covered by this chapter was one that was critical for Palmer's professional development, and also for the establishment of the frame of mind that later was to enable him to discover a spiritual purpose in the painting of landscape. Yet it is a period that is little documented. This is hardly surprising, given the fact that Palmer was at the time an unknown youth in his early teens. The small amount that is known comes largely from Palmer's own reminiscences and from records preserved by Palmer and his family.[4] It was this material that was drawn upon by Palmer's son, A.H. Palmer, in his biography of his father,[5] and that has remained the principal source for subsequent biographers.

The present chapter aims to augment such accounts by drawing upon material hitherto little referred to or completely ignored. This includes the standard reference materials used by topographical historians and genealogists; the rate books, trade directories, court records and related documentation that provide such a rich source of information about London and Londoners in the early nineteenth century. It also includes direct records by contemporaries. The most important of these is the diary of Benjamin Wrigglesworth Beatson, a youth two years older than Palmer who was a pupil at Merchant Taylors' School – the school that Palmer briefly attended in 1817 – and who was a regular visitor to the Palmer household throughout the period covered by this chapter.[6] Although the picture that emerges is not radically opposed to that already commonly known, it does have some strikingly different details. It suggests, furthermore, that Palmer's circumstances as a child and adolescent were significantly more urban and impoverished than is normally supposed. This fact in itself puts his attachment to idyllic rural landscape in a different light.

Perhaps the most significant feature to emerge is that Palmer was living, throughout this period, not in the leafy near-rural suburb in which he was born (Surrey Square, Walworth) but in one of the most deprived parts of the inner city: Houndsditch. Running along the eastern limit of the City of London, Houndsditch had a long history of impoverishment and murky dealings. Its very name is believed to have been derived from the habit of citizens of throwing dead dogs in the ditch just outside the city wall. At the time that Palmer lived there it had a substantial immigrant population – largely Jewish – and abounded in second-hand shops and cheap clothing establishments. It was emphatically not the place for those aspiring to genteel life to be living. It must have been a great come-down for Palmer's family to have moved there from the salubrious suburb that they had formerly inhabited.

The fact that Palmer's family had at one time an address in Houndsditch is not hard to discover. The address 126 Houndsditch was given in the catalogues of his first exhibited works, at the Royal Academy and the British Institution in 1819.[7] Yet Palmer's biographers have been extremely reluctant to dwell on the fact or to explore its implications. Neither Palmer nor his son made any reference to Houndsditch. In the case of Palmer's letter to *The Portfolio* this is a pardonable omission, since he talks of his childhood in the broadest manner and doesn't specify any residences. A.H. Palmer's account, in his *Life and Letters,* is more misleading, since he mentions Palmer's residences both before and after Houndsditch and implies that the family moved from one to the other without having spent any time in an insalubrious part of the City. He opens his first chapter by providing an idyllic account of the houses in Surrey Square: 'From the upper windows might be caught pleasant glimpses of sylvan Dulwich, and the southerly wind came fresh from many a neighbouring copse and meadow…'.[8] In his subsequent description of Palmer's birth and upbringing he makes no reference to any change of address. Only when he comes to the move to Bloomsbury in 1820 does he record a change: 'In 1820 he was again successful in getting a picture accepted at the Academy, and we find from the index of the catalogue that the family had migrated to No.10, Broad Street, Bloomsbury.'[9] Since A.H. Palmer consulted the Royal Academy catalogues when compiling the life of his father, he would of course have seen that the address given for the exhibits the previous year, in 1819, was 126 Houndsditch. The suppression of this fact must have been deliberate.

Twentieth-century biographers have acknowledged the Houndsditch address, but usually in the briefest manner. In his seminal *Samuel Palmer: The Visionary Years* (still the finest account of Palmer's early life), Geoffrey Grigson does mention that by 1817 the Palmer family had moved from Surrey Square 'to the less pleasant district of Houndsditch'.[10] However he does not comment beyond this. Raymond Lister, the author of the most substantial biography on Palmer in recent times, moves the arrival of the family in Houndsditch to 1818 and again has no further comment to make. He simply tucks the fact into a phrase in a sentence that moves his narrative along by two years; '… soon after Martha's death [Palmer's Mother; died January 1818], Samuel Palmer Senior [Palmer's father] had moved to 126 Houndsditch and then, in 1820, he again moved his home and bookshop to 10 Broad Street, Bloomsbury…'.[11]

Quite why Lister believed that the family only moved to Houndsditch after the death of Palmer's mother in January 1818 is unclear. It is all the more puzzling since in the same year that he published his biography of Palmer, Lister also published the first volume of his compilation of Palmer's letters. The first of these, written by Palmer and his mother to Palmer's father when they were on holiday in Margate, is addressed 'Mr. Palmer / 126 Houndsditch/ London'. The date of the postmark is June 13/14 1814.[12] It is possible that Lister believed that the Houndsditch address was, at that time, only a business address. However, he also includes a letter by Palmer addressed to his mother at 126 Houndsditch, dated 18 January 1815.[13] Certainly there could be no doubt that the Palmer family was living in the Houndsditch area by May 1817, since this is the time that Beatson began to record visits to them there in his diary.[14]

The first extant letter of Samuel Palmer makes it clear that the family was already living in Houndsditch when he was nine. In fact they may have been there some time before that. For according to the Rate Books of St Mary's ,Newington, the family had already moved out of their Surrey Square residence by 4 November 1808.[15] This means that Palmer, born 27 January 1805, must have left Surrey Square before he was four. There is no evidence that they moved straight from Surrey Square to Houndsditch. However, there is no evidence that they lived in any other place. It would also seem that there may have been a clear professional reason for Palmer's father to make a move involving a serious change in fortune in 1808. 1808 was the year in which Palmer's paternal grandfather, Christopher Palmer, died. Christopher Palmer had been a prosperous hatter, a partner of the firm Moxon, Palmer and Norman in Cannon Street.[16] Palmer's father had begun his professional life by working in this firm, but appears to have left soon after the death of his own father, Christopher.[17] Since Palmer's father was notoriously unbusinesslike it seems highly likely that the other partners of Moxon, Palmer and Norman would have been happy with this turn of events and may even have encouraged it.

Leaving Surrey Square meant more than simply abandoning a pleasant neighbourhood. It also meant abandoning an area where the Palmers had strong family connections. Surrey Square was surrounded by relatives on both sides of the family. Christopher Palmer, the prosperous hatter, had lived in a substantial property in Crosby Row on the Walworth Road.[18] William Giles, the banker and father of Samuel Palmer's mother Martha, lived in an equally grand building in Apollo Buildings in East Street, which runs just north of Surrey Square between the Walworth Road and the Old Kent Road. Like Christopher Palmer, William Giles had moved into the neighbourhood in the later eighteenth century when it began to be developed with grand late Georgian mansions, transferring the district from its former function as a provider of market gardens. Walworth had the attraction at the time of combining a still largely rural environment with easy access to the City, via Borough and over London Bridge. It remained a salubrious area until the mid-nineteenth century, after which it rapidly went downhill.[19] William Giles also had a house at Margate (the town from which his wife originated), but he retained his residence in Walworth until his death in 1825.[20] Apart from being a successful banker William Giles was also a fervent Baptist and author of a number of moral tomes, one of which, *A Guide to Domestic Happiness*, had sufficient reputation to be treated as a classic in the nineteenth century.[21] Known in the family as 'the author', he was the most authoritative figure in Palmer's early life.

In the opening sentences of his book, A.H. Palmer dwells on the rural nature of his father's birthplace. He implied some antiquity to the building, something that encouraged Lister later to describe their home as 'an old house in Surrey Square'.[22] However it was far from being this. The house Palmer was born in was part of the new urban expansion. It was in a grand new layout (never actually completed as a square) put up by the speculative builder Thomas Clutton and the architect Michael Searles in 1792. Still standing, it remains one of the finest examples of later Georgian architecture in the area.

Far from being a 'young bookseller' as A.H. Palmer describes him at the beginning of his life of Palmer, Palmer's father was a junior employee in his father's hatters firm at the time of the artist's birth. It seems surprising that a man of such a modest position should occupy one of the most handsome modern residences in the area. The surprise is ameliorated to some degree by the discovery that Samuel Palmer senior was not the person responsible for the payment of rates – and therefore, presumably, not the leaseholder or official tenant of the property. The person responsible listed in the rate books of St Mary's Newington was William Giles. This could either have been Palmer's grandfather 'the author', who lived round the corner in Apollo Buildings; or it could have been the author's son, who was also named William Giles and was making his way in the world as a stockbroker. William Giles had a double marital bond with Samuel Palmer senior, for while Samuel Palmer senior had married his sister Martha, *he* had married Samuel Palmer senior's sister, Sarah. It seems quite likely that these two pairs of Palmers and Giles all lived in the one house, with William Giles being the leaseholder. As this situation suggests, the Palmers and Giles were a closely knit family, and one that had doubtless joined together as prosperous city merchants and bankers with strong Baptist affiliations. Samuel Palmer was always to remain particularly close to the cousins that emerged from the union of William and Sarah Giles. One of them, John Giles, was to become a member of The Ancients and to be one of Samuel Palmer's most constant and enthusiastic patrons.

The linkage between the two families may have originated from a professional connection since William Giles 'the author' had been a hatter, like Christopher Palmer, prior to becoming a stockbroker and banker.[23] By the 1790s the links seem to have involved both older and younger members of the families. One further instance of this is that the house in Surrey Square in which Samuel Palmer was born had been the responsibility, prior to being that of William Giles, of Nathaniel Palmer, Samuel Palmer's uncle and the brother of Samuel Palmer senior. Nathaniel Palmer was a corn factor, and a man of considerable wealth. He was ratepayer for 42 Surrey Square from 1798 to 1803.[24] After that he moved to 12 Aldermanbury in the City, where he was partner in the firm of Scott, Garnett and Palmer and where he remained until his death in 1840.[25] William Giles therefore took over a residence that had formerly been the responsibility of Nathanial Palmer. The relation with this other Palmer seems to have been a cordial one, since William and Mary Giles named their fourth son Nathaniel Palmer Giles.[26]

Nathaniel Palmer is given a bad press by A.H. Palmer. He describes him as a 'shrewd, cold, determined man utterly impervious to persuasion or argument and utterly indifferent to ties of kinship'.[27] Nathaniel Palmer did, it is true, persuade his eccentric brother, Samuel Palmer senior, to give up his unsuccessful bookselling business in 1826 and go and live in the country. On the other hand he did pay his brother a regular allowance – hardly the action of one 'utterly indifferent to ties of kinship'.

While the date at which the Palmers arrived in Houndsditch is not known, the time of their departure from Surrey Square can – as has already been mentioned – be set. This was in 1808. We can surmise this because this was the year in which the ratepayer changed. In the rate book for 4 November 1808 William Giles' name is crossed out and replaced by that of one Alfred Smith. There is, furthermore, a note in pencil against William Giles' name saying 'left and not paid'.[28] So it would seem there was no likelihood of a continuance of residency. Whether the cessation of this tenancy was due to some event in the Giles family or – as has been surmised above – to a change in the fortunes of Samuel Palmer senior is not known. In any case the departure seems to have been somewhat precipitous and may well have been traumatic for the family. We may have a glimpse of this in a recollection of Palmer's, given in his autobiographical letter of 1871 and repeated by every biographer ever since. After having cited the influence of his father in instilling in him a love of literature and deep involvement in religion, he turned to another key childhood influence, his nurse Mary Ward; 'I remember too, the priceless value of a faithful and intelligent domestic, my nurse, who, with little education else, was ripe in that without which so much is often useless or mischievous; deeply read in her Bible and *Paradise Lost*.' Palmer records a momentous occasion when

As I was standing with her, watching the shadows on the wall from branches of elm behind which the moon had risen, she transferred and fixed the fleeting image in my memory by repeating the couplet

'Vain man the vision of a moment made,
Dream of a dream, and shadow of a shade.'
I never forgot those shadows, and am often trying to paint them.[29]

In his autobiographical letter Palmer says that he was 'less than four years old' when this event took place.[30] This would have been precisely the time when the family was having to leave Surrey Square, presumably heading for less salubrious quarters in the City. If this was so, then this might have given particular poignancy to Mary Ward's utterance about vanity and transience, made in the knowledge that a disadvantageous move was about to be forced on the family. It might also explain why this event was lodged so firmly in Palmer's mind. It was the only specific event in childhood that he refers to in his autobiographical letter.

While Palmer's family left the Walworth area most probably when he was three, and undoubtedly before he was nine, he did not lose all contact with the area. His grandfather and his favourite cousins still lived there and he must have made frequent visits back. Perhaps these also intensified the sense of loss that he must have experienced in his new surroundings in Houndsditch.

Although there is no mystery, given the family connections with the area, why Samuel Palmer senior should have begun his married life in Surrey Square in Walworth, the reasons for moving to Houndsditch seem obscure. It may be that he left with debts. This is certainly believable, given the note in the St Mary's Newington rate book about the rate having been left unpaid. As a beneficiary of his father Christopher Palmer's will, one would have thought that he would have some funds. However, while he died in 1808, Christopher Palmer's will was not proved until 20 February 1811. This seems largely to have been due to complications in reaching a settlement in relationship to his partnership in the hatters firm.[31] It may well have been the case, therefore, that Samuel Palmer was particularly short of funds during the three years between the death of his father and the proving of the will. He had, after all, left his job in his father's hatters business, and had not yet been compensated by receiving the inheritance mentioned in his father's will.

It was presumably after the proving of the will that Samuel Palmer had the funds to set up his bookshop. Extrapolating from notes left by A.H. Palmer, Lister states that, soon after leaving the family firm he 'set up in business as a bookseller and stationer, in a dingy little City shop with a stall outside'.[32] However, there is no documented reference to the existence of the shop prior to May 1817. This reference is in the diary of Beatson. It is also clear from the diary that the bookshop was in Houndsditch, as he states 'At Mr. Palmers Houndsditch' in the first record of his visit there.[33] Beatson's father was a warehouse manager and the family lived at 11 Pancras Lane, Queen Street, just south of Cheapside. Houndsditch was within easy walking distance. However, Pancras Lane was in the City and a far superior address.

Houndsditch seems a curious location for a bookshop, given its general reputation for poverty and for cheap and second-hand goods. However it seems that, while Samuel Palmer senior set up his shop there, this might not have been his reason for moving into the area. That might have had more to do with his previous occupation as a hatter. For there is evidence that, during the early part of his residence in Houndsditch at least, he worked in a clothing establishment. Such is the distaste of Palmer's biographers for the fact that the family address in this period was 126 Houndsditch, that none of them seem to have enquired what was actually going on at that place. Given that it can be established – on the evidence of Beatson – that Samuel Palmer Senior's bookshop was in Houndsditch it would seem natural to assume that this would have been at 126 Houndsditch. But it was not. Consultation of the trade directories of the period show that throughout the time the Palmers lived in Houndsditch, Number 126 housed a very different activity. It was a cheap clothing establishment run by the brothers Thomas, Joseph and Sargent Smith.[34]

Cheap clothing establishments – or 'slop shops' as they were inelegantly called at the time – abounded in the Houndsditch area. They typically sold bespoke clothing much used by sailors and working people – and also by impecunious youths, such as apprentices and students. It must be supposed that the Palmers had lodgings at this address, although it was also possible that it was simply used as a post-restante. In any case there seems to have been a clear professional connection. For it appears that Sargent Smith's 'slop shop' was, for a time at least, actually Samuel Palmer senior's place of work. This astonishing probability can be deduced from the record of an Old Bailey trial of 1815.[35] In this year Sargent Smith was witness in an action against a seller of leather breeches, Matthew Rowland, for what was termed a 'misdemeanour'. In his statement in court Smith said;

I am a slop-seller. I have a servant of the name of Samuel Palmer, and another
of the name of Joseph Mason. We were in the habit of purchasing leather
breeches from the prisoner. I have two partners, Thomas and Joseph Smith.[36]

Samuel Palmer is not that uncommon a name and it is just possible that Smith had a servant named Samuel Palmer who was not the father of the artist. However the fact that Smith's address was the one that Samuel Palmer senior used as his postal address greatly stacks the odds in favour of Smith's servant and Samuel Palmer senior being one and the same person. It is not an improbable occurrence. Samuel Palmer senior, after all, had begun his professional career in his father's hatters business and had even, on 8 May 1805, purchased the Freedom of London as a feltmaker.[37] Although he may well by 1815 have already been running a bookshop as well, he could also have maintained a trusted position with responsibility for financial affairs in Smith's slop shop establishment. The trial in which his name was mentioned was one in which he had paid a fraudulent bill that had been presented to him by Matthew Rowland. His testimony was as follows;

SAMUEL PALMER. The prisoner produced a bill to me, on the 23rd of
September, for the amount of three pounds five shillings and ninepence;
that bill purported to be signed by J. Mason, who is shopman and
foreman to the prosecutors. I paid the prisoner in three one-pound
Bank of England notes, a dollar, and three pence in halfpence.

In the trial Mason affirmed that the signature was a forgery and Rowland received the surprisingly light sentence of one month's imprisonment.[38]

It seems likely that Samuel Palmer senior combined a post at Smith's slop shop with the running of his bookshop. As already noted, it is quite possible that he did not actually live at 126 Houndsditch but used it as a postal address. Rather intriguingly, there is a Samuel Palmer registered at this period at Duke Street, which runs into Houndsditch. This is only a few yards from the junction with Houndsditch and close indeed to 126.[39] However, given the commonality of the name, one cannot be certain that this was where Samuel Palmer senior had his shop, and/or housed his family.

Unfortunately there are no printed documentary records of Samuel Palmer senior's bookshop prior to its removal to Bloomsbury in 1820.[40] His business appears in none of the trade directories of the period. It was presumably too modest to merit this kind of advertisement. There are, however, intriguing references to it in the unpublished diary of Beatson. The first reference occurs on Friday 2 May 1817: '6-9 At Mr. Palmers Houndsditch, called on Mr. Brounger : saw at Palmers [unreadable word] Greek/ Testament and many others.'[41] This entry interestingly establishes that Palmer's bookshop was indeed in the Houndsditch area. There is also no doubt that 'Mr Palmer' is Samuel Palmer's father since Samuel Palmer himself soon emerges in subsequent visits. A further interesting reference is that to 'Mr. Brounger'. This was the man who ran a substantial 'slop shop' on the corner of Duke Street and Houndsditch.[42] Presumably Beatson was visiting it to purchase cheap clothing, as an adolescent student might do. The mysterious Samuel Palmer recorded in the land rent payments in Duke Street would have lived just two doors away from Brounger's emporium, something that strengthens the supposition that this might indeed have been the same as Samuel Palmer senior.[43]

As well as establishing a location for Palmer senior's business, Beatson's diary is also interesting for the glimpse it gives of the bookshop's stock. Beatson was a student in the sixth form of Merchant Taylors' school. He was subsequently to gain a scholarship to Cambridge where he eventually became a classics don.[44] At this time he was learning languages prodigiously. Apart from Greek and Latin he was also gaining the rudiments of Hebrew and Syriac. He seems to have been drawn to 'Mr. Palmer's' shop because it contained many esoteric items, as well as a good range of modern classics. Many of the works mentioned by Beatson suggest that the stock in Palmer senior's shop extended well beyond the 'general stock of good quality' that Grigson reported from his perusal of the sale of its contents in 1827.[45]

In the period between 1817 and 1821 Beatson made habitual visits to Samuel Palmer senior's shop and his diary contains interesting references to works of theology and language, as well as some modern classics. Much of the works bought by Beatson were doubtless related to his school studies, as with the copies of Herodotus and Livy that he bought on 4 December 1819.[46] In a similar category can be placed the mathematics books he acquired, such as Miles Bland's *Geometrical Problems* on 22 March 1820.[47] Beatson was evidently a keen mathematician, since he recorded that he ordered the book (which had only recently been published) 'with great delight'. It would seem, in fact, that Palmer senior shared Beatson's enthusiasm for mathematics, for on a number of occasions he demonstrated the properties of magic squares and other puzzles to the budding scholar.[48] Since Palmer senior had undertaken the teaching of his own son at home it seems he was probably experienced and interested in instructing the young. He also introduced Beatson to new inventions and pastimes, such as the Kaleidoscope.[49] The first Kaleidoscope was patented by the Scottish scientist Sir David Brewster in 1817, and it was a highly topical innovation at the time. The bookshop also contained rarities. Soon after his first recorded visit Beatson was admiring 'a facsimile of the Alex/andrian Manuscript'.[50] This was presumably the Codex Alexandrinus in the British Museum, a fifth-century Greek manuscript of the bible.[51] Given Beatson's devotional interests and clerical ambitions this must have been a particularly interesting volume.

Beatson's scholarly studies extended beyond his school and Palmer's bookshop seems to have provided him material for these, too. On Wednesday 5 January he recorded he 'looked at several Syrian grammars'.[52] Beatson's appetite for languages relevant to classical studies and his biblical interests was prodigious. In 1817 he was learning Hebrew from a Mr Levy. It would seem that Mr Levy also lived in the Houndsditch area since he met him while visiting Palmer on 12 November 1817: 'Met Mr. Levy in going out with S. Palmer / ret~d to attend his instructions'.[53] The meeting with Mr. Levy is a reminder that, as well as being an area of poverty and second-hand goods, Houndsditch was also a place of learning for the Jewish community. The seventeenth-century Synagogue of Bevis Marks (the first to be established in Britain after the return of the Jews under Cromwell) lay in the next street and was a centre of scholarship. It may be that Palmer senior's bookshop was welcome in this community for its stock of biblical material and Middle Eastern languages.

While Samuel Palmer junior appears to have had little connection with Beatson's biblical and linguistic studies, they did appear to share interests in modern literature. They exchanged volumes of Maria Edgeworth's *Popular and Moral Tales*.[54] These works, which preached moral virtues and stressed the duties that the wealthy had towards the poor, were very widely circulated at the time and would have been influential on Palmer in emphasizing those conservative values that were later to be so central to his life. In Edgeworth's writing could be found the reactionary designation of progressive movements of the period as heartless and destructive to the fabric of society.[55]

During the course of 1817 Beatson gradually became more intimate with the Palmer family and would often stay to supper. His records of these meals add confirmation to the fact that the Palmers were not well off. Something of a serious trencherman, Beatson made regular records of what he ate. Normally he would have a substantial meal in the middle of the day, usually well furnished with meat. When at home it was usually something filling, such as 'boiled beef and mashed potatoes' (1817, 30 October).[56] Supper was a more modest affair, but typically contained some cold meat or sausages.[57] When having supper at the Palmers, all he got was either eggs, or bread and cheese.[58]

While intimate with the Palmer family, Beatson records little interest in their life or fortunes. It is striking that he makes no reference in his diary to the most devastating occurrence that Palmer experienced. This was the death of his mother on 19 January 1818, which happened when Palmer was away from home, staying with relatives in Margate. Palmer recorded that the news, when he heard it, 'pierced him like a sharp sword'.[59] Yet there is no mention of the event or its aftermath in Beatson's diary. The first diary entry recording a visit to the Palmers after Martha's death was only a few weeks later, on 16 February. Yet all Beatson comments on is the fact that he has borrowed a book on chemistry![60] This lack of concern is all the more surprising since Beatson had been sufficiently close to the family to be invited to Palmer's younger brother William's birthday on Tuesday 9 December 1817: 'Went to Palmers. W. Palmers birthday… at Palmers had 3 or 4 cakes.'[61] Beatson was invited to William's birthday party again the next year. This time the occasion seems to have been not an altogether happy one: '9 December 1818; 6 ½ - 9 Tea at Palmers. William will be murdered!'[62] Later in life William's wayward behaviour was to be a sore trial to Samuel. It seems that even at this age he was something of a problem. Yet one cannot help but feel some sympathy for a boy just turned eight who had only recently lost his mother.

While Beatson may first have been attracted to Palmer senior on account of the stock in his bookshop, it is clear that he was also interested in his religious activities. A convinced Baptist, Palmer senior was already active at this time as a lay preacher. Beatson was a devout youth and later became a Church of England clergyman. It seems probable however, that he was at this time also a Baptist.[63]

Both Palmer senior and Beatson were not restricted by denominational orthodoxy in their choice of places to worship. Like many in London at the time, they were in the habit of seeking out popular preachers from all kinds of non-conformity. One of their first outings was recorded on Wednesday 19 November 1817: '6-7. tea. Went with father of S.P. to Long Acre / Chapel – heard Mr. Howell'.[64] This was the evangelical Welsh clergyman William Howels who obtained the Episcopal Chapel of Long Acre in 1816 where he became popular for his preaching.[65] Other preachers mentioned included the Scottish divines Thomas Chalmers, whose *Astronomical Discourses* were causing a current stir,[66] and Alexander Crombie.[67] It is not surprising, perhaps, that given this climate of charismatic and radical speakers, Palmer senior did not measure up particularly well when he entered the pulpit. In 1818, the year after Beatson began to frequent the Palmers' residence, he began to note negative views on Palmer senior's preaching. '1818 Sunday April 5.

10-1 Heard Mr. Palmer his sermon dated.'[68] This view of Palmer senior's sermon as 'dated' is interesting as the first recorded use of the word in a pejorative sense.[69] An even more negative opinion was implied when Beatson recorded wishing to hear one of the Scottish divines rather than Palmer senior: '1818 Sunday September 20 10 ¼ - 1 Heard Mr. Palmer (Mr. Crombie being where I wish I was) Came home with S Palmer.'[70] Beatson's emerging view of Palmer senior as uncharismatic and out of date seems to coincide with a changing relationship with the Palmers. Beatson continued to make visits until at least 1821, but the tone of his opinions became more dismissive and he may have kept up the relation largely because Palmer senior could continue to provide him with the books he wanted.

There is no doubt, however, that for a time at least Beatson was intrigued both by Samuel Palmer's artistic skills and also by evident eccentricities in his character. Samuel Palmer was two years younger than Beatson. They first appear to have come into contact when Beatson began to frequent Palmer senior's shop in May 1817. Indeed, it is even possible that Beatson may have encouraged Palmer senior to send his son to Merchant Taylors'. For it was at the end of that month, on 26 May, that Samuel Palmer was entered into the school, in the second form.[71] Beatson was by that time already in the sixth form, yet he appears to have taken a personal interest in the new boy. On 26 May, the day that Palmer was recorded as having entered the school, Beatson noted in his diary that he 'led up S. Palmer' in the Latin class.[72]

There are, in fact, no further direct references to Palmer at school. The time was, we know, a most unhappy one, and he only lasted there six months, leaving for good in December 1817.[73] The period must have been traumatic, and it has been supposed by all biographers that it had been one of unrelieved misery. Certainly life at the Merchant Taylors' School at that time could be grim. A gruesome record of the school is provided by a near contemporary, the actor Charles James Matthews, who was at the School 1813-15.[74] Interpolating from a remark about 'big boys' in a letter to F.G. Stephens dated August 1875, Lister surmises that Palmer thought of the older boys in the school as 'baboons'.[75] Yet while this might have been the case, it is clear from Beatson's diary that he found one friendly acquaintance there, and that from among the older students.

While all biographies of Palmer mention Palmer's unhappiness at school, it is usually supposed that this is because he was too sensitive and delicate a child to cope with the tough world of Merchant Taylors'. This may indeed be the case, but perhaps there was also another reason why the experiment did not work. It may be that, having been taught before at home, he simply did not have the grounding to cope with the level of understanding of classical languages and literature expected. This fact may be hinted at obliquely by a remark made in Beatson's diary on 2 January 1818, soon after Samuel Palmer had withdrawn from Merchant Taylors': '8-11½ breakfast with newspaper –

took it to show / Mr. Palmer an advertisement by Mr. Smith / my ever honoured tutor at Mill Hill now / established in Store Street.'[76]

Beatson's showing of an advertisement by his former tutor to Samuel Palmer senior may have been spurred by the knowledge that Palmer had now left school and was in need of further instruction. Presumably Palmer senior would not have taken up such a suggestion for financial reasons. But it does also hint at what might be the main reason why Palmer left Merchant Taylors'. There are no records of his schoolwork there, but it is quite likely that he had difficulties as he had not been prepared beforehand for the rigorous learning of classical texts that were then the basis of instruction there.[77] Beatson, by contrast, had been tutored before going to Merchant Taylors'. Samuel Palmer had only had the doubtless erratic and unsystematic instruction of his father before being thrown into the rigours of school life.

This is only a surmise, yet it seems highly likely that, quite apart from any unhappiness at bullying from older boys (not all of whom, as Beatson's presence makes clear, were unsympathetic to him) that he was having difficulties with the schoolwork. In his autobiographical letter Palmer states that his parents '… thinking me too fragile for school, gave me at home the groundwork of education; sound Latin, so far as it went, with the rudiments of Greek'.[78] Yet how 'sound' was this education likely to have been from a kind but weakly mother and an indulgent and eccentric father? Palmer's 'so far as it went', shows that he himself was uncertain of the extent of the value of his Latin instruction. We know from his later life that he was immensely wide in his reading and also continued to have ambitions as a translator of Latin – an ambition finally achieved at the end of his life with the translation of Virgil's *Eclogues*.[79] But even at that stage he required assistance, first from his son Thomas More and then from his friend Edward Calvert, both of whom had had thorough classical educations at school.

It seems that the debacle of the Merchant Taylors' School may have laid to rest once and for all what Palmer had hinted in his own autobiographical letter as his first ambition. For when he described how, at the age of thirteen 'It was thought right that I should attempt painting as a profession' he continues, 'Perhaps this arose from misinterpreting an instinct of another kind, a passionate love – the expression is not too strong – for the traditions and monuments of the Church.'[80] It may well be that part of the original attraction between the two boys was that Beatson also had ambitions to go into the Church. In Beatson's case these were fulfilled after he had won a scholarship to Cambridge. He was ordained in 1828.[81]

While clearly mainly interested in intellectual and religious matters, Beatson did show some interest in art on his visits to the Palmers: '1817 wed 12 november 5-8½ at Mr Palmers he drew ships and gave / Anby 10 paints'. From this is would seem that Palmer senior also had some artistic gifts and interests. It would also seem that Palmer senior stocked paints in his shop. This is not altogether surprising, since Palmer senior's shop is recorded as having been a stationers as well as a booksellers. It would also seem that Palmer senior dealt to some degree in prints. Over the next two years Beatson made several references to acquiring paints and brushes from Palmers, either for himself or for his younger brother Anby. It would seem that colours were quite pricey for young students in those day and individual acquisitions were often noted as something special, as when on 9 December 1817 he recorded 'Purple and Green added to my collection'.[82] Often these were related to what must have been school projects, such as colouring maps.[83]

The first direct reference to Samuel Palmer's own art also occasioned the first reference to the artist's temperamental behaviour. This was the 'awful row with Palmer' that occurred on 18 November 1817. The day was also memorable for the burial of Princess Charlotte. As usual, Beatson is laconic, but it must have been a key event since he recorded it in three separate places; in the main body of his diary and in the two synopses of key events that he wrote out to summarize the occasion. The two synoptic references are as follows: 'Pr. Charlotte buried – awful row with Palmer.'[84] 'Palmer came and made an awful row.'[85] The significance of the day being the funeral of Princess Charlotte was that the boys were allowed a day off school. This gave them the chance to meet socially in the daytime. Palmer seems to have availed himself of this to come and make some kind of protest. The protest was followed by Palmer showing Beatson some of his pictures. There seems to have been a reconciliation since they later went to chapel in the company of Samuel Palmer senior and the day ended with Palmer presenting Beatson with a picture. The full day is recorded in Beatson's diary as follows:

> Wednesday Nov. 19, 1817 (holiday)
> 6-9½ Breakfast. The Bakers sold no rolls.
> 9½-11 Rare fun in the warehouse Anby platted string – made a map
> 11-1 Heard Mr. Watkins at S. Swithins
> 1-3 S.Palmer came, made an awful noise he bro[t] us paint box,
> brush drawing book & pencils shewed us several drawings
> 3-4 Dinner Roast Beef. P.C. [Princess Charlotte] buried today
> 4-6 Played in my room, looked over Hebrew
> 6-7 Tea. Went with father & S.P. to Long Acre chapel – heard Mr. Howell
> 7-9½ went home with S.P. changed III vol of Popular Tales for
> I of Popular and Moral tales he gave me a picture.[86]

By this time other evidence suggests that Samuel Palmer was already prized for his art. The earliest sign of this is a drawing done in 1812 and preserved by his mother.[87] However this work hardly suggests precocity. The next direct reference comes from the first surviving letter which contains Samuel Palmer's writing. This was at the end of a letter written by his mother Martha to Palmer Senior when she and her children had arrived in Margate for a holiday, dated

13 June 1814. In this Martha reports that 'Sam has been writing half a copy and taking a sketch of Margate Church for Mr. Samson Covell.'[88]

For the most part there is no account by Beatson of the subjects of drawings by Palmer that he saw and occasionally acquired. However, the one record of a subject is surprising as it is different from the kind of topographical work that Palmer is known to have been doing at that time. '1818 Wednesday 23 September … 6 - 8½ Palmer came, made him draw a / steampacket heard of the map handkerchief.'[89] This reference is of interest as steampackets had only started running on the Thames in 1815.[90] Beatson had a strong interest in ships and was himself a keen boatman, so it is not surprising that he coerced Palmer into making a drawing of this novel form of nautical transport.

After 1818 Beatson's interest in art seems to have declined – perhaps because this was no longer a requirement in his school work – and he makes no further reference to this side of Palmer's life. This is all the more striking, since this was precisely the time when Palmer was beginning to develop a professional competence in art, under the guidance of the art tutor William Wate.[91] Although continuing to go to Palmer senior for books, Beatson makes no reference to the dramatic success that Samuel Palmer had in getting his work accepted by the British Institution and the Royal Academy, nor does he comment on the fine if conventional watercolours and wash drawings Palmer was now producing. His comments on Palmer seem to relate now only to his peculiarities – as when he referred 'S. Palmers prejudices'.[92] Perhaps he thought by this time that Palmer was too full of himself; very much the confident young man about town, as recorded by one of Palmer's new artistic friends, Henry Walter, in a drawing now in the British Museum dated July 1819.[93] There is some evidence that Palmer was making efforts to continue the relationship. There are a number of records in 1819 of him visiting Beatson for tea and on one occasion, on 31 July, he made what seems to have been a characteristic extravagant remark: '5-6 Tea. S. Palmer here. Canister [?] for £500 / for which he would not give 6~d.'[94]

The growing distancing between Palmer and Beatson seems to have increased after Palmer senior moved his shop from Houndsditch to 10 Broad Street, Bloomsbury. This is usually given as having taken place in 1820, when the first printed references to the new premises occur.[95] However it might be inferred from an entry in Beatson's diary that the move had already taken place: '1819 Thur 23 December … 8-10 Trotted to Mr Greens 21 Marybone str / and back, called at Mr Palmers for the / Adventurer – knocked a long time at / last S. Palmer appeared.'[96] Marylebone Street, being in the West End, would indeed have been quite a 'trot' from Beatson's home in the city and Bloomsbury would have been on the way back, whereas Houndsditch would have been quite in the opposite direction. The fact that Beatson had trouble raising anyone at the shop mid-morning a couple of days before Christmas suggests that the establishment was not being very well run at the time. Perhaps this is yet another sign of Mr Palmer's poor business sense; or maybe things were in disarray because the move had been so recent. In any case he seems to have been disappointed in his quest, since he returned on 5 January 1820 to purchase *The Adventurer* for 8/-.[97]

Beatson continued to visit the Bloomsbury shop, and also kept some social contact with Palmer, at least until the summer of 1820. One of the last references to Palmer is also the most fulsome. It is the account of a trip made up river from London Bridge to Brentford and back on Wednesday 28 June. It was clearly an important adventure, and Beatson records it in great detail from the time he went down to London Bridge before breakfast 'to know if there was any wind', to their return at 9.30 in the evening when they enjoyed sailing in the swell of a steamship.[98] Beatson recorded the places they stopped – such as Battersea for a beer and Chiswick for swimming – and minor mishaps such as his getting sunburnt and his brother Anby getting a splinter in his hand. But while the general tone of the account is good humoured, it contains one damning judgement. This is in relation to Palmer. For near the end of his account he made the following comment: 'Palmer / a fool and cannot row nor steer.' This failure of Palmer's might have been all the worse since Beatson was clearly a keen waterman much given to rowing. There are several mentions of rowing, for example, when on holiday in Margate.[99]

After this references to Palmer gradually peter out. As Beatson intensified his classical studies in preparation for his time at Cambridge, and Palmer began to develop artistic friendships in his new Bloomsbury home, they seem to have had increasingly less reason to be in contact with each other. There is no sign, either, that Beatson took any interest in Palmer's subsequent career, even though he lived to 1872, by which time Palmer was a successful exhibiting watercolourist and also had a certain status in the literary world as a witness to the final years of William Blake. Perhaps they had never been that close. The contact with Palmer senior and the books he could provide was probably always more valuable to Beatson than contact with the artistic and eccentric son. Nevertheless his comments – brief though they are – can provide valuable glimpses of Palmer and his home environment in his formative years, and help to give some substance to a period about which we know all too little.

Notes

1.   A.H. Palmer, *The Life and Letters of Samuel Palmer, Painter and Etcher*, London: Seeley, 1892, p. 8.

2.   Letter sent to F.G. Stephens, editor of *The Portfolio*, 1 November 1871. Published in *The Portfolio*, no. 35, November 1872, pp. 163-4.

3.   *Portfolio*, p. 164.

4.   The most significant of these are now in the Linnell archive at the Fitzwilliam Museum, Cambridge.

5.   Palmer, *Life and Letters*.

6.   This diary is now in Pembroke College, Cambridge, Acc. Nos: 29.I.11, 29.I.12. As the pagination is not continuous, references are to the dates of entries. I am grateful to the Master and Fellows of Pembroke College for permission to publish quotations from the diary here.

7.   These are listed in Palmer, *Life and Letters*, pp. 405, 407.

8.   Palmer, *Life and Letters*, p. 3.

9.   Ibid., p. 8.

10. Geoffrey Grigson, *Samuel Palmer; The Visionary Years*, London: Kegan Paul, 1947, p. 8.

11. Raymond Lister, *Samuel Palmer. A Biography*, London: Faber and Faber, 1974, p. 27.

12. Raymond Lister (ed.), *The Letters of Samuel Palmer*, Oxford: Clarendon Press, 1974, vol. 1, 1974, p. 5. The original letter is now in the Linnell Archive, Fitzwilliam Museum, Cambridge.

13. Lister, *Letters*, p. 5.

14. Beatson Diary. The first reference is 2 May 1817.

15. St Mary Newington, *Assessment for the Relief of the Poor and for other purposes…*, 1808, November, p. 12. The Rate Books are now preserved in the Southwark Local History Library.

16. Lister, *Biography*, p. 18; Lister refers to Christopher Palmer as a feltmaker. However the firm is described as a Hatters in contemporary trade directories. For example, *Kent's Directory for the Year 1794. Cities of London and Westminster, & Borough of Southwark* lists 'Moxon, Palmer & Norman, Hatters, 40 Cannon Street' (p. 130). The confusion arises as hats at this time were principally made from felt. In the eighteenth century a hatter had to be a freeman of the Feltmakers' Company in order to trade in the City of London. This was confirmed by a Charter in the age of George III. See R.J. Blackman, *The Soul of the City: London's Livery Companies*, London: Sampson Low, 1931, p. 130.

17. Lister, *Biography*, p. 18.

18. Christopher Palmer is listed as a ratepayer at that address in the Poor Rate Books of St Mary's Newington from at least 1790 to 1808, the year of his death. In 1809 the ratepayer named was G. Jones, which implies that the Palmer family had vacated the property after Christopher Palmer's death.

19. Mary Boast, *The Story of Walworth*, London Borough of Southwark, 2005, pp. 8-9.

20. St Mary Newington Rate Books, Grigson, *Visionary Years*, p. 3. In his will, proved in 1827, William Giles gives his address as Apollo Buildings.

21. These details are recorded by Samuel Palmer in a letter of 1880. See Lister, *Letters*, pp. 1021-3.

22. Lister, *Biography*, p. 19.

23. See Lister, *Letters*, p. 1021.

24. St Mary Newington Rate Books 1797-1802.

25. Nathaniel Palmer is first recorded as paying the land tax for 12 Aldermanbury in the year 1802/3. See land tax returns, Cripplegate Within, 1802/3. Ms 11, 316/310. Guildhall Library London.

26. The family genealogies are given by Palmer himself in a letter to a cousin, the Rt Rev. Monsignor William Giles, 9 August 1880; Lister, *Letters*, pp. 1021-3. The three elder sons all had family names – respectively William, Christopher and Edward (the name of one of Palmer's uncles). None of the others, however, included the name Palmer in their names.

27. Lister, *Biography*, p. 18.

28. St Mary Newington Rate Book.

29. Lister, *Letters*, p. 283.

30. Ibid., p. 823.

31. Will of Christopher Palmer, 1808. Public Record Office. Prob. 11/1491.

32. Lister, *Biography*, p. 19.

33. Beatson Diary, 2 May 1817.

34.   This information can be found in the land tax books in Guildhall Library.

35.   The Proceedings of the Old Bailey. Ref: t18151025-68.

36.   Proceedings of the Old Bailey. Eighth session 1815, p. 454.

37.   Lister, *Biography*, p. 18.

38.   Rowland had in fact delivered twelve pairs of breeches and had then replaced the receipt that he had received for these with one for 18 pairs. The lightness of the sentence makes one think something was odd here, and Palmer senior certainly could be seen as having been naive in paying the bill without having checked it properly. This would fit in with his reputation of being dreamy and bad with money.

39.   Land Rent payments for Houndsditch – Guildhall library.

40.   Grigson speculates that Palmer Senior might have taken over from another Palmer running a bookshop in Bermondsey Street in the period, but gives no reason why he should suppose this. Grigson, *Visionary Years*, p. 2.

41.   Beatson Diary, 2 May 1817.

42.   Land Rent payments for Houndsditch – Guildhall library.

43.   Land Rent payments for Houndsditch – Guildhall library.

44.   *Oxford Dictionary of National Biography* (ODNB), Oxford: Oxford University Press, 2004, vol. 4, p. 562.

45.   Grigson, *Visionary Years*, pp. 2, 146 (n. 2). Unfortunately the copy of the sale catalogue consulted by Grigson at the British Library appears to be no longer available.

46.   Beatson Diary, 4 December 1819.

47.   Beatson Diary, 22 March 1820. Miles Bland, *Geometrical problems deducible from the first six books of Euclid...*, Cambridge, 1819. His *Algebraical Problems* (1812) was a very popular school textbook; a ninth edition was published in 1849. *ODNB*, vol. 6, p. 165.

48.   E.g. '1817 thur 30 October Mr. Palmer made me a magic square'; 31 March 1819 'Magic squares – feast with S.Palmer', Beatson Diary.

49.   E.g. '1818 Friday 1 May... 6½ - 10 At Mr Palmers – Kalidoscopes', Beatson Diary.

50.   Beatson Diary, 26 May 1817.

51.   *The Codex Alexandrinus*, London, British Library, MS Royal 1. D. V-VIII.

52.   Beatson Diary, 5 January 1820.

53.   Beatson Diary, 12 November 1817.

54.   For example; '1817 wed nov 19. 7-9 ½ went home with SP changed III vol of / Popular Tales for I of Popular and Moral Tales'.

55.   Edgeworth also set a personal example. She was tireless in her support of the local Irish community on her father's Irish estate and was one of those few among the Anglo-Irish who campaigned vigorously for the relief of the Irish during the potato famine.

56.   E.g. 'boiled beef and mashed potatoes' (1817 30 October).

57.   E.g. 19 Sept 1820 'supper sausages', 20 Sept 1820 'supper cold pork'.

58.   E.g. 'two eggs' (1817 May 26), 'supper eggs' (1817 21 October), 'bread and cheese' (1818 15 July).

59.   Palmer *Life and Letters*, p. 6.

60.   'Monday 16 February ... 5½ - 9 At Palmers borrowed Parkes' chemistry'. Presumably the book was Samuel Parkes, *Rudiments of Chemistry; Illustrated by Experiments*, London, 1810. This was an abridgement of his popular *Chemical Catechism* (London, 1806) intended for school use. It ran into many editions in the early nineteenth century.

61.   Beatson Diary, 9 December 1817.

62.   Beatson Diary, 9 December 1818.

63. This fact seems to be confirmed by the fact that both Beatson and his brother were baptized as adults at Barnard Castle in Durham. Beatson was baptized there 22 January 1828. It is possible that the baptism took place in Barnard Castle to avoid attention being drawn to the fact that he was not yet baptized. Interestingly, 1828 was the year that Beatson was ordained as an Anglican priest. [GEN UKI. Barnard Castle Baptism Records 1813-37 – Transcribed by Major L.M. Kenyon-Fuller. genuki.cs.ncl.ac.uk/Transcriptions/DUR/XBAR_A-C.html]

64. Beatson Diary, 17 November 1817.

65. ODNB, vol. 28 pp. 513-14.

66. ODNB, vol. 10, pp. 879-87.

67. ODNB, vol. 14, pp. 284-6.

68. Beatson Diary, 5 April 1818.

69. The Oxford English Dictionary records the first use of the word in the pejorative sense as 1900.

70. Beatson Diary , 20 September 1818.

71. Records at Merchant Taylors' Hall. See Grigson, *Visionary Years*, p. 141, note 18.

72. Beatson Diary, 26 May 1817.

73. Grigson, *Visionary Years*, p. 141, note 18.

74. Charles Dickens (ed.), *The Life of Charles James Matthews*, 2 vols, London: Macmillan 1879, pp. 8, 26-7.

75. Lister, *Biography*, p. 23.

76. Beatson Diary, 2 January 1818.

77. For the school curriculum in the early nineteenth century see F.W.M. Draper, *Four Centuries of Merchant Taylors' School, 1561-1961*, London: Oxford University Press, 1962, pp. 122-3.

78. Lister, *Letters*, 1974, p. 822 (1871 (1)).

79. William Vaughan, Elizabeth E. Barker, Colin Harrison et al., *Samuel Palmer (1805-1881): Vision and Landscape*, London: British Museum Press, 2005, pp. 240-43.

80. Lister, *Letters*, p. 823 (1871 (1)).

81. *ODNB*, vol. 4, p. 562.

82. Beatson Diary, 9 December 1817.

83. '1817 Wednesday 22 October (doctors day).... 7-9 Palmer bt. Some tints for color maps. Supper'. (Beatson Diary.)

84. Beatson Synoptic Diary (29.I.11), p. 21.

85. Beatson Synoptic Diary (29.I.11), p. 21.

86. Beatson Diary, 19 November 1817.

87. This is now in the Huntington Library, San Marino. (66.5). See Raymond Lister, *A Catalogue Raisonné of the Works of Samuel Palmer*, Cambridge: Cambridge University Press, 1988, p. 25, no. 1.

88. Lister, *Letters*, p. 3. Samson Covell was a relative of Mrs Palmer's.

89. Beatson Diary, 23 September 1818.

90. The interest in this new form of transport is recorded in a publication of 1819; 'In 1815, a new and interesting mode of travelling commenced on the Thames in steam packets. These vessels are provided with steam-engines and wheels, called paddles, to propel the vessel with greater rapidity, even against wind and tide, and over stormy seas. From the costliness of these vessels, their extensive accommodations, and splendid decorations, they are now universally designated "STEAM YACHTS".' *Leigh's New Picture of London*. Printed for Samuel Leigh, 18, Strand by W. Clowes, Northumberland Court, 1819.

91. Palmer, *Life and Letters*, p. 7.

92. Beatson Diary, 31 March 1819.

93.   Vaughan, Barker, Harrison et al., *Vision and Landscape*, no. 3, pp. 68-9.

94.   Beatson Diary, 31 July 1819.

95.   For example in the Royal Academy catalogue of that year. See Palmer, *Life and Letters*, p. 8.

96.   Beatson Diary, 23 December 1819.

97.   Beatson Diary. *The Adventurer* seems to have been the periodical to which Samuel Johnson contributed a number of celebrated essays. It was reprinted several times in the later eighteenth century.

98.   Beatson Diary, 28 June 1820.

99.   Beatson Diary, 16 August, 4 September 1817.

2

Ancients and moderns: Samuel Palmer and the 'progress of water colours', 1822-1833

Greg Smith

Looking at the earliest works of Samuel Palmer, there is nothing in the conventional landscape studies produced by the young artist to prepare one for the highly idiosyncratic sepia landscapes of 1825 such as 'A Rustic Scene' (Ashmolean Museum), or the intense 'Self Portrait' (Ashmolean Museum) of about the same date, that signal the outset of his major contribution to British art. The material is not copious, but beginning with the evidence of a youthful vocation for landscape watercolour in the form of a tiny drawing by the seven-year-old Palmer, 'Windmill and House' (The Huntington Library, Art Collections, San Marino), there is enough to suggest a typical development of a young landscapist, albeit largely self-taught. A sketchbook from 1819 contains the sort of studies that one might expect from a budding watercolourist at this date, including pencil sketches made from London scenery, drawings of animals, and cloud effects worked in watercolours with supplementary written notes. An oil sketch from nature, 'Syon Park' (1819, Yale Center for British Art, New Haven), and, from 1821, a watercolour study of a 'Storm Approaching, Hailsham, Sussex' (Yale Center for British Art) suggest an assiduous training as an observer of natural effects. Then there are two studies of buildings, also plausibly dated to 1821, which, with their picturesque compositions, are thoroughly conventional. 'Evening' (Victoria and Albert Museum, London) is close to the aquatints produced after David Cox's sepia drawings for a drawing manual entitled *A Treatise on Landscape Painting and Effect in Water Colours: From the First Rudiments to the Finished Picture* (1813-14), where the technique is used to teach students effects of light and shade prior to engaging with the more complex use of full colour.

The startling shift from these conventional works to the radically different sketchbook of 1824 and the sepia landscapes of 1825 is made all the more so by a complete gap in the visual record from 1822-23. This is especially frustrating given the evidence of Palmer's letters and diaries of the time, which indicate a heady cocktail of new and unconventional influences: the prints of Dürer and Bonasone; the works of early northern masters, as well as his older contemporaries John Linnell and William Blake; and the efforts of the other Ancients. These were amongst the last artists that one might have expected a young watercolourist to look to, and their influence resulted in a complete disruption of what appeared to have been a hitherto well-trodden career path. But, whilst much attention has been paid to the art that helped to fuel the radical, albeit off-stage shift in his work, what Palmer termed the 'pit of modern art' from which he claimed to have been rescued, following his meeting with Linnell in 1822, has tended to be overlooked.[1] The specific character of this 'modern art' is, however, worthy of careful consideration because, without a sense of what it was that Palmer was reacting against, we are in danger of losing sight of the strangeness of the landscapes of the Shoreham period. Moreover, Palmer's work in the period up to c.1833, as well as comments in his letters and sketchbooks, takes on a more radical edge in the context of the discursive norms of the landscape watercolour as a modern and progressive art. More specifically, it was the newly-christened commodity, 'the modern English style of painting in water colours' – defined as a distinct alternative to the older 'tinted drawing' – which fuelled Palmer's search for an 'ancient' alternative.[2] The landscape watercolour, as it was characterized within progressive critical, historical and pedagogical discourses, was, I contend here, the 'modern practice' of painting which provided the crucial counter influence on Palmer's work during the Shoreham period.[3]

The period during which Palmer went absent from the historical record, that is between 1822-24, coincided with a new level in the celebration of watercolour as a modern progressive art, making Palmer's subsequent reaction all the more dramatic. The first stage in the development of a new critical identity for the watercolour medium had occurred in the second half of the 1790s, with the exhibition at the Royal Academy of the landscapes of Thomas Girtin and J.M.W. Turner, as well as the historical subjects of Richard Westall. Large scale works such as Turner's 'Caernarvon Castle' (private collection) or Girtin's dramatic and sublime 'View near Beddgelert' (National Museums and Galleries of Wales, Cardiff), both shown to considerable acclaim in 1799, were widely welcomed as marking a new epoch predicated on watercolour equalling or even surpassing the qualities of oil painting.[4] With the foundation of the Society of Painters in Water Colours in 1804, and the early critical and commercial success of their exhibitions after 1805, a more complex picture of progress emerged, particularly within a new type of fashionable cultural journal exemplified by the *Beau Monde* and Rudolph Ackermann's *Repository of Arts*.[5] The 'painting in water colours', it was said, was the outcome of a progress driven by technical and material improvements directed towards a broadly naturalistic agenda of a landscape of light and atmospheric effects.

Broader historical judgements, however, had to wait until a series of exhibitions which showed contemporary works in the context of earlier material for the first time. The example was set by the collector Walter Fawkes who opened his London home in Grosvenor Square in 1819; his spectacular collection of English watercolours, dominated by Turner, amounted to a retrospective of a career in that medium which had developed away from the walls of the Royal Academy and which consequently appeared all the more startling to public and critics. This was followed in 1822-24 by three loan exhibitions organized by the engravers and publishers George and William Bernard Cooke in their gallery in Soho Square, which again featured Turner at the apex of contemporary achievement. Works such as the dazzling 'Sunrise: Whiting Fishing off Margate' (private collection, dated 1822 and exhibited in 1823), which was made for engraving in the Cookes' *Marine Views*, were praised in the press as the epitome of the landscape watercolour of effects.[6] Substantial groups of works by John Robert Cozens, Thomas Girtin and others allowed the Cookes to promote what they called 'a connected view of the Progress of the Art of Drawing in this Country, from the time of Paul Sandby, to the present day'.[7] Palmer would have been well aware of such developments, for George Cooke himself was known to have been a visitor to the family home and the youngster would therefore have had an opportunity, hitherto denied to generations of watercolourists, of seeing an overview of the development of their art.

Palmer may also have seen the retrospective loan exhibition organized by the Society of Painters in Water Colours (SPWC) itself in 1823 in response to the success of the Cookes' shows. This included works by Cozens and Girtin, as well as contemporary members, producing what the *Examiner* called 'an entertaining example of the progressive advance of a fascinating branch of painting'.[8] The exhibition was also significant for the impetus it provided for a series of articles by William Henry Pyne entitled 'The Rise and Progress of Water-Colour Painting in England', which were published in 1823-24 in the *Somerset House Gazette*. Pyne's description of a chain of innovative landscape artists provided the model for numerous progressive accounts of the medium in the following decade. A series of pioneering artists, went Pyne's argument, had transformed the humble tinted outline into the full blown 'painting in water colours' and this, he continued, manifested a triumph for the 'British school for this modern art' without equal abroad.[9] Of course, this simplistic model breaks down at a number of points, confusing as it does the different functions of watercolours; there were large paintings in watercolours in the 1760s and outline with touches of colour remained a key part of sketching practice in the 1820s; but it fulfilled the professional need of watercolourists, and the patriotic agenda of their supporters, for a triumphant history and proof of their positive role in the cultural and commercial life of the nation.[10] The exhibitions in the period 1822-24, together with the texts they inspired, made visible the fact that small incremental changes of watercolour practice across fifty years could now be promoted as a self-evident progress that the nation could be proud of.

The rapid adoption of the progressive model of watercolours and its widespread acceptance was made possible by the fact that Pyne and others based their arguments on an authoritative paradigm. Progress by stages, the result of the gradual refinements of individuals, had been the ordering principle behind art history since Giorgio Vasari writing in the sixteenth century; in turn, he had patterned his model on classical precursors who celebrated the progress of painting as gradual shift from line to tone, to colour. Within academic discourse James Barry, Henry Fuseli and others followed this paradigm, beginning with the story of the Corinthian Maid and the origin of painting in outlines, moving to others who 'have an idea of light and shadow', and concluding with the full use of colour.[11] Most writers described this progress within broader cycles of improvement and decline, but from the standpoint of England in 1824, such a model had a less ambiguous message. An art supposedly newly minted in England and still improving had no need for renewal and was not subject to the corollary of progress: decline.

There were, nevertheless, some dissenting voices: a conservative type of critic in the 1790s, opposed to any form of artistic innovation at a time of fears of revolution; supporters of oil painting in the first decade of the new century who felt threatened by the commercial success of the new commodity, the 'painting in water colours'; and established watercolourists who continued to work in old-fashioned styles.[12] However, it was quite another matter for a young artist to reject quite so decisively the comforting consensus of a newly established national triumph. We can get some idea of Palmer's dissatisfaction with the dominant aesthetic of the day from a now lost memorandum of a trip to Dulwich, undertaken sometime in 1823-24 and which was recorded by the artist's son A.H. Palmer in his *Life and Letters*. The text describes a trip to what was then the only public gallery in the country, where Palmer studied a copy of a Leonardo head and shoulders (now attributed to Piero di Cosimo) and landscapes by Dutch masters. Further comments on two contemporary watercolourists, David Cox and George Barret the younger, as well as the older deceased master, Thomas Girtin, indicate a visit to a second location nearby. Given the uncertainty of the date, it is possible that it was even the 1823 SPWC retrospective, where all three artists were heavily featured, though perhaps a more likely candidate was the collection of John Allnutt in nearby Clapham Common. He was a major lender to the 1823 retrospective, and works he owned by the three watercolourists tally closely with Palmer's comments.

The first point to make regarding Palmer's only surviving comment about contemporary watercolourists from outside his circle is that he selected three artists whose subject matter – pastoral themes, rural retirement and twilight – matched his own interests, ignoring, in the process, a wide range of more highly thought of artists, including, of course, Turner. David Cox, in particular, barely figured in the critical record at this time, though Palmer knew his drawing manual as a young man. The Cox watercolour Palmer referred to may have been the 'Scene in Herefordshire' (private collection) shown at the 1823 retrospective, lent from Allnutt's collection, and now identified as 'Dindor Hill and Rotheros Woods'.[13] This type of scene, conceded Palmer, is 'pretty ... sweet', but 'not grand, not profound. Carefully avoid getting into that style', he admonished himself; it 'is elegant and beautiful but too light and superficial'.[14] The combination of a topographical view and a concern with atmospheric effect meant for Palmer that the pastoral scene cannot fulfil its potential as a vehicle for moral sentiment; in Cox's hands it is 'not learned enough', he concluded. This too was the problem with the work of George Barret the younger, whose more idealized 'Retirement' (private collection) was shown at the 1823 retrospective, again on loan from Allnutt.[15] The reclining figure amongst the trees in the middle left is a familiar motif from Palmer's work, and, indeed, there are a number of parallels with other works by Barret then in the Allnutt collection, including an untraced composition titled 'Evening' and another listed as 'The Happy Valley'.[16] This work, Palmer reflected, has a 'beautiful sentiment and it is derived from Nature; but', he continued, 'Nature has properties which lie still deeper, and when they are brought out the picture must be most elaborate and full of matter'. Palmer's 'The Valley Thick with Corn' (Ashmolean Museum) of 1825, a Christian, Gothic reworking of Barret's classical retirement theme, illustrates what he meant by 'full of matter'. Such a superior picture, he added, must 'be most simple of style, and be what would have pleased men in the early ages, when poetry was at its acme, and yet men lived in a simple, pastoral way'.[17] The critique of Barret revolves around a typical primitivist inversion, whereby commonly accepted signifiers of modernity – a highly sophisticated technique, and a style which, instead of enumerating individual parts, emphasizes breadth, unity and easy transitions within a rational composition redolent of the seventeenth-century landscape masters – are dismissed as superficial and corrupt in contrast to a distant ideal identified as the 'early days'.

It is telling that Girtin's earlier 'twilight' subject is, in contrast to the works of Barret and Cox, unambiguously characterized by Palmer as being 'beautiful'. The 'twilight' subject from the Allnutt collection that fits Palmer's comments is a version of 'The Stepping Stones on the Wharfe' from c.1800 (private collection). The deeper and simplified palette, and a sparer, even severe style, coupled perhaps with Girtin's early position in the progressive chain, made him less open to censure in subjects such as this. Nonetheless, it still prompted Palmer to pose the question 'did he know the grand old men?', and to admonish himself in turn to remember to 'Look at Albert Dürer'.[18] As Pyne noted in his account of Girtin's early training with Edward Dayes and then at Thomas Monro's house, the earliest masters he looked to were eighteenth-century Venetian view painters and recent British topographers and architectural draftsmen.[19]

Palmer's alienation from the modern art of 'painting in water colours' went far beyond a search for stylistic alternatives, however. Indeed, as his comment about the attractions of a 'simple style' commensurate with 'men in the early ages' suggests, it reflected a rejection of the broadly positive contemporary view of the links between the progress of society and the arts.[20] This is certainly the tenor of the autobiographical passage in which Palmer claimed that his meeting with Linnell in 1822 had rescued him from the 'pit of modern art'. The passage appeared in a now lost sketchbook quoted by A.H. Palmer, and it presumably dates from 1824-25. The artist began by outlining a two-stage journey 'in the pursuit of grand art', beginning with what he termed the 'primitive and infantine feeling with which we set out'. Looking to 'my very early years', he claimed, 'I felt the finest scenery and the country in general with a very strong and pure feeling'. From this primal state, however, learning 'arithmetic and grammar' meant that 'my feeling and taste left me' and that 'by the time I had practised for about five years I entirely lost all feeling for art'. And it was then that 'it pleased God to send Mr. Linnell as a good angel from Heaven to pluck me from the pit of modern art'. Eighteen months of struggle later, and, he continued, 'I have just enough cleared my eyes from the slime of the pit to see what a miserable state I am now in'. With the beginning of a new sketchbook, he concluded, I must 'try to work with a child's simple feeling and with the industry of humility'.[21]

This passage can be read in various ways, ranging from a parable of Christian redemption, to the primitivist trope of the innocent child, symbol of nature, corrupted by knowledge. However, I want to concentrate on a more specific artistic level, whereby Palmer claimed to reverse the progressive development of a conventional watercolourist, characterizing it instead as a decline. Palmer's target here was the contemporary commonplace that the training of the student watercolourist, and increasingly the amateur through the medium of a new type of drawing manual which appeared in the first decade of the new century, should, like the historical progress of watercolours, be based on a series of progressive steps; what he dismissed as the 'arithmetic and grammar' of art.[22] These included moving from simple to complex forms and from copying to invention; but, more importantly, students were also encouraged to progress from drawing simple outlines, to studying light and shade as in Palmer's sepia study 'Evening', and only then to move on to seek to master colour. As Sir Joshua Reynolds stated, the 'progress of an individual Student bears a great resemblance to the progress and advancement of the Art itself', and for the young watercolourist this meant leaving behind the outline drawing and the sepia or Indian ink tonal study on the progressive road to maturity.[23] According to Palmer, however, such a training without the counter influence of a Linnell or 'the very ancient Italian and German masters' whom he claimed he 'would have admired and imitated' had he discovered them sooner, meant being driven along the road to a sterile modern art at the expense of a primal personal vision.[24] The 'Windmill and House', produced by the seven-year-old Palmer, was therefore not a point of departure but a sign of artistic integrity and a touchstone of 'primitive and infantine feeling'.

Palmer's opposition to the notion of progress in the arts did, of course, have some important precedents. William Hazlitt's articles on 'Why the Arts are not Progressive', dating from 1814, for instance, are well known today. In a passage that might be read as a prophetic critique of Pyne's progressive history of watercolours, he argued that anything which 'admits of gradual improvement' through 'the accumulation of borrowed advantages' must be mechanical, whilst 'true excellence ... depends on 'the genius, taste and feeling of the artist'.[25] Still better known, though even less typical of the period, was Blake's attack in his *Descriptive Catalogue* of 1809 on the critic who 'Pretends to Improve Fine Art'.[26] Blake argued that there can be no progress on two grounds. First, it is impossible to go beyond the 'perfect and eternal' works of a Michelangelo or a Shakespeare – a view shared by Palmer who talks in a letter of 1828 of the perfection of an 'eternal style, immutable by all the fashions of manners of opinion'.[27] And, second, since the first term in Blake's primitivist history of the arts is perfect, progress is by its nature impossible, decline inevitable.[28] What is often overlooked in considering Blake's arguments, however, is that they actually responded directly to the progressive discourse of watercolours with its emphasis on colour over line: 'the distinction that is made in modern times', he complained, 'between a Painting and a Drawing proceeds from ignorance of art'.[29] He even included in his 1809 exhibition a watercolour, 'The Angels Hovering Over the Body of Jesus in the Sepulchre' (Victoria and Albert Museum), to illustrate the modern fallacy that 'losing and obliterating the outline constitutes a Picture'.[30] Blake's attempt to counter the progressive paradigm of watercolours was in part a defence of his own artistic practice, but it also provided an inspiring example of how a passionate opposition to the dominant discourse of progress might engage with a contemporary manifestation in the new art of 'painting in water colours'.

Blake's emphasis on the fallacy of 'obliterating the outline' of a work is also a useful reminder that the modern landscape watercolour was characterized by a number of formal characteristics, which Palmer had to negate in order to forge an alternative language which might be 'most simple of style'. The autobiographical passage from 1824-25 again provides a good starting point, for it makes clear that Palmer sought above all to distance his art from 'what the moderns ... mean by what they call their "effects"'.[31] What he called, in the context of earlier Venetian and Flemish artists, those 'miserable varieties of imitation, spiritless and castrated, blind wanderings and glaring impudence'.[32] The modern landscape artist, it was widely accepted, was synonymous with a commitment to capturing and portraying the changing light and atmosphere of the British climate. By extension, the weather itself was deemed to support the artist in his or her vocation. Turner's statement as Professor of Perspective at the Royal Academy in the second decade of the century, that the English landscape painter is blessed by 'our variable climate where [all] the seasons are recognisable in one day, where all the vapoury turbulence involves the face of things, where nature seems to sport in all her dignity ... dispensing incidents for the artist's study', was crudely deterministic, but was a truism nonetheless for supporters of a triumphant national school.[33] The notion that landscape itself, seen through the ever changing effects of light and atmosphere, formed the basis of a national art was even more significant for supporters of watercolours. The nature of the medium, argued Pyne, was inherently suited to capturing 'an endless variety of effects' of 'light, shadow, and vapour'.[34] This was true both as a sketching medium, he continued, where 'coloured studies' alone might keep 'pace with the variable effects of atmosphere throughout the day', and for finished works, where the 'clearness, delicacy, and transparency' of the medium matched the effects of light and atmosphere which alone might transform a simple topographical subject.[35] Water, as the medium for the pigment, was therefore locked in a mutually reinforced relationship with the 'humid atmosphere of England' that it depicted.[36] As Amédée Pichot, a French visitor to Britain in the early 1820s admitted, the 'astonishing water-colour drawings' of the new school depended for their success on depicting 'the variations of the atmosphere at the different hours of the day, the accident of light and shade in clear and cloudy weather, or the effects of storm, and the difference of seasons'.[37]

Palmer's view of the landscape of effects, and his ambivalence to the contemporary vogue for sketching from nature was nicely caught in his 1828 letter to George Richmond, in which he mocked the well-known patron of watercolourists, Dr Thomas Monro. For Pyne and the earliest historians of watercolour, Monro was an heroic figure who provided a generation of young artists with support, access to his collections, and what amounted to an 'academy' for them to work in. He employed Turner and Girtin to copy the outlines of John Robert Cozens, for instance, and he accompanied the young John Varley on his earliest sketching trips. Monro's support for what Palmer dismissed as 'some of the first-rate housepainters and sky sloppers and brush blotters' was detrimental, however, because the patron demanded that they study directly from 'Nature', 'that great goddess Diana of nightmen, atheists, and bad artists', according to Palmer.[38] He was particularly scornful of the amateur's efforts to teach and ridiculed one sketching expedition with a young protégé and associate of his, Welby Sherman. These bold 'picturesque tourists', Palmer wrote, set out from Monro's cottage at Bushey, near London, where they settled to study neither 'sylvan simplicity or unadorned grandeur', but that 'admixture of nature and of art in which great critics assert perfection to consist'. This, he mocked, amounted to no more than a 'brick field'.[39] The landscape of effects is thus dismissed as an essentially suburban and debased form of nature. It is the province of the shallowest type of interfering amateur who dares to impose the limits of his vision on artists who are valued only for their literal, but inferior, accuracy – 'first-rate housepainters', or their indisciplined use of the medium – 'sky sloppers and brush blotters'.

An art which sought to capture transient effects through the bravura use of the brush was anathema to Palmer's belief that the highest form of landscape should transcend 'General nature'.[40] The humid atmosphere depicted by the modern landscape painter obscures individual parts, creates ambiguity and comes between the object and the spectator. However, as sketches such as 'A Barn with a Mossy Roof' (Yale Center for British Art) make clear, 'the drawing of choice positions and aspects of external objects is one of the varieties of study requisite to build up an artist'.[41] But that is all, since, as Palmer continues, 'the general characteristics of Nature's beauty not only differ from, but are, in some respects, opposed to those of Imaginative Art'.[42] 'General nature is wisely and beneficently adapted to refresh the senses and sooth the spirits of general observers', but it is inferior to a 'loftier vision' where 'art is the standard of nature'.[43] Here Palmer could not be more specific in his inversion of the central truism of the progressive watercolour that 'nature', as William Henry Pyne contended, is 'the prototype' of art.[44] All of the technical innovations and improvements highlighted by Pyne were directed towards the removal of conventions such as the prominent outline which obscured the convincing depiction of nature and her myriad effects. The contrast between the cloudscape of Constable's 'Tillington Church' (1834, British Museum, London) with the 'glorious round clouds' of Palmer's 'The Bright Cloud' (Tate, London) of a year or two earlier is instructive of the distinction. The latter, according to Palmer, 'an example how the elements of nature may be transmitted into the pure gold of art', the former, an assured exercise in the rapid use of watercolour washes to capture the effect of a sky which must change within moments.[45] As Palmer claimed, he may have made studies of the 'Shoreham scenery' for Linnell, but 'I will never be a naturalist by profession'.[46]

It was, however, Palmer's abandonment of colour, perhaps even more than his eschewing of natural effects, that marked out those of his works which were actually accepted for the Royal Academy's annual exhibitions from those of his contemporaries.[47] It is not always possible to identify which works were shown, but they included a number of the Oxford sepias such as the 'Rustic Scene' (1825), and some of what he called 'my blacks' which he submitted in 1832. One example of these Indian ink drawings is 'The Bright Cloud', which was perhaps exhibited as 'The Sheepfold' in 1832.[48] The 'Rustic Scene' may have been among the 'amazing' works which so shocked the critic of the *European Magazine* in 1825, prompting the writer to question the sanity of the

Hanging Committee and to suggest that the artist himself should be exhibited as a curiosity.[49] Of course, Palmer did not avoid colour in studies such as 'In a Shoreham Garden' (Victoria and Albert Museum) and other works which he painted for himself. But the artist maintained a strict distinction between finished works such as 'The Bright Cloud, which were submitted for public scrutiny, and those studies which were kept in the portfolio. Palmer thus chose to be judged by works which avoided the most obvious charm of the modern watercolour. Monochromes such as Michael 'Angelo' Rooker's 'Caesar's Tower, Warwick Castle' (Royal Academy of Arts, London) would have appeared old fashioned when they were shown at the Academy as early as 1794 and the next obvious precedent for Palmer's exhibits were the varnished brush-and-ink compositions shown by Alexander Cozens in the 1760s and 1770s such as 'Italian Landscape' (1766, Leeds City Art Gallery).[50] Moreover, the use of Indian ink had a further pejorative association for proponents of the 'progress of water colours', for it was commonly used for the neutral underdrawing of the humble 'tinted drawing'. The abandonment of the monochrome underpainting and the use instead of local colours in areas of shadow was, William Henry Pyne, stressed, the key technical innovation which made possible the emergence of the 'painting in water colours'.[51]

Palmer, though, looked beyond the narrow national and chronological limits of the progressive model of watercolours to the severe style of Michelangelo and Leonardo who, he claimed, provided 'models of light and shade so profound, subtle, intense, and commanding'.[52] And, amongst his contemporaries, Palmer preferred the 'mystic and dreamy glimmer' of Blake's wood engravings to the 'gaudy daylight of this world'.[53] Dusk scenes may have remained an essential subject for the modern watercolourist, but for critics in the 1820s and early 1830s, the special 'look of daylight' and the 'fresh clear natural mid-day tint of English scenery' was, in contrast to old-master gloom, the characteristic triumph of the modern medium and that required the colour that Palmer eschewed.[54] It would have taken a sharp-eyed visitor to have noticed, however, that whilst Palmer's exhibited watercolours were in monochrome they actually displayed, as Sarah Herring has argued, a number of technical features derived from the latest watercolour practice.[55] The use of extensive scratching out in 'The Bright Cloud', for instance, cannot be found in the work of Rooker's generation or earlier and it was a significant feature of Turner and Girtin's major exhibition pieces after 1797. Furthermore, the way in which Palmer often built up rich effects with superimposed washes of ink, the addition of gum arabic, and with areas of paper left bare for the highlights, or, alternatively, employed bodycolour for highlights as 'In a Shoreham Garden' (Victoria and Albert Museum), is unthinkable without the innovations in handling associated with the modern 'painting in water colours'. The resulting surface richness may have been typical of modern practice, but the lack of colour and the fact that Palmer's exhibits were consistently small in scale meant that, even as framed objects on public display, their origins in an art associated with the book were still evident. The shift from the 'tinted drawing' to the 'painting in water colours' was specifically characterized by Pyne and others as the development of a larger commodity suitable for close framing, rather than mounting for storage in a portfolio, though it was the even earlier association of watercolour with miniatures and book illustrations that Palmer would have evoked in his exhibits.[56] This would have been even clearer when the Oxford sepias were exhibited in their original, and subsequently discarded mounts, which were inscribed by Palmer with verses from Milton and other literary texts.[57] The progress of the 'painting in water colours' meant moving on from an art suited to the portfolio or the book, but even as Palmer's works incorporated some new stylistic elements they resisted this key functional change.

Any signifiers of modernity employed by Palmer, would, in any case, have been overwhelmed for contemporary viewers by the presence in his work of strong bounding lines between forms. This feature, together with an often disorientating absence of aerial perspective, would have linked his works with reproductive prints in a way which flatly contradicted the basic assumption of the 'progress of water colours': that it was an art of painting. The association of his watercolour practice with prints was made explicit by Palmer himself, for in his 1824 sketchbook he described the use of outline, 'which cannot be too black', as one of the keys to the 'much hoped for & prayed for revival of art'.[58] In a passage that anticipates the Oxford sepias such as 'The Skirts of a Wood', he called upon himself to 'insert those masses of little forms like the leaves of a near tree which serve instead of shadows & themselves make a tint all this while fattening up the outline, till as near as you can ... make it like the prints of the Georgics'. Presumably referring to Blake's wood-engraved illustrations to Thornton's *Pastorals of Virgil* from 1821, Palmer was reversing the popular truism that watercolour approached closest to its essence as it shed the linear language of the print.[59] The passage which begins 'Remember that most excellent remark of Mr. B's' also indicates that he had in mind Blake's broader argument about the primacy of outline for an imaginative art opposed to the blurring of lines within the landscape of effects; what Blake termed the modern error of 'losing and obliterating the outline' led, he claimed, to 'chaos' and the absence of 'character'.[60] 'The great and golden rule of art', Blake argued in the *Descriptive Catalogue*, is 'That the more distinct, sharp, and wiry the bounding line, the more perfect the work of art'.[61] Our familiarity with such idiosyncratic statements, and with the outline drawings of Flaxman and other figurative artists from what is now commonly termed the neo-classical period, again obscures the radical nature of Blake's position as it was adapted by Palmer for the landscape watercolour. Since, not only was the move away from line sanctioned by recent historical precedent, but evident line in this context had a series of mechanical and unpalatable associations.

Outline was thus the basis for processes of mechanical replication employed, for instance, with map-making and cheap hand-coloured prints, and with utilitarian practices such as sign painting, silhouettes and cut paper, and coach painting.[62] The strong outlines of 'A Rustic Scene' may today signify a radical primitivist agenda derived from early Northern European woodcuts, but for contemporary watercolourists the association with reproductive prints would have appeared perverse if not damaging to professional aspirations based on the superior status of the painter.

Palmer soon jettisoned some of the more extreme stylistic features of the Oxford sepias, such as the obsessive linear detail within the forms, but strong outlines remained in both the colour sketches and the Indian ink compositions, whether finished works such as 'The Bright Cloud' or studies such as 'Evening: A Church Among Trees' (Tate, London). As Sarah Herring has again noted, this meant that the link with prints remained strong, simply shifting ground from woodcut and wood engraving to mezzotint.[63] This tonal technique, which required working from dark to light by scratching out the dark tones on the copper plate, suited Palmer's favoured evening subjects where complex forms might be reduced to simple silhouettes. This emphasis remains even in daytime scenes such as 'A Young Man Yoking an Ox' (Ashmolean Museum), where Palmer's use of the archaic convention of a series of scene-like flats stepping back into the distance makes a startling contrast with the contemporary employment of an increasingly complex aerial perspective. Works such as this therefore reject both the conventional progression of space, determined by the logic of the Claudean composition employed by George Barret in his 'Retirement', and the careful gradation of tone to create the illusion of space found in watercolours such as Turner's 'Margate'. Palmer's response to the modern watercolour landscape as a triumph of aerial perspective – of melting and illusive distances – again recalls Blake in its insistence on the primacy of the self-contained object. Referring to a favoured view near Dulwich, Palmer noted in a lost sketchbook that 'the distant hills seem the most powerful objects in colour, and clear force of line', concluding that 'we are not troubled with aerial perspective in the valley of vision'.[64]

Such a view was self-evidently absurd to contemporary commentators such as Pyne, who argued that the progressive drive towards the eradication of line in the watercolour landscape was sanctioned by the fact that it is 'entirely at variance with nature'.[65] John Robert Cozens owed his position in the progressive chain to precisely his perfection of 'aerial perspective' at the expense of a landscape of bounded forms.[66] In fact, Palmer agreed that 'There is no line in nature', though there is 'excessive sharpness', but he could invert progressive norms because he believed that 'Nature is not at all the standard of art, but art is the standard of nature.' Artists in search of the 'revival of art' must therefore 'all be', what he called, 'severe outlinists' and thus, by definition, outsiders.[67]

Palmer's formal language may have marked him out as an outsider, but equally did his conduct as an artist. The ancient artist in his contemporary guise in Shoreham was as widely differentiated from the modern professional watercolourist as his works were stylistically distinct. The progressive project was centred on the highly commercialized venture of the Society of Painters in Water Colours, which was dedicated to the production and sale of attractive commodities whilst simultaneously promoting the professional respectability of its members. The practitioners were, in turn, supported by a variety of commercial interests, including print publishers, the sellers of art materials and dealers, all centred on London. Palmer, at the centre of a rural-based community, distanced himself from the art world in general, and the newly emergent specialist watercolour profession in particular. It is true that he submitted works to the Academy, but they included unconventional if not eccentric compositions such as 'Ruth Returning from Gleaning' (RA 1829, Victoria and Albert Museum), which the artist himself did not expect to be accepted since they displayed what he termed his 'wonted outrageousness'.[68] Nor was he prepared to compromise in order to attract purchasers. After making a sale in 1825, Palmer declared that 'I will no more ... seek to moderate for the sake of pleasing men', and he later reaffirmed that 'By God's help I will not sell away His gift of art for money; no, not for fame neither, which is far better.'[69] Of course Palmer was not just blessed by God, but also had 'a small independence [which] made me heedless, for the time, of further gain', and he was thus free to affect a lofty disdain for the commercial world of art and the 'barbarous condition' of the times.[70]

Looking back from 1871, Palmer characterized the Shoreham period as the idyllic interregnum of a dilettanti, where 'literature and art and ancient music wiled away the hours'; certainly, he was able to act more like an amateur than a professional necessarily motivated by prosaic financial needs.[71] This short-lived idyll was ended, Palmer later asserted, by the assumption of family responsibilities and a move back to London, where, he later admitted, his 'Real life began'.[72] In turn, he came to embrace the artistic language and the logic of the 'painting in water colours' in works such as 'A View of Modern Rome' (1838, Birmingham City Museums and Art Galleries), and he successively sought to cultivate a place in the market place, embark on a teaching practice, and, ultimately, accept membership of the Society of Painters in Water Colours. Palmer's later recollections, in which he played down the significance of the Shoreham period in the larger picture of his career, is a striking reminder of the shifting basis of all progressive accounts, including Palmer's own biography. As always, the crucial point with any account of declines, progresses, falls and improvements is the choice of the time frame. 'Samuel Palmer 1805-1822' shows a not untypical self-taught student's progress. 'Samuel Palmer 1822-1833' encompasses a rare revolt against progressive norms. Whilst 'Samuel Palmer 1805-1881' might be characterized as a prolonged youth leading to a long professional career of solid if unspectacular achievements, or, as is more commonly thought today, a career which saw a decline from youthful genius, albeit with a partial recovery in the later Miltonic subjects. Palmer himself came to favour the first version of the latter narrative, describing his activities during the Shoreham period as 'eccentric' and deluded and, tellingly, he kept his more innovative early works aside, lodged privately in what he called 'The Curiosity Portfolio'.[73] Palmer was right to suggest that he had been in a fortunate position to oppose the artistic norms of watercolour practice, but his later offhand manner should not obscure the singleness of purpose and independence of mind that was also required. The older artist's views do, however, underline what, in the longer term, was the ambiguous significance of the modern in relation to watercolour practice. On the one hand a historically specific consensus against which he reacted; and, on the other, a twentieth-century construct to which his wilfully primitivist Shoreham works came to be seen as a major contribution, and which, in turn, continues to colour readings of his works and career.

Notes

1.   A.H. Palmer, *The Life and Letters of Samuel Palmer, Painter and Etcher*, London: Seeley, 1892, p. 14.

2.   James Elmes, *A General and Bibliographical Dictionary of the Fine Arts*, London: Thomas Tegg, 1824, p. 323.

3.   William Marshall Craig, *A Course of Lectures on Drawing, Painting and Engraving*, London: Longman, Hurst, Rees, Orme, and Brown, 1821, p. 425. The paradox is, of course, that it was the resulting primitivist elements that saw his Shoreham work later reassessed as proto-modernist.

4.   Greg Smith, *The Emergence of the Professional Watercolourist: Contentions and Alliances in the Artistic Domain 1760-1824*, Aldershot: Ashgate, 2002, pp. 134-41.

5.   See Anon., 'Rise and Progress of Painting in Water Colours', in *The Repository of Arts*, vol. 9, 1812-13. The anonymous author of the series of articles has been identified as William Henry Pyne.

6.   *Examiner*, 9 June, 1823, p. 379.

7.   *Exhibition of Drawings, No.9 Soho Square*, London, 1822.

8.   *Examiner*, 14 July 1823, p. 460.

9.   *Somerset House Gazette*, 8 November 1823, p. 65.

10.   Needless to say, Pyne had not travelled abroad and was ignorant of foreign watercolour practice.

11.   James Barry, *An Inquiry into the Real and Imaginary Obstructions to the Acquisition of the Arts in England*, London: T. Becket, 1775, pp. 41-2. See Smith, *Emergence of the Professional Watercolourist*, pp. 197-200.

12.   Smith, *Emergence of the Professional Watercolourist*, pp. 38-9; p. 142; pp. 211-14.

13.   A similar 'Pastoral Scene in Herefordshire' was shown at the 1824 SPWC exhibition as was his 'Shepherd Collecting their Flocks'.

14.   Palmer, *Life and Letters*, p. 15.

15.   The work was shown at the Royal Academy exhibition *The Great Age of British Watercolours. 1750-1880* (1993) wrongly entitled 'Solitude' (no. 6), but descriptions in the numerous reviews of the watercolour at the Society of Painters in Water Colours in 1823 indicate that it was the exhibit entitled 'Retirement' and which was bought by Allnutt for sixty guineas.

16.   Barret's exhibits at the SPWC include numerous compositions entitled 'Moonlight', 'Retirement', 'Twilight', 'Evening' which parallel Palmer's, as well as more specific titles in common including 'English Pastoral' and 'Harvest Moon' (exhibited in 1829).

17.   Palmer, *Life and Letters*, p. 15.

18.   Ibid.

19.   *Somerset House Gazette*, 8 November 1823, p. 65.

20.   The relationship between views of progress in the arts and civil society is ably summarized in David Spadafora, *The Idea of Progress in Eighteenth-Century Britain*, New Haven and London: Yale University Press, 1990.

21.   Palmer, *Life and Letters*, p. 14. Palmer was primarily self taught and so the familiar romantic trope of oppressive tradition is not institutionalized so much as self inflicted through ignorance.

22.   See Smith, *Emergence of the Professional Watercolourist* , pp. 117-18.

23.   Robert R. Wark (ed.), *Sir Joshua Reynolds. Discourses on Art*, New Haven and London: Yale University Press, 1975, p. 152.

24.   Palmer, *Life and Letters*, p. 14. Linnell's influence here is not stylistic in the sense that his works provided a model to follow, and there is little to be gained from comparing their works of this date. Looking back from 1871, Palmer claimed that Linnell had rather more prosaically made him embark on a 'course of figure drawing', much of it undertaken in the British Museum (Raymond Lister (ed.), *The Letters of Samuel Palmer*, Oxford: Clarendon Press, 1974, vol. 2, p. 824). Irrespective of any stylistic influence, this was enough to save young artists from the 'modern' obsession with the landscape of effects.

25.   P.P. Howe (ed.), *The Complete Works of William Hazlitt*, London and Toronto: Dent, 1930-34, vol. 18, pp. 5-10.

26.   Geoffrey Keynes (ed.), *Blake Complete Writings*, London: Oxford University Press, 1976, p. 593.

27.   Ibid., p. 579; Lister, *Letters*, vol. 1, p. 9.

28.   For Blake's position, see Morris Eaves, *William Blake's Theory of Art*, Princeton: Princeton University Press, 1982, pp. 99-111 and Morris Eaves, *The Counter-Arts Conspiracy. Art and Industry in the Age of Blake*, Ithaca and London: Cornell University Press, 1992, pp. 92-102. The broader context of the challenge to progress is discussed in Lois Whitney, 'English Primitivistic Theories of Epic Origins', *Modern Philology*, vol. 21, no. 4, May 1926; Gabriel A. Almond, Marvin Chodorow, Roy Harvey Pearce (eds), *Progress and its Discontents*, Berkeley: University of California Press, 1982; Christopher Lasch, *The True and Only Heaven: Progress and its Critics*, New York: Norton, 1991.

29.   Keynes, *Blake Complete Writings*, p. 584.

30.   Ibid., p. 585.

31.   Palmer, *Life and Letters*, p. 14.

32.   Ibid., p. 37.

33.   John Gage, *Colour in Turner: Poetry and Truth*, London: Studio Vista, 1969, p. 213.

34.   *Somerset House Gazette*, 1 November 1823, p. 62.

35.   *Repository of Arts*, vol. 9, January 1813, p. 26.

36.   *Somerset House Gazette*, 1 November 1823, p. 62.

37.   Amédée Pichot, *Historical and Literary Tour of a Foreigner in England and Scotland*, London: Saunders and Otlay, 1825, pp. 111, 131.

38.   Lister, *Letters*, vol. 1, pp. 42-3.

39.   Ibid., p. 44.

40.   Ibid., p. 49.

41.   Ibid., p. 47.

42.   Ibid.

43.   Ibid., pp. 49-50; Palmer, *Life and Letters*, p. 16.

44.   *Somerset House Gazette*, 22 November 1823, p. 98.

45.   Lister, *Letters*, vol. 1, p. 50.

46.   Ibid., p. 36.

47.   He submitted as many as eight works a year, but only twenty-one were accepted between 1824 and 1833.

48.   Lister, *Letters*, vol. 1, p. 57. Alexandra Greathead has usefully distinguished between sepia as a medium which was derived from cuttlefish and which was used by Palmer in the Oxford series and Indian ink, employed in the 'blacks' in the same collection, and which might be loosely described as sepia in colour. ('Samuel Palmer's Materials and Techniques: The Early Years' in William Vaughan, Elizabeth E. Barker, Colin Harrison et al., *Samuel Palmer (1805-1881): Vision and Landscape*, London: British Museum Press, 2005). The same catalogue is elsewhere, however, inconsistent and confused in its description of the media Palmer used. The issue is complicated by the fact that the sepias have changed colour from black to a warm brown and Indian ink itself can be used in a more dilute form to give a lighter colour.

49.   *European Magazine*, new series, vol. 1, September 1825, p. 85. A critic in *John Bull* (8 May 1825, p. 150) also reviewed the works, claiming that they were 'unrivaled' in their 'skill and power of execution' and had a 'clear and brilliant light and a vivid style of colouring which it would be vain for any other artist to hope to equal'. As Timothy Wilcox has argued, this was heavily ironic (*Samuel Palmer*, London: Tate Publishing, 2005, p. 45).

50.   Two of Alexander Cozens' drawings were shown in the Cookes' 1822 exhibition.

51.   *Somerset House Gazette*, 3 January 1824, p. 193.

52.   Palmer, *Life and Letters*, p. 36.

53.   Ibid., pp. 15-16.

54.   *Bell's New Weekly Messenger*, 25 May 1834, supplement, p. 41.

55.   Sarah Herring, 'Samuel Palmer's Shoreham Drawings in Indian Ink. A Matter of Light and Shade', *Apollo*, vol. 148, November 1998, pp. 38-9.

56.   See Simon Fenwick and Greg Smith, *The Business of Watercolour: A Guide to the Archives of the Royal Watercolour Society*, Aldershot: Ashgate, 1997, pp. 3-6. Few are bigger than 18 × 28 cms and many are much smaller.

57.   Vaughan, Barker, Harrison et al., *Vision and Landscape*, pp. 87-93.

58.   Martin Butlin (ed.), *Samuel Palmer. The Sketchbook of 1824*, London: Thames and Hudson, 2005, p. 158 (page 140); p. 54 (page 28).

59.   Ibid., p. 136 (page 114).

60.   Ibid., p. 54 (page 28); Keynes, *Blake Complete Writings*, p. 585.

61.   Ibid.

62.   See Smith, *Emergence of the Professional Watercolourist*, 2002, pp. 51-71.

63.   Herring, 'Shoreham Drawings', 1998, pp. 39-41.

64.   Palmer, *Life and Letters*, p. 17.

65.   *Repository of Arts*, vol. 8, November 1812, p. 260.

66.   Ibid.

67.   Palmer, *Life and Letters*, p. 16.

68.   Lister, *Letters*, vol. 1, p. 54.

69.   Palmer, *Life and Letters*, p. 13; Lister, *Letters*, vol. 1, p. 36.

70.   A.H. Palmer, *Samuel Palmer. A Memoir*, London: Fine Art Society, 1882, p. 6.

71. Lister, *Letters*, vol. 2, p. 824.

72. Ibid.

73. Palmer, 1892, p. 37; Martin Hardie, James Laver and A.H. Palmer, *Catalogue of an Exhibition of Drawings, Etchings & Woodcuts by Samuel Palmer and Other Disciples of William Blake*, exhibition catalogue, Victoria and Albert Museum, London, 1926. This was a view that Palmer's son was particularly keen to emphasize.

3

'This very unstudent-like student':
Palmer and the education of the artist

Martin Postle

Samuel Palmer's early career coincided with a period of increasingly contested academic ideologies in the British art world. Palmer grew up in the shadow of Reynoldsian discourse, and had first-hand knowledge of the academic teaching of Henry Fuseli and John Flaxman. During his childhood the veracity of the Parthenon sculptures was debated, defended and challenged; within the Royal Academy there were heated debates over the relative role in the curriculum of the antique, anatomy and the living model. More generally, there was a fundamental sea-change in the canon of European art, with the emergence of an appreciation of earlier Italian painting (the so-called 'Primitives') and the rise in appreciation of seventeenth-century Dutch and Flemish art. In all these matters Palmer took a keen interest and expressed strong opinions. Although Palmer himself had little formal training, in later years he devoted a great deal of his time to teaching art. Indeed, as he matured, his educational method was characterized by a *furor pedagogicus*, fuelled by his fascination with art practice and theory, and a desire to compensate for the shortcomings in his own art education. In view of his artistic development outside the parameters of the academy, and the unorthodox nature of his early 'visionary' oeuvre, it is tempting to assume that Palmer was 'anti-academic' in outlook and in practice. In fact, he was, as this chapter suggests, among the most deeply academic artists of his generation.

Palmer's was a sheltered and relatively pampered childhood. He had little formal education, aside from a brief spell at Merchant Taylors' School, which he left after only two terms. Instead, he preferred to follow his scholarly pursuits in the comfort of his own home, supplied with a wide range of literature from his father's bookshop.[1] In terms of his early artistic training, Palmer, too, was an avowed autodidact. As his son recalled, around 1815-17, when Palmer was about thirteen years old: 'Instead of being made to attack the all-important rudiments of draughtsmanship and anatomy (a discipline of which he afterwards well knew the value) he was allowed to copy laboriously, prints of the Campo Santo frescoes, engravings of "botanical minutiae" and even architectural drawings.'[2] The reference to the engravings of the Campo Santo is of particular interest. Carlo Lasinio (1759-1838), Conservatore of the Campo Santo in Pisa, first published a series of engravings from fifteenth-century frescoes there in 1812 (Figure 3.1).

As William Holman Hunt was to recall, these engravings had been of seminal importance to the founders of the Pre-Raphaelite Brotherhood, who pored over them in 1848, according to Hunt, 'with the determination that a kindred simplicity should regulate our own ambition'.[3] It is reasonable to assume that the Campo Santo had a similar impact on the young Palmer some twenty years earlier, not least because he would have been attracted to their linear qualities, profusion of detail, 'simplicity', and their Christian content; artistic values that were certainly upheld by Palmer and the Ancients a decade or so later.

Following the death of his mother, when he was thirteen, Palmer was tutored at home by the professional drawing master, William Wate, who exhibited a series of Thames-side and southern English landscapes at the Royal Academy and the British Institution until his untimely death from cholera in 1832.[4] At an age when his peers from less well-off backgrounds were serving apprenticeships, Palmer's early teenage tutelage by Wate was more reminiscent of a genteel young lady than an aspiring male professional painter. In 1819, encouraged by Wate, Palmer exhibited his first works at the Royal Academy, including 'Cottage scene – Banks of the Thames, Battersea', a subject similar to one exhibited by Wate at the Royal Academy three years earlier.[5] (Although they have not been identified, both Wate's and Palmer's exhibits were probably oil paintings rather than watercolours.) Earlier in 1819, Palmer had sold his first picture, a 'landscape' priced at seven guineas, shown at the British Institution.[6] Then aged only fourteen, Palmer was a year younger than Turner had been when he had shown his first watercolour at the Royal Academy in 1790. By the same age, however, Turner was already enrolled in the Royal Academy Schools and pursuing a professional career. As it is often remarked, Palmer was virtually the only member of his immediate artistic circle who did not train at the Royal Academy Schools. It is also worth remarking that those artists of a slightly older generation, to whom Palmer looked up in early adult life, were among the brightest stars of the Schools, notably John Linnell and William Mulready. These young artists were thoroughly drilled and skilled in drawing from antique sculptures, anatomical figures and the living model. Palmer particularly admired, for example, Mulready's 'thoroughness and love of conscientiousness', and in later life was to urge his own pupils to draw with 'exactness'.[7]

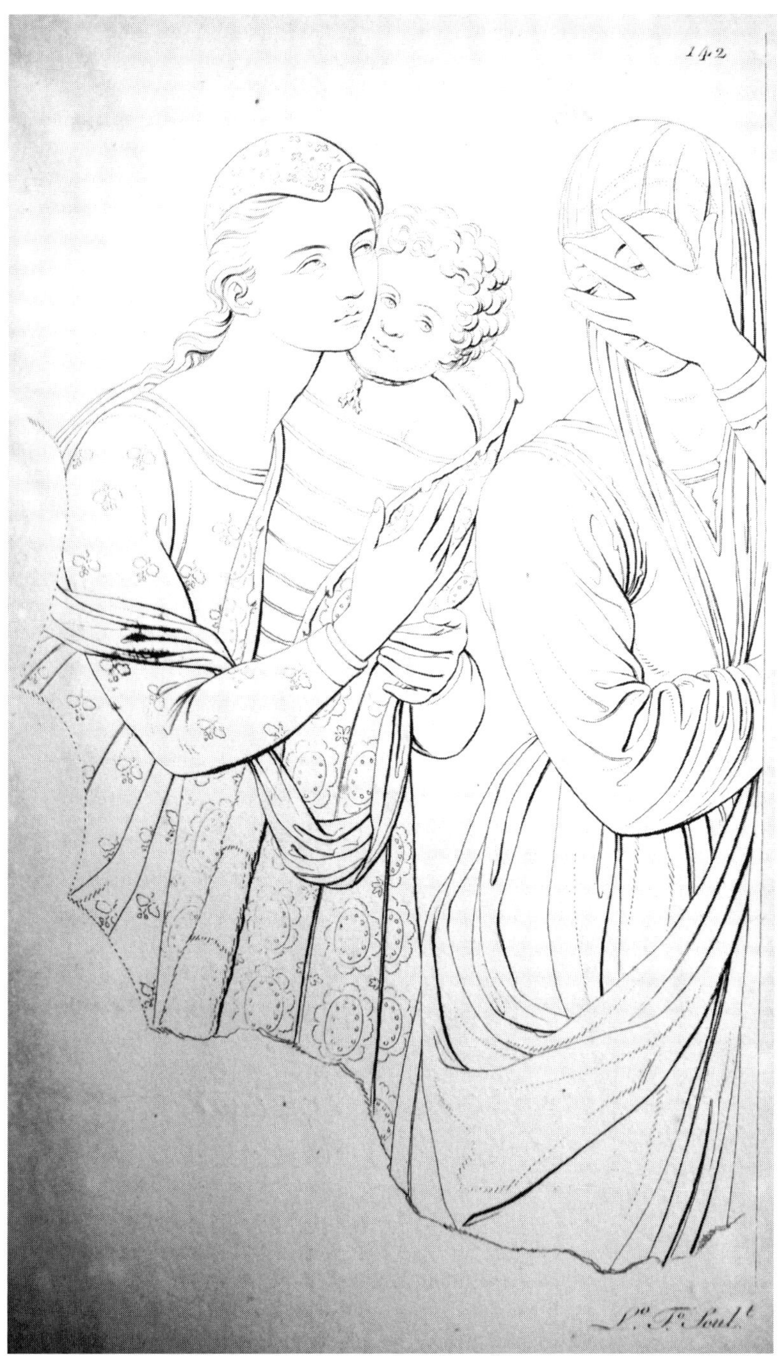

3.1 Carlo Lasinio, illustration from *Descrizione delle Pitture del Campo Santo di Pisa*, Florence 1816. © The Trustees of the British Museum, BM 1847.10.9.14 (5).

So why did Palmer refrain from undertaking a formal art education through the free training offered by the Royal Academy Schools? One factor, I would suggest, was his rather isolated and cosseted middle-class upbringing, which may have engendered in him a suspicion that the majority of art students were, despite their aspirations to gentility, engaged through their routine copying exercises in a merely mechanical process. Certainly, 'class' was an important issue for Palmer in later life, not least when he forced his son to give up printing 'because it was a trade'.[8] Perhaps, too, the young Palmer did not feel emotionally or physically robust enough to endure the rough and tumble of the Academy's schools: as Henry Fuseli told his students famously, 'By G-d! you are a pack of d-d wild beasts, and I am your bl-st-d keeper!'[9]

Another, more deep-seated reason for Palmer's disinclination to follow the traditional academic path related to his preoccupation with theory over practice. As his son, Herbert, recalled, 'my father was without the healthy emulation of the schools, where he might have profited by seeing the workmanship of those more experienced than himself. So, at a time when he should have contented himself with the alphabet of art, he was full of theories and speculations more suitable to the most learned professors.'[10] Even so, while Palmer did not learn to draw at the Schools, he had potential allies within the Academy, not least his maternal grandfather's friend, Thomas Stothard (1755-1834), who as well as being a senior Academician was, in 1814, appointed Librarian. Stothard apparently gave the young Palmer 'plenty of good advice'. He also provided him with tickets to attend the lectures given by leading Academicians, notably Fuseli, Professor of Painting, and John Flaxman, who had been appointed as the Academy's first Professor of Sculpture in 1810.[11]

Like Flaxman, Palmer was a devout Christian, attracted to 'the traditions and monuments of the Church; its cloistered abbeys, cathedrals, and minsters'.[12] And, among Royal Academicians, it may have been Flaxman in particular who most influenced the formation of Palmer's taste during these early years. Flaxman's first lecture as Professor of Sculpture was devoted to English sculpture, including, notably, later medieval sculpture.[13] In subsequent lectures he continually affirmed his reverence for Michelangelo and for Donatello, both of whom were greatly admired by Palmer. And while we cannot be sure which lectures Palmer attended (they were only published posthumously in 1829), it is perhaps relevant that, in comparison to his fervent admiration for Michelangelo, Flaxman's attention to classical sculpture was, as David Irwin has noted, often 'more dutiful than passionate' – a response shared by Palmer, who, on the whole, found classic Greek art 'too mild and pure'.[14]

Fuseli's impact upon the young Palmer is in no doubt. Palmer must have attended his lectures, and read the first six lectures on their publication in 1820. In his 1824 notebook Palmer carefully copied a passage from Fuseli's fifth lecture on composition, relating to Raphael's use of light and shade in his frescoes in the loggia of the villa Farnesina in Rome.[15] And, even in later years, Palmer continued to read Fuseli's Royal Academy lectures, which he regarded as the 'best' of their kind.[16] One reason why Fuseli in particular appealed to the young Palmer was, I would suggest, the cerebral nature of his discourse. Fuseli, despite his position as a teacher in the Royal Academy Schools, had scant respect for the routine aspects of practical training, with its plethora of awards and diplomas, and its association with the manufacture of trivial art for a debased contemporary consumer society. 'If it be', as he stated in his twelfth and final lecture, 'out of our power to furnish the student's activity with adequate practice, we may contribute to form his theory.'[17] While such views must have appealed to the youthful Palmer, later in life he became convinced that the role of art education was to shape practice as well as theory.

While Palmer resisted the Royal Academy Schools, and restricted his attendance at Somerset House to the occasional lecture, under the tutelage of John Linnell, whom he met in September 1822, he was eager to broaden his knowledge of the history of art. In this respect, he was attracted especially by the opportunity to educate his eye in London's museums and art galleries. Palmer was fortunate in being among the first generation of young artists to benefit from the burgeoning museum culture in the capital: old-master prints, drawings and classical sculpture in the British Museum, a visit with Linnell to Charles Aders' celebrated collection of Flemish and German primitives in Euston Square, as well as the annual exhibitions of contemporary art at the Royal Academy, which, on one celebrated occasion, he attended with William Blake. In the notebook he kept at that time Palmer made notes on a variety of artists, including Dürer, Raphael and Lucas van Leyden, as he urged himself to look for 'Van Leydenish qualities in real landscape, and look hard, long and continually'.[18] An important resource for Palmer, in terms of his exposure to old-master painting, was Dulwich Picture Gallery, which he also visited with Linnell.

Founded in 1811, Dulwich Picture Gallery, London's first public art gallery, opened its doors in 1817, preceding the National Gallery (opened in May 1824) by seven years. At Dulwich, Palmer particularly admired a Renaissance head-and-shoulders portrait of a young man: 'The copy of Leonardo da Vinci at Dulwich is merely a head and shoulders. How amazingly superior it is in style to any portrait there. The tone of the flat blueish sky is wonderful, though it is nothing of itself.'[19]

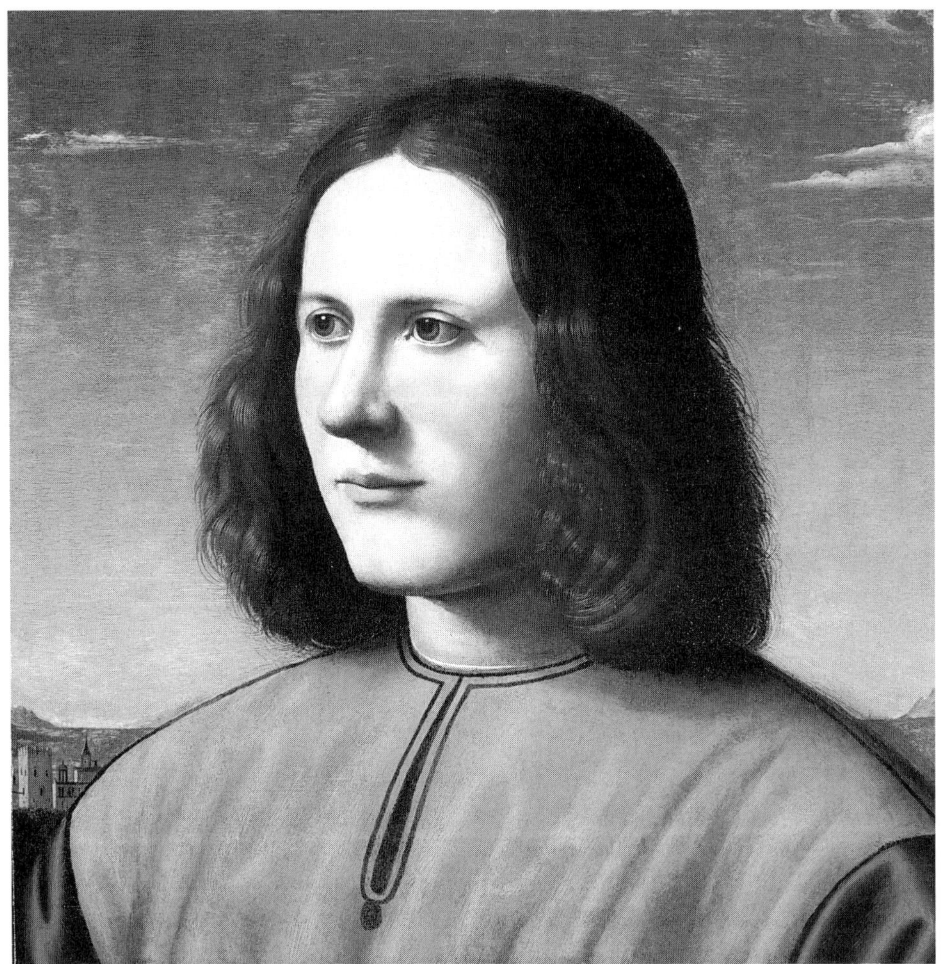

3.2   Piero di Cosimo, 'Portrait of a Young Man', c.1500. Oil on panel, 41.2 × 41 cm. Dulwich Picture Gallery.

The work, of around 1500, and now attributed to Piero di Cosimo, is the earliest painting in the collection. In Palmer's time it was attributed to Leonardo da Vinci – although interestingly Palmer refers to it as a copy.[20] As with his admiration of Lasinio's engravings of the frescoes in the Campo Santo, Palmer, under Linnell's watchful eye, once more demonstrated an affiliation to earlier Italian art which was beyond the bounds of orthodox British academic taste, but which paralleled that of the Nazarene movement of German painters in Rome. At Dulwich, Palmer also admired the Dutch seventeenth-century landscape painters, Ruisdael, Hobbema, Potter, and Cuyp, which were then very much in vogue. It was a type of art for which he retained a respect, as many years later, in 1864, Palmer advised one of his pupils to visit 'sweet, quiet Dulwich College' to copy Dutch paintings including 'a very fine Cuyp, very few cows, one black, or spotted with black; church tower I *think* on the opposite bank: you will know it by the amber sky'.[21] The painting was probably Aelbert Cuyp's 'View on a Plain', the work in the collection that most closely fits his description. He also directed the same pupil towards *Jacob's Dream*, then thought to be by Rembrandt, but subsequently discovered to be by Arent de Gelder. In the second instance the choice of picture was perhaps more personal as the painting is far closer to the visionary aspect of Palmer's own art.

Despite his admiration for the technical accomplishments of seventeenth-century Dutch artists, Palmer's greatest admiration was reserved for the High Renaissance, as embodied in the art of Michelangelo. Here Palmer's response was passionate and deeply personal, as one can gauge from his response to the taste championed by Richard Payne Knight, one of the country's foremost arbiters of taste. In his annotations to Knight's *Analytical Inquiry into the Principles of Taste* (published in 1805), Palmer responded vigorously to Knight's criticism of Michelangelo's 'vast and turgid compositions of the Sistine Chapel', and Knight's preference for works such as 'The Raising of Lazarus', in which the artist had sensibly 'lowered the tone of his invention'.[22] (The latter painting was subsequently found to be by Michelangelo's follower, Sebastiano del Piombo.) Palmer railed against the measured criticism of Knight, which he believed to be antagonistic towards the Michelangelesque sublime: as he remarked sarcastically, 'our taste is Dutch; Rembrandt is our Da Vinci, and Rubens our Michelangiolo!'.[23] Palmer detested Knight's dispassionate approach, which demanded moderation and equilibrium; and which appeared to be suspicious of any spark of individuality. As a devout Christian, he was also at odds with Knight's fundamentally secular aesthetic, which promoted the classical aesthetic above all others, and claimed that a true appreciation of art lay ultimately with an educated, intellectual, elite.

In the late autumn of 1822 John Linnell, conscious of Palmer's lack of academic training, urged him to 'begin a course of figure drawing', which was, according to Geoffrey Grigson, 'less sensibly carried out by doing it in the antique galleries of the British Museum'.[24] Yet, as Grigson concedes, the British Museum was by this time used extensively by art students, especially those who used the occasion to prepare drawing for submission for entry to the Royal Academy Schools. It was also a social venue: it was there, for example, in 1843 that the young John Everett Millais first met William Holman Hunt: it was there also, some twenty years earlier, that Palmer first met George Richmond. While Richmond, a consummate professional, took to the task with assurance, Palmer struggled. Yet, it was not merely lack of confidence in his own technical competence that held him back, but the mental turmoil these antique fragments occasioned, as uncompromising material objects. As he recorded in his notebook of 1824: 'N.B. in my attempts to copy the Antique statues to try and draw most severely, and to cry out for more and more form; and then I shall find in the Antique more than I can copy, if I look and look and pry into it earnestly for form. I shall not be easy till I have drawn one Antique statue *most severely*. I cannot execute at all.'[25] The struggle between the duty to record what he observed with the utmost precision and the desire to express his more imaginative impulses was something that was to remain with Palmer throughout his life, and was to shape his own pedagogical instincts.

Among the classical statues in the British Museum particularly admired by Palmer, at least in later years, was a Roman statue of a youth called Endymion, part of the celebrated collection purchased from the estate of Charles Towneley on his death in 1805. 'More than two thousand years ago', he stated, ' the sculptor bade that marble live. It lived, but slept, and it is living still.'[26] Yet, during the later 1820s Palmer, who had made 'sedulous efforts to render the marbles exactly, even to their granulation',[27] formed an aversion to classical sculpture. He found that the exercise of copying, far from increasing his admiration for these objects, had instilled in him a sense of their sterility, which was in opposition to inspiration he gained from other artistic sources, and from his new mentor, William Blake. And, in a pointed reference to increasing disagreements with John Linnell, his erstwhile mentor, and future father-in-law, who had exhorted Palmer to study from the antique, Palmer told George Richmond in 1828: 'I have not yet opened the campaign against the smooth antiques.'[28]

A generation older than Palmer, Linnell took an orthodox stance on art education, valuing the work ethic associated with traditional academic training. (He sent all his sons to the Royal Academy schools and ran his studio, or workshop as he preferred to call it, with ruthless efficiency.) Thus, in addition to broadening his taste in old-master paintings and prints, Linnell urged Palmer 'to learn figure drawing professionally, to know every bone and every muscle, however superficial'.[29] In 1824, in deference to Linnell, Palmer informed him, albeit tongue-in-cheek, that he had been a 'good boy' and had recently made two life studies on grey paper, 'a head on grey paper life size and tinted, also another sketch of the same person smaller'. Yet, such exercises in direct observation, he confessed, countered his instinctive interest in Mannerist art, for 'when I am drawing from Nature vision seems foolishness to me – the arms of an old rotten tree trunk more curious than the arms of Buonaroti's Moses – Venus de Medicis finer than the 'Night' of Lorenzo's tomb and Jacob Ruysdael a sweeter finisher than William Blake'.[30] At this time Palmer was also in the habit of visiting the Royal Academy to admire Michelangelo's chalk drawing of Leda and the Swan (a work now attributed to Rosso Fiorentino). 'I wonder', he observed, 'whether anybody in London has got a real bit or two of Mike's drawing, in the Leda style – her brawn was the richest treat I ever had … The chastity of most of the Antique is too mild and pure for my gross appetite to relish thoroughly – I dare say people have a very refin'd pleasure in boiled chicken, but give me the *"rich experience"* of a roasted goose, which is to chicken what Mike is to the antique ...'.[31] Here Palmer extols the emotional, erotic, appeal of Michelangelo's figure drawing, a taste which was fostered being shaped and influenced by his new-found association with Blake.

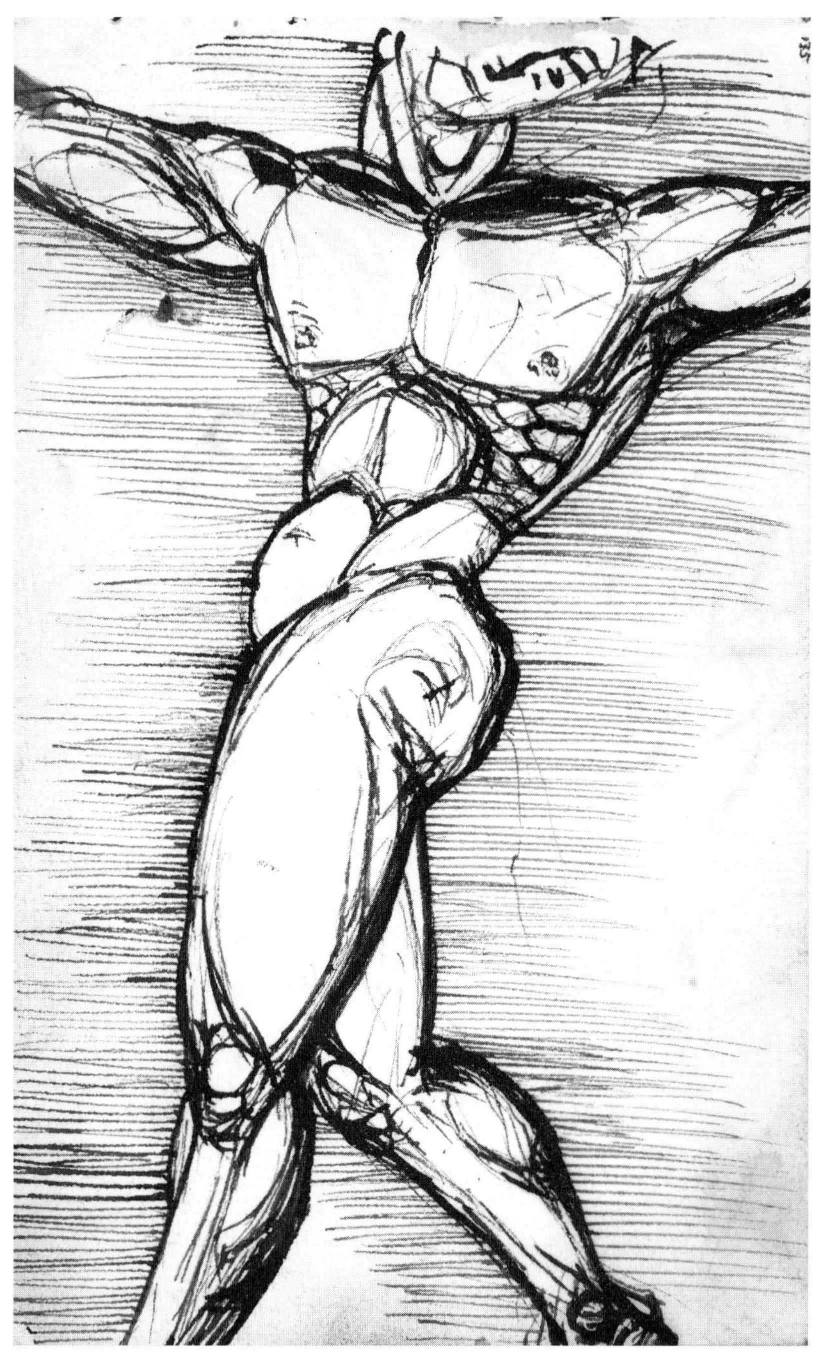

3.3   Samuel Palmer, *Sketchbook*, 1824, page 135, male nude figure. Pen and brown ink, 11.6 × 18.9 cm. © The Trustees of the British Museum.

There are very few surviving figure drawings by Palmer, aside from a small series of male torsos in the 1824 sketchbook.[32] Alfred Herbert Palmer referred presumably to these or similar drawings made by Palmer while in Shoreham: 'The works', he recalled, 'to which this very unstudent-like student was labouring to give birth and for whose sake he turned his back on London are remarkable for exaggerated attitude, unwieldy muscular form, and a nightmare composition for which even the teaching of Blake could not be held responsible.'[33] Yet, these figures were clearly influenced by Fuseli and Blake, with musculature worn like body armour in emulation of Michelangelo's heroic nudes. (A specific influence upon the figure in Palmer's sketchbook with outstretched arms may have been Blake's 'Pestilence: The Death of the First-Born', of around 1805, which it closely resembles.) Indeed, as his son was forced to concede, Palmer had indeed 'spurred his hobby onwards by means of his unmeasured admiration of Michael Angelo, Fuseli and Blake, till in some instances, in seeking the sublime he sank to the ridiculous'.[34]

Samuel Palmer met William Blake in 1824, through an introduction by Linnell. Palmer was then nineteen and Blake in his late sixties. Palmer was awe-struck, referring many years later to their first meeting as 'my never-to-be-forgotten first interview'.[35] On subsequent visits to Blake's house he kissed the door-handle before entering. As Raymond Lister has noted, in Blake, Palmer 'encountered a being in whom were centred all the aspirations, artistic and moral, for which he had been groping'.[36] And, much as he admired the gifted and hard-working Linnell, Blake offered an alternative 'academic' role model, a living artist who was, he considered, the equal of Michelangelo; a modern Mannerist who could counter the blandness of the Graeco-Roman paradigm which still held sway within the Royal Academy. Like Linnell, Blake had attended the Royal Academy Schools. However, his few known drawings from the living model are perfunctory – or deliberately perverse.[37] After only a few months of attendance, Blake appears to have drifted way from the Schools. Even so, it was through the Royal Academy that he formed friendships with John Flaxman and Thomas Stothard, Academicians who were also to influence and assist the young Palmer in later years.[38] More significantly, Blake's brief exposure to the curriculum and prevailing ethos of the Royal Academy engendered in him a disdain for its educational principles, not least the preference for Reynoldsian eclecticism over Blake's own 'single-minded intensity'.[39] At a crucial moment in Palmer's life, in the mid-1820s, the example and inspiration provided by Blake must have quelled any residual thoughts in Palmer's mind that he should either submit himself to the strictures of the Royal Academy's educational system or its academic authority. Indeed, his association with Blake must have served to have given him confidence to develop the essential facets of his own artistic doctrine.

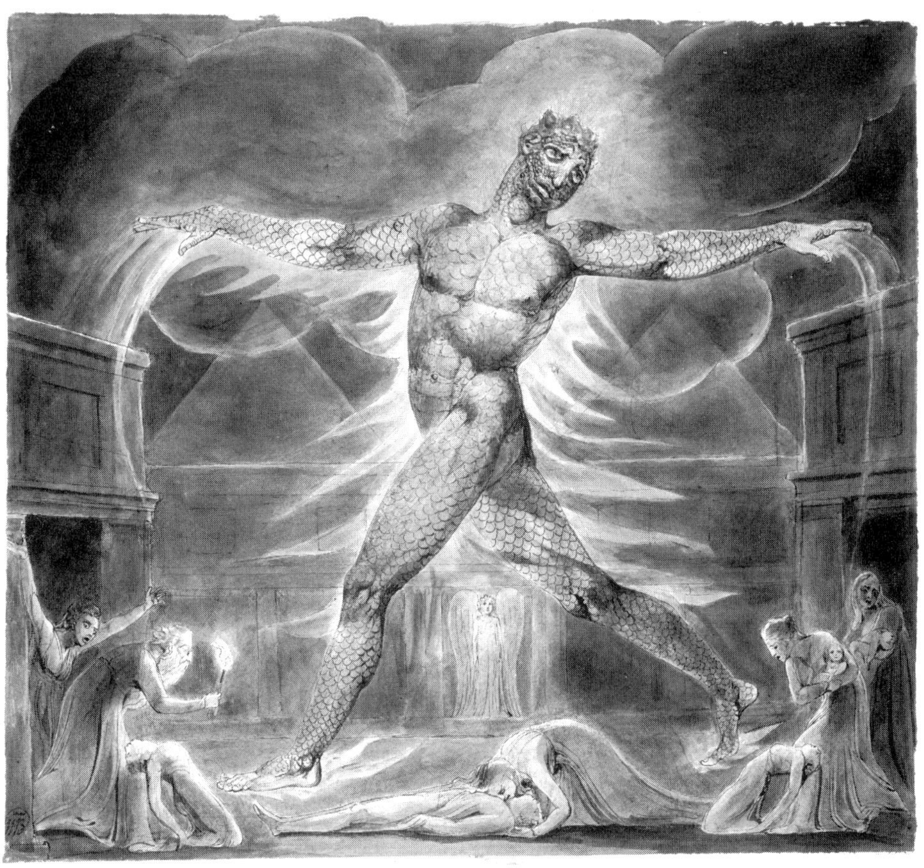

3.4   William Blake, 'Pestilence: The Death of the First-Born', c.1805. Pen and watercolour over graphite on paper, 30.4 × 34.2 cm. © Museum of Fine Arts, Boston.

In 1832, at the age of 27, Palmer established himself at 4 Grove Street, Lisson Grove, in northwest London, where he began his career as a professional art teacher. Already, he was inclined towards pedagogy, telling George Richmond a few years earlier how he longed to make 'faithful transcripts of true gems of art' that would when engraved form basis of 'a drawing book for young students of other kind than the execrable trash with which their first appetite is gorged, their taste perverted, their intellectual eyes jaundiced, and their very fingers tortured almost out of the power of drawing a single line or shape of real beauty'.[40] He imagined himself in Italy working hard on making accurate drawings after Michelangelo and Donatello, stating that he would rather see 'really fine copies' of Donatello statues 'on white or grey paper, than highly finish'd pictures from most of Raffaell's frescoes'.[41] Yet, certain aspects of Palmer's Italian 'honeymoon' of 1837-39, following his marriage to Linnell's daughter, turned out to be more of a nightmare as he laboured to make copies after Raphael in the Vatican loggias (the so-called 'Loggia struggle'[42]) and assist his wife in colouring and correcting Linnell's lithographs after the Sistine ceiling. At the same time, however, Palmer also regarded his Italian sojourn as an opportunity to complete his own art education, and to think 'a great deal', as he told his friend, Edward Calvert, 'about the principles and practice of art'.[43] He worked hard, investigating the landscape techniques of the old masters, notably Giorgione, Titian and Bellini, and sketched extensively from nature. He also looked upon the time spent in Italy as preparation for his future professional life, conscious of the need to make a living through his art and produce saleable products to support himself and his family. 'Real life began' in Italy, as he later recalled many years later.[44] It was also upon his return from Italy that Palmer was transformed from art student to art teacher.

In England, Palmer increasingly supplemented his income through teaching. Indeed, his teaching practice intensified rapidly, so that by 1848 it comprised two-thirds of his income. And, when he himself became a father (his first child was born in 1842), it is clear that he felt a strong personal responsibility for educating others, and not just in the matter of art. As he freely admitted some years later, 'it would be mock modesty to say that I have not studied the subject of education – it has been my hobby'.[45] As he aged, Palmer became increasingly proscriptive, spurred on by memories of his own casual attitude towards art training in his youth and the enduring guilt he suffered due to his self-image of slothfulness and inactivity. As he stated with respect to his earlier inattention to anatomy and his ignorance of bones and muscles: 'I wished I had been well flogged when somewhat younger, and made to copy every one of them.'[46] Palmer expressed his views on the nature of art education in regular letters to his pupils, including George Richmond's daughter, Julia, and the philanthropist, Louisa Twining, whose notebook containing her lessons in watercolour from Palmer survives in the Ashmolean Museum, Oxford.[47] In several long letters to Twining, Palmer provided detailed advice on drawing and watercolour technique, as well as his thoughts on the principles of art education for young children.[48] Much of what he had to say was practical commonsense, balancing the importance of sketching from nature with the need for close observation and accurate draughtsmanship. 'All educational acquisitions which have not exactness', he told Julia Richmond at the commencement of her art studies, 'are in my opinion worse than useless.'[49]

In the later 1860s Palmer became involved in a wide-ranging discussion on art education, which extended well beyond his own immediate experiences. It related to the proposed foundation of an entirely new school of art in London, which was to become the Slade School of Fine Art. The Slade was founded at University College in 1871 through the legacy of Felix Slade, a collector with strong liberal principles, who had died in 1868, leaving £45,000 to be shared between the universities of Oxford, Cambridge, and London for the promotion of the Fine Arts. The Slade was characterized, as David Bindman has noted, by its 'bias towards the French academic system, with its emphasis on drawing and painting from the living model, the exercise of a critical intelligence, and an awareness of art history'.[50] The ethos of the Slade was championed by its first Professor of Art, the French-trained, Edward Poynter. However, many of the practices and ideas usually credited solely to Poynter, had already been shaped by University College over previous decades through the vision of a rather less well-known individual, Edwin Wilkins Field.

Edwin Field was born in 1804, a close contemporary and later a friend of Samuel Palmer. The son of a dissenting minister and schoolmaster he went on to become a champion of Chancery reform and religious toleration for dissenters. A keen amateur draughtsman, Field extended his interest in reform to the sphere of art education, including the teaching of drawing and perspective to working men. In the 1840s and 1850s Field continued to promote the cause of Fine Art at University College, and in 1868 Felix Slade's legacy allowed Field to fulfil his ambition. Palmer's involvement in discussions surrounding the foundation of the Slade School was a direct result of his friendship with Edwin Field, who was, among other things, a fellow-member of the Old Watercolour Society. Until recently Palmer's sole connection to the issue of the foundation of the Slade, was to be found in a passing comment made in a letter to Julia Richmond early in 1869, where he noted the lack of progress in the scheme.[51] In the same letter Palmer even considered calling on Ruskin to lend his weight to the proposal, although he confessed that he did not wish to intrude upon the great man's time.

In the summer of 1868 Field sent out a printed circular letter to various friends and colleagues – mostly professional artists – summarizing his views on the ethos and curriculum of the putative art school. Their replies are contained in an album, which now belongs to the College Records Office at University College London.[52] Besides Palmer, the album contains letters by John Linnell, Charles West Cope, and Richard Redgrave. There is also correspondence from Palmer's fellow members of the Old Watercolour Society. Field's correspondents aired a wide variety of differing opinions on the nature of the art academy. One common bond which united many of them was an antipathy towards the system of art training then offered by the Royal Academy, viewed as reactionary and cliquish. A significant number of Field's correspondents were watercolourists. Not only were these individuals independent from the Royal Academy through their network of sketching clubs and exhibitions, but they were, like Palmer, teachers and drawing masters.

While many of Field's correspondents were suspicious of the idea of a new art school in London, Palmer's was a lone voice of optimism, fully endorsing Field's ambitious scheme 'because it is so large and hopeful'. In his first letter to Field, dated 1 September 1868, Palmer envisioned 'a vast gallery of casts from the finest antique statues – like that beautiful new court at Brompton where Michael Angelo's David stands – plenty of light, plenty of room'. There should be, he noted, 'another large room with the best prints from the great Italian masters glazed and framed in single beads so that students should not get their first notions of engraving from Woolett & Strange but from Marc Antonio & Bonasoni'.[53] William Woollett (1735-85) and Robert Strange (1721-92) were both eighteenth-century British engravers who made prints after the old masters. Here, therefore, Palmer stressed the importance of going back to Renaissance masters of line, highlighting his admiration for Marcantonio Raimondi (1480-c.1534) and Giulio Bonasone (c.1498-1574). In addition to plaster casts and old master prints Palmer also advocated 'an anatomical drawing school and an Art Library like that at Brompton – and last, but not least, a fine draughtsman, a master of the figure who could teach the drawing from the antique and teach the students how to make use of your neighbouring anatomical school'.[54] Palmer, however, made no mention of the living model, which was to be the cornerstone of the Slade's pedagogy.

Following his initial letter to Edwin Field, Palmer wrote once more, a week later. 'Don't think me lukewarm about the Slade business, which beside its importance to Art itself, will somewhat raise the status of every artist in England. Connection with the Universities is national recognition.' At the same time, Palmer's letter made clear that the National Art Training Schools recently established at South Kensington should also be the model for the Slade. 'I believe that S. Kensington in several ways is doing more for art than has been done since its decline after the Reformation, and if your first steps are well considered, there is no knowing what may not be done in Gower Street.'[55] Palmer's views on the structure of the Slade – an art school where the study of the antique, old master prints, and anatomy took precedence – reflected the increasingly conservative views on art education that Palmer had adopted since at least the 1840s, as well as his own personal preferences for Michelangelo and Renaissance engravers.

Palmer's views were also shaped by personal friendships, not least his association with Richard Redgrave. Born a year earlier than Palmer, Redgrave had begun his artistic career as a drawing master. By 1851 he had been elected a Royal Academician, and like Palmer's other close friend in the Academy, Charles West Cope, was an expert etcher. A prolific writer on art, Redgrave was a major force in art administration, as Director of the National Art Training School, Director of the South Kensington Museum, and Surveyor of the Queen's Pictures. Given his pre-eminent position at South Kensington, Redgrave queried what could be done by the proposed art school at University College to 'supplement and complete' that which had already been achieved at the Government Schools of Art, which 'teach the figure at least as well as it could be taught in a class of University College'.[56] The only hope for the Slade, in Redgrave's view, was to foster high art in an age of increasing mediocrity. 'Our art gets meaner and meaner. Even in landscape art we have lost all those artists who had a conception of it as something more than mere imitation – Turner Constable Callcott Collins Stanfield are gone – only Linnell is left.'[57] As for Linnell, he was dismissive of the idea of an art school inside a university, as he told Edwin Field. 'The only teacher required is one to teach method of work & method of study leaving the student to adopt what is to his own taste and powers … only let the best work be accessible to the student and he can do without a professor who generally methinks professes too much.'[58] Linnell was also insistent that any teaching offered at University College should, like the Royal Academy Schools, be at little or no cost to the student. It was a view not shared by Palmer, who endorsed the middle-class bias of the Slade and felt that students should pay their way.

Palmer's views on art education in the late 1860s were inextricably linked to the future career path he was then carving out for his son, Alfred Herbert Palmer. Herbert, Samuel Palmer's younger, and only surviving son, was born in 1853. According to Herbert, having been neglected emotionally and intellectually by his father in early childhood, he became the focus of his father's pedagogical passion. And despite Herbert's own preference for entymology, he was for over fifteen years, as he recalled, 'gradually taught S.P.'s views on the principles of Art; on composition; on clouds and skies; the imperative importance of linear and aeriel perspective; and a host of other matters which went to form his great tests of good and bad in Art – to form his intensely earnest creed'.[59] Inevitably, the intensity of Herbert Palmer's education was in inverse proportion to that of his father. A sickly child, Herbert was given a course of military drill by a former sergeant major in the Grenadier guards. He was also drilled in the art of copying antique figures, at first under his father's own tutelage, and then under his godfather, Charles West Cope, Cope's son, Arthur, as well as the life class in the Royal Academy Schools. Family friends, including Richard Redgrave, George Richmond, and the Linnells, also proffered advice. Alfred Herbert Palmer was, it is fair to say, among the most intensively tutored art students of his generation.

In September 1868, at very time he wrote to Edwin Field, Samuel Palmer was planning to train Herbert to be a professional artist; what he termed 'a great Christian duty'.[60] He therefore sent Herbert to study at the National Art Training Schools at South Kensington, from where he was to graduate to the Royal Academy Schools. During this time Palmer provided Herbert with detailed advice on the best means to study geometry, perspective, and anatomy. And while he encouraged him to work hard at his studies, he also encouraged Herbert to temper the 'machinery' of South Kensington's rigorous curriculum through regular free-hand sketching.[61] It was presumably with Herbert in mind that Palmer subsequently summarized his messianic approach to art education:

In entering the Brompton Schools, the pupil explains his aim. In this case it would be, of course, the figure; because the plaster teaches drawing in a tenth of the time required by other courses of study; nor do they answer the end after all. Of course success requires energy – bull-dog tenacity. 'O! well and happy shall they be' on whose funeral tablets we might inscribe, each by each, HE WAS A CHRISTIAN BULL-DOG.[62]

For his part, Herbert endured the well-meaning paternal onslaught, recalling many years later, how he had become the reluctant focus of his father's educational beliefs, or what he referred to as his 'intensely earnest creed'.[63]

In 1909, prior to starting a new life in Canada, Herbert Palmer destroyed a large proportion of his father's life's work, in the belief that 'no one would be able to make head or tail of what I burnt'.[64] Through these bonfires, which apparently lasted for days, Herbert deprived posterity of material that would have allowed a fuller and more balanced insight into the artistic and personal life of Samuel Palmer. Herbert's motives remain obscure, other than that they contained material 'never intended to be seen', combined with a hint of embarrassment over his father's 'mental condition', which was 'neither sufficiently masculine nor sufficiently reticent'.[65] Following the destruction of so much of his own father's work, Herbert admitted that he was also prepared to consign material relating to his own art education to the incinerator, 'things I learnt from my father, Hook, Leighton, Redgrave, Cope, etc. – privately or as an R.A. student'.[66] Beyond the consideration of Herbert's pyromaniacal tendency, the contrast between Palmer's own free-spirited art education (his 'free pasture', as he described it) and the rigid academic straitjacket into which he forced his own son, is remarkable – and quite tragic. In his determination to provide Herbert with the formal art education that he had denied himself, Palmer paradoxically engendered in his son a distrust of the more imaginative aspects of his own art, as well as contributing inadvertently to the wilful destruction of so much of his own creative output.

Notes

1.   Raymond Lister, *Samuel Palmer: His Life and Art*, Cambridge: Cambridge University Press, 1987, pp. 3-7.

2.   A.H. Palmer, *The Life and Letters of Samuel Palmer, Painter and Etcher*, London: Seeley, 1892, p. 6.

3.   See Elizabeth Prettejohn, *The Art of the Pre-Raphaelites*, London: Tate Publishing, 2000, p. 27.

4.   For Palmer's friendship with Wate and his death see Raymond Lister (ed.), *The Letters of Samuel Palmer*, 2 vols, Oxford: Clarendon Press, 1974, vol. 1, pp. 54, 60.

5.   In 1816 Wate exhibited at the Royal Academy, 'Study from nature; Banks of the Thames, Battersea'.

6.   Palmer, *Life and Letters*, p. 7. The work was purchased by a Mr Wilkinson of 4 Beaumont Street, Marylebone.

7.   Palmer, *Life and Letters*, p. 8.

8.   Lister, *Letters*, vol. 2, p. 765, n. 2.

9.   John Thomas Smith, *Nollekens and his Times*, London: Henry Colburn, 1829, vol. 2, p. 425.

10.   Palmer, *Life and Letters*, p. 8.

11.   Ibid.

12.   Ibid., p. 6.

13.   See David Irwin, *John Flaxman 1755-1826. Sculptor, Illustrator, Designer*, London: Studio Vista/ Christies, 1979, pp. 204-5.

14.   Ibid., p. 213; Lister, *Letters*, vol. 1, p. 54.

15.   See Martin Butlin (ed.), *Samuel Palmer. The Sketchbook of 1824*, London: Thames and Hudson, 2005, pp. 94-5.

16.   Lister, *Letters*, 1974, vol. 2, p. 893.

17.   Ralph N. Wornum, *Lectures on Painting by the Royal Academicians. Barry, Opie and Fuseli*, London: H.G. Bohn, 1848, p. 558.

18.   See Geoffrey Grigson, *Samuel Palmer. The Visionary Years*, London: Kegan Paul, 1947, p. 15.

19.   Palmer, *Life and Letters*, p. 15.

20.   See Peter Murray, *Dulwich Picture Gallery. A Catalogue*, London: Sotheby Parke Bernet, 1980, pp. 90-91. The painting was attributed to Leonardo da Vinci until 1854. The present attribution to Piero di Cosimo was made in 1879.

21.   Samuel Palmer to Miss Louisa Twining, 22 November 1864. See Lister, *Letters*, 1974, vol. 2, pp. 717-18. Lister notes that Palmer was either referring to the present work (DPG 4) or Cuyp's *Herdsmen with Cows* (DPG 128).

22.   Palmer, *Life and Letters*, p. 35.

23.   Ibid., p. 36.

24.   Grigson, *Visionary Years*, p. 12. See also Lister, *Letters*, vol. 2, p. 824.

25.   Palmer, *Life and Letters*, p. 13.

26.   Lister, *Letters*, vol. 2, p. 706. See also William Vaughan, Elizabeth E. Barker, Colin Harrison et al., *Samuel Palmer (1805-1881): Vision and Landscape*, London: British Museum Press, 2005, pp. 210-11, fig. 29.

27.   Palmer, *Life and Letters*, p. 14.

28.   Lister, *Letters*, vol. 1, p. 37.

29.   Lister, *Letters*, vol. 1, p. 13.

30.   Ibid., p. 8.

31.   Lister, *Letters*, vol. 1, p. 54.

32.   See Butlin, *Sketchbook*, pp. 154-6.

33.   Palmer, *Life and Letters*, pp. 34-5.

34.   Ibid., p. 37.

35.   Lister, *Letters*, vol. 2, p. 574.

36.   Ibid, vol. 1, p. 23.

37.   See Ilaria Bignamini and Martin Postle, *The Artist's Model. Its role in British Art from Lely to Etty*, Nottingham: Nottingham University Art Gallery, 1991, pp. 56-7.

38.   David Bindman, *Blake as an Artist*, Oxford: Oxford University Press, 1977, p. 19.

39.   Ibid., p. 21.

40.   Lister, *Letters*, vol. 1, pp. 33-4.

41.   Ibid., p. 35.

42.   Ibid., vol. 1, p. 339.

43.   Ibid., vol. 1, p. 216.

44.   Ibid., vol. 2, p. 824. See also Vaughan, Barker, Harrison et al., *Vision and Landscape*, p. 14.

45.   Lister, *Letters*, vol. 2, p. 618.

46.   Ibid., vol. 1, p. 805.

47.   Ibid., pp.129-30, and Vaughan, Barker, Harrison et al., *Vision and Landscape*, pp. 208-10.

48.   Lister *Letters*, vol. 1, pp. 519-22, vol. 2, pp. 580-82, 715-19.

49.   Ibid., vol. 1, p. 527.

50.   David Bindman, *The Thames and Hudson Encyclopaedia of British Art*, London: Thames and Hudson, 1985, p. 247.

51.   Lister, *Letters*, vol. 2, p. 791.

52.   See Martin Postle, 'The Foundation of the Slade School of Fine Art: Fifty-nine Letters in the Record Office of University College London', *The Walpole Society*, 1995/96, vol. 58, pp. 127-230.

53.   Ibid., p. 171.

54.   Ibid.

55.   Ibid., p. 175.

56.   Ibid., pp. 171-2.

57.   Ibid., p. 172.

58.   Ibid., p. 169.

59.   Lister, *Letters*, vol. 2, p. 765, n. 2.

60.   Ibid., vol. 2, p. 765.

61.   Ibid., vol. 2, pp. 844-52.

62.   Ibid., vol. 2, p. 1065.

63.   Ibid., vol. 2, p. 765, note 2.

64.   Ibid., vol. 1, p. xiv.

65.   Palmer, *Life and Letters*, p. 18.

66.   Ibid.

4

'Dreaming of the marriage of the land and sea': Samuel Palmer and the coast

Christiana Payne

> *Why, from childhood onwards, are we ever dreaming of capes and caves,*
> *and islets and headlands, and the marriage of the land and sea?*
> Samuel Palmer to James Clarke Hook, May 1863

Samuel Palmer is not usually thought of as a painter of the sea. However, his son A.H. Palmer included five coastal scenes amongst the 22 illustrations of his *Life and Letters*, and described one work, 'Storm and Wreck on the North Coast of Cornwall', as 'one of the best of [his] sketches from nature'.[1] The coast features in a number of the elaborate exhibition watercolours of the mid-century, such as 'Robinson Crusoe guiding his Raft into the Creek' (1850, City Museum and Art Gallery, Stoke on Trent) and 'Farewell to Calypso' (1848-49, Whitworth Art Gallery, University of Manchester). In addition to these, exhibition records show that in the 1850s and 1860s Palmer exhibited a considerable number of paintings which focus on the contemporary life of the British coast. In many cases we know these works only from their titles, because they sold very well, and disappeared into private collections straight after the exhibitions. Palmer evidently shared the preoccupations of other artists of the time: he made detailed studies of wave movements, and explored narrative subjects drawing on the life of the British fisherfolk, with all its anxieties and dangers.

These works are from the middle period of Palmer's life, which has been unduly neglected by art historians. The standard account of Palmer focuses on the visionary Shoreham years, which came to an end in the early 1830s, and the 'vision recaptured' in the Milton and Virgil illustrations of his last years, starting in 1865. Yet Palmer produced many works of great beauty between the mid-1830s and the mid-1860s, in which he showed himself to be fully aware of recent artistic developments. As Timothy Wilcox has recently pointed out, our understanding of the historical Palmer has become distorted by the needs and desires of the artists who 'rediscovered' him in the 1920s, and were keen to reconstruct him as a painter who relied on his inner visions and had little contact with the society of his own day: 'The more Palmer's work resembled observed nature, or the style of other artists, past or present, the less valid it was considered.... Having had little to do with the nineteenth century, Palmer could all the more readily adapt to the twentieth.'[2] In contrast, this chapter aims to restore the balance by focusing on the sketches and exhibition watercolours inspired by Palmer's visits to the North Devon and Cornish coasts, particularly those dating from the late 1840s, 1850s and early 1860s. It will explore those aspects of his career which were uncongenial to his admirers amongst the neo-Romantics: his close study of nature and the parallels between his work and the activities of his contemporaries.

Palmer loved the coasts of North Devon and Cornwall. The richly wooded valleys plunging down towards tiny fishing villages in Devon, and the bleaker, wilder coast of Cornwall, recreated for him some of the intimacy of the Shoreham landscape, in places remote from the railway network where he could feel that the primitive pastoral life was still being lived. Near Tintagel in Cornwall, where he stayed in July 1848, he 'found the people ... very human and civilised' and spent 'a very pleasant week in a lone cottage among the hills, close to a rocky, sea cove. The goat was milked in the kitchen, and two pigs always came up to be scratched the wrong way of the bristles.'[3] To get to Clovelly in Devon, where he spent at least a month in the June and July of 1849, he had to take the train to Exeter, followed by a coach to Bideford, and then travel a further eleven miles, presumably on foot. Once he was there, he enjoyed visiting the 'ancient little church' where 'the service was all chanted even the litany' and he found that 'Clovelly agrees with its natives, who are said scarcely ever to [be ill], and who live to a great age.'[4] In August 1859 he was 'living in a most remote lovely valley', at Berrynarbor near Ilfracombe.[5] These quotations are from letters to Edward Calvert and George Richmond, who had been his companions at Shoreham, and to his much-loved son Thomas More Palmer. They suggest that Devon and Cornwall had become, to some extent, a substitute for the experiences he had living amongst the villagers of Shoreham in the company of the Ancients. In July 1849, he even invited George Richmond to come and join him in Clovelly.[6]

As at Shoreham, his visits to the coast offered plentiful opportunities for study of what he called the 'visible creation'.[7] He was able to escape from his normal routine of teaching private pupils and concentrate fully on observing, and sketching, the landscape around him. Closely detailed drawings of waves breaking on the beach, and systematic observations of the sun setting over the sea, were amongst the sketches he brought home from these expeditions. They became the essential raw material for the exhibition watercolours of the 1850s and 1860s which have coastal settings and themes of parting and return, of storm and danger.[8]

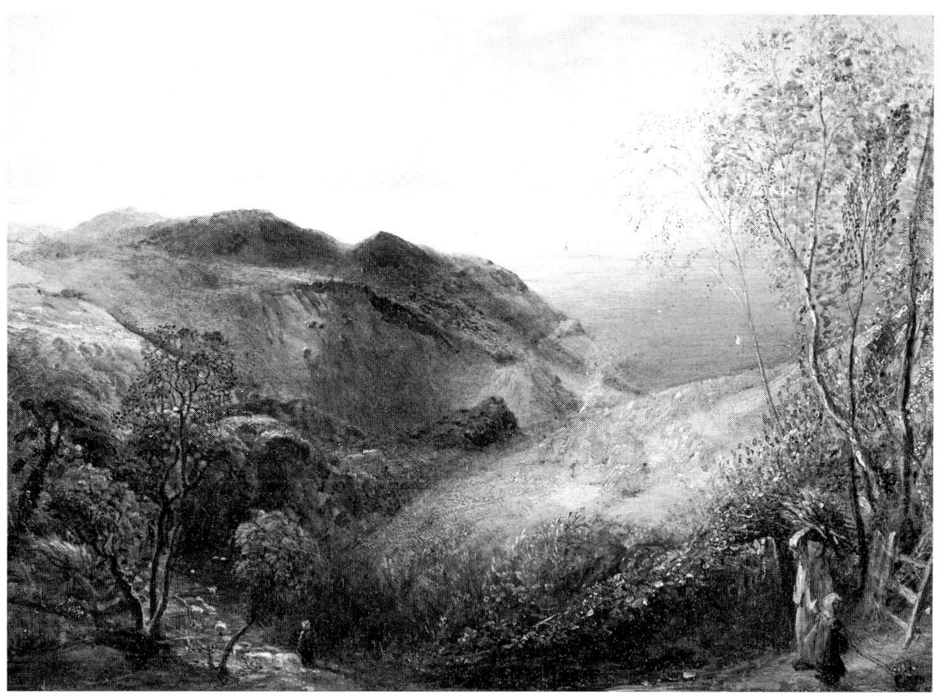

4.1   Samuel Palmer, 'A Scene from Lee, North Devon', 1835. Oil on canvas, 26.7 × 38.1 cm. Fitzwilliam Museum, Cambridge.

It is not easy to reconstruct Palmer's visits to Devon and Cornwall: none of the surviving sketches are dated, and A.H. Palmer's notes on them are often rather vague.[9] An additional problem is that many of the exhibited coastal scenes are untraced, or known only from an old photograph. Palmer first visited Devon in the 1830s, between his Shoreham period and his Italian honeymoon. He mentions his Devon studies in a letter to George Richmond in October 1834, and there are a number of sketches in Raymond Lister's *Catalogue Raisonné* which Lister dates to two visits, in 1834 and 1835, although he writes elsewhere that Palmer visited Devon in 1833 and 1835.[10] However, since Palmer himself did not date these drawings, it is impossible to be certain that they date from this time, or even that there were two visits in the 1830s. In 1835 he exhibited two oil paintings at the Royal Academy, 'A Scene from Lee, North Devon' (Figure 4.1) and 'The Cornfield'. 'The Cornfield' is now thought to be the painting in the Ashmolean Museum known as 'A Pastoral Scene', while 'A Scene from Lee' is the painting in the Fitzwilliam Museum formerly known as 'On Chaldon Down, Dorset'.[11] 'The Cornfield' still has many characteristics of the Shoreham works, with its use of tempera, although it combines several motifs from the coastline of north Devon, including a (much exaggerated) depiction of the rocky outcrops west of Lee, near Ilfracombe, and a view on the left of a narrow valley which could be Lee itself, or Berrynarbor. The sea is prominent in the distance of the painting, and even more so in the related drawings.

The 'Scene from Lee', as its specific title suggests, is a more topographically accurate view of the downland to the west of Lee. In this painting there are still Shoreham-like motifs in the foreground of harvesters, sheep and a girl carrying faggots, but the area given over to the sea, and its shimmering reflection of light, is much greater. In both these paintings, and in all the drawings dated by Lister to this first visit or visits, the sea is in the distance, seen from cultivated fields high above; in his later views of Devon and Cornwall, Palmer would come down to sea level and explore the lives of fisherfolk rather than farm labourers.

In the second half of the 1830s, Palmer continued to study coastal scenery, but in Wales and Italy, rather than Devon and Cornwall. In the summers of 1835 and 1836 he travelled to North Wales. Most of the studies he made here were of inland scenery, but he also sketched Harlech Castle in its seaside location, a view which became the basis for 'The Guardian of the Shores – Twilight after Rain', exhibited in 1844 but untraced since 1926. A.H. Palmer describes this as 'one of [his] largest and most solemn water-colour drawings'.[12] The various versions of the composition focus on the castle itself, seen from above with a distant view of sea and mountains beyond, or else from a low viewpoint, towering over the spectator. In each case the effect is one of grandeur, reminiscent of Turner's depictions of the subject. The views of Harlech were one of a series of studies from this trip of castles and ruined abbeys, traditional 'picturesque' subjects for artists.

In 1837, Palmer married John Linnell's daughter Hannah, and the couple set off on their Italian honeymoon, which was to last for over two years. In the summer of 1838 they were staying on the Bay of Naples, regarded by many people as the most beautiful coastal landscape in the whole of Europe. Palmer concurred with this view: 'on the shores of this bay one feels that one has at last discovered the climate and the land of joy and of enchantment ... I caught a distant glimpse [of Baiae] which realised the enchanted islands we have sometimes dreamt of and "cried to sleep again"', he wrote to George Richmond, who was not so enthusiastic about the area.[13] He considered that 'a months stay (sic) would furnish distances for life'.[14] Palmer painted several watercolours of the bays of Naples and Baiae, most of which are untraced.[15] Being in an area where both Turner and Claude Lorrain had painted, his thoughts turned naturally to these artists' renditions of coastal subjects, encouraging the development of grander compositions, with broad sweeps of water between framing rocks or trees.

Palmer never returned to Italy after 1839, although he had hoped to make Italian visits a regular feature of his life. Instead, he had to make do with the West Country, so that Devon and Cornwall became for him substitutes for the Bay of Naples, as well as for Shoreham. A.H. Palmer says that his father made four visits to Devon and Cornwall between 1848 and 1858.[16] Palmer himself often refers to Devon or Cornwall in his letters, but the evidence is patchy, and complicated by the fact that he liked to go back to places he had visited in previous years. On the basis of dated letters, we can say with certainty that he was in Trebarwith and Tintagel, in Cornwall, in July 1848; in Clovelly, Devon, in June and July 1849; and at Berrynarbor, near Ilfracombe, in August 1859.[17] Titles of some exhibited works provide further clues: in 1858 he exhibited 'The Honeymoon – in the Background the Rocks of Kynance', so he presumably had travelled as far south in Cornwall as the Lizard by 1857 or earlier. In 1859 he exhibited 'The Comet of 1858, as seen from the skirts of Dartmoor' – proof that he was in Devon in early October 1858.[18] At some stage he made a visit to Cornwall (including Kynance Cove) with his son, Thomas More, perhaps in 1857.[19] More would then have been fifteen. It may have been on this visit that he got as far as Land's End, which he refers to in his letters, though it must have been a brief visit since there are no surviving sketches of the area.[20] 1859 was probably his last visit; after Thomas More's death in 1861 he wrote that he could not bear to go again.[21] So there were perhaps five trips in all between 1848 and 1859. As far as we know, he never took Hannah to Devon and Cornwall – or even considered taking her: these visits were an escape from domesticity and a chance for Palmer to revert to a younger self, more like the person he had been in Shoreham. There were also, of course, practical reasons why he left Hannah at home: money was always tight, and travelling on his own or with Thomas More, he could lodge with poor families, as he had done at Shoreham, rather than having to pay for a hotel.

On a professional level, Palmer valued these visits to the West Country for the opportunities they afforded for intensive open-air sketching. Writing to Thomas More in 1861, Palmer referred to 'my most valuable piece of past study … the doing each sunset for three weeks over the *same* piece of rock and sea'.[22] A sheet in Princeton is usually assumed to be one of this series, and dated to 1849 (A.H. Palmer dates it only as 'Kensington period').[23] However, the location of this study is in the hills to the west of Lee, near Ilfracombe in Devon, which would imply a three-week stay in that village which is otherwise unrecorded. It is also quite a long walk from any house in which Palmer might have been staying. It is more likely that the series Palmer refers to was actually made at Trebarwith Strand in Cornwall, where there were plenty of rocks, and where we know that he also made systematic studies of the waves: he was there in 1848, and wrote of it in 1864 as 'a good place for watching storms and studying waves'.[24] There is a pub just above the beach which would probably have been there in Palmer's day, a useful shelter for watching storms over the sea, and there are also houses nearby, in one of which he might have lodged. In the same letter to Thomas More in which he refers to the three-week study he also writes: 'If I sit out of doors during and after sunset, I *rue* it – as I had reason to do in Cornwall.' In further letters, dated 1866 and 1880, he mentions a violent cold he caught sketching three or four feet above the sea after sunset in Cornwall, and three weeks of dry weather which he once experienced in Cornwall. In addition, A.H. Palmer describes the series of sunsets and says that they were made in Cornwall in July 1848.[25] Unfortunately, this series, which must have consisted of at least eighteen studies, perhaps more, appears not to have survived: A.H. Palmer might have destroyed it, although this seems unlikely since he was generally approving of works by his father which showed careful study from nature. It may be that some watercolours of sunsets over the sea languish unattributed in private or public collections, since they are unlike the usual view of the 'visionary' Palmer who painted from his imagination.

It was also on this visit to Cornwall in 1848 that Palmer made several studies of the coast around Tintagel, as well as a detailed study of King Arthur's Castle which became the basis for a finished watercolour of the same subject, now in the Ashmolean Museum.[26] In the latter, Palmer included a huge anchor being transported along a road in an ox-cart, and two goats in a cave, perhaps a reminiscence of the goat he had encountered being milked in the kitchen of his lodgings. Apart from the earlier watercolours of Harlech Castle, this was the only time Palmer produced a watercolour of a well-known coastal feature, a site that had earlier been depicted (though with greatly exaggerated proportions) in Turner's 'Picturesque Views on the Southern Coast'. Palmer admired Turner's work, but he was critical of this exaggeration: 'It strikes me that Turner injured his grand version by unreality in the rocky bluff – but how well he used the crane-work on the round slate wharf!'[27] Like his views of Harlech, Palmer's paintings of Tintagel are depictions of a grand castle which happens to be by the sea, rather than explorations of the human life and natural topography of the coast.

On a later visit to Trebarwith, Palmer made systematic studies of the waves of the sea. A drawing, 'Study of Waves breaking upon the Seashore, Cornwall' (Figure 4.2), usually dated to 1858, must have been made from the beach at Trebarwith Strand: the characteristic Gull Rock is easily recognizable on the left, and the rocks in the foreground are topographically accurate.

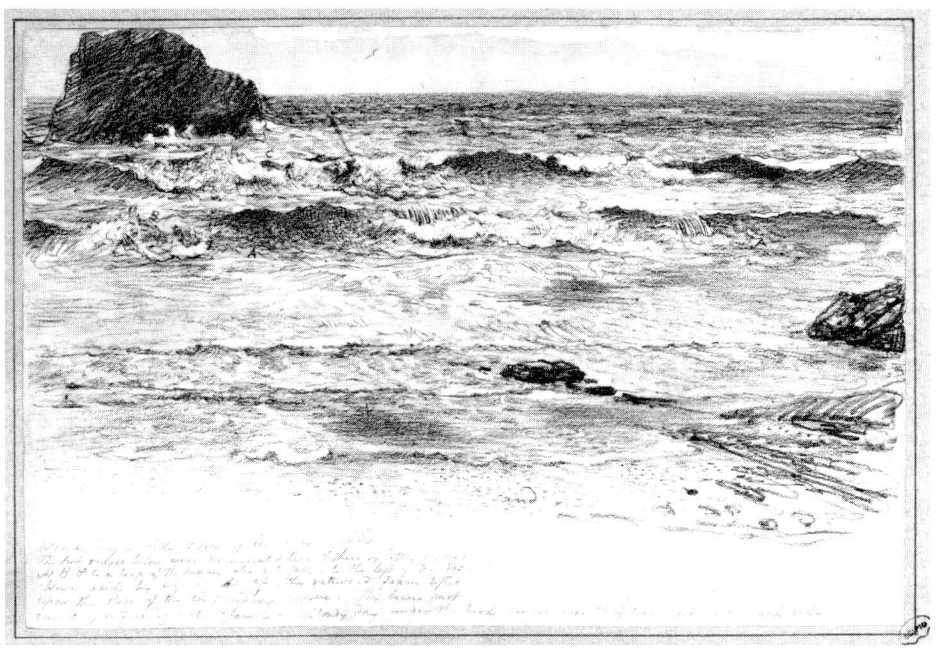

4.2   Samuel Palmer, 'Study of Waves breaking upon the Seashore, Cornwall', c.1857. Black chalk and graphite on wove paper, 16.8 × 25.2 cm. National Gallery of Canada, Ottawa. Photo © National Gallery of Canada, Ottawa.

There are also detailed studies of waves in the Yale Center for British Art and in Manchester City Art Gallery; others are recorded in sales from A.H. Palmer's collection in 1909.[28] Palmer's drawing of the waves in Figure 4.2 is remarkably detailed and accurate, subjecting the structure and movement of the waves to close scrutiny. His annotations show an interest in the effects of wind and water that we might more readily associate with 'scientific' artists such as John Constable or John Brett, rather than the visionary, imaginative Palmer:

Windy Day – tide coming in over sands / the two ridges below even terminated here & there by little waves / At B & C a leap of the foam about to fall – at the left of D do: / blown aside by wind. At AA the returned foam lifted / upon the slope of the impending wave. The lower part / consists of returning water & foam. Cloudy day under the bird (?) central weight of foam pushing up each side.

While there appears to be no definite evidence that he was in Trebarwith again in 1858, the style of the drawing, with its copious annotations and use of A, B, C to mark key details, is similar to dated drawings of 1855 and 1856.[29] Perhaps the sunsets were done in 1848 and the wave studies on a second visit, with Thomas More, in 1857. If this is so, then they would have been done in the summer following the exhibition of Gustave le Gray's photographs of the sea,

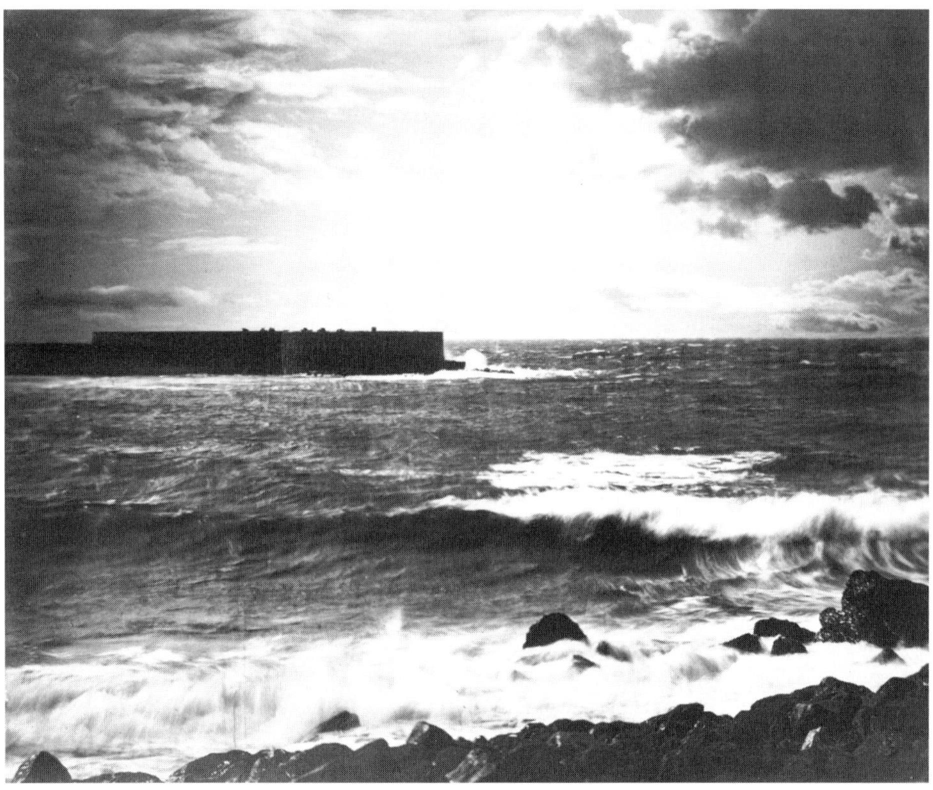

4.3   Gustave Le Gray, 'The Great Wave, Sète', 1857. Albumen print, 34.3 × 41.2 cm.
© Victoria and Albert Museum, London.

shown in London in the winter of 1856-57. Palmer's drawing is uncannily
similar in its composition to Le Gray's photograph, 'The Great Wave, Sète'
(Figure 4.3), recently dated to April 1857.[30]

There was intense interest in the appearance of the waves of the sea in the
1850s. This was the period when photographers were first able to capture the
movement of the waves. As early as 1853, a Welsh amateur photographer,
John Dillwyn Llewelyn, succeeded in taking photographs of breaking waves
using the wet collodion process. These were included in the first exhibition
of the Photographic Society in London, early in 1854. In 1855 a set of four
of his photographs was exhibited under the title 'Motion' at the Exposition
Universelle in Paris, and he was awarded a silver medal of honour.[31] In the
following year, 1856, the French photographer, Gustave Le Gray, created a
sensation in London with his photographs of the sea. These pioneers were
rapidly followed by other practitioners of instantaneous photography, who
for the first time were able to fix effects which had been offering technical
challenges to artists for centuries.

While there is no definite proof that Palmer was aware of these developments, we do know that he was interested in photography.[32] The photographic exhibitions were visited by many painters and reported in the press. They created a climate in which it would seem natural for an artist to devote time to meticulous drawings of waves, and the experience of seeing instantaneous photographs made it easier to grasp the basic forms of an element in constant motion. Henry Moore, who was to make his name as a painter of the sea, first recorded his observations of waves at Clovelly in 1857, and first showed seascapes in 1858.[33] Palmer, therefore, was amongst the pioneers of a new development in naturalistic landscape at this time. Murray's guide to Cornwall and Devon, which was published in the 1850s and used by Palmer on his travels, specifically mentions Trebarwith Strand as 'deservedly a favourite spot with artists; for not only is it intrinsically beautiful as coast-scene, but it offers facilities for the study of the sea in its greatest purity, the billows being unsullied by earthly particles held in suspension'.[34]

In his 1864 letter, Palmer mentions 'watching storms' at Trebarwith, presumably in 1857,[35] and in some of his exhibited works of the late 1850s and early 1860s he took up the theme of shipwreck, with an emphasis on lifesaving. Here, too, he was in tune with contemporaries such as Thomas Brooks, an artist from Hull, who produced several paintings showing lifeboats being launched from the shore. Critics generally preferred such paintings when they showed a successful rescue, and they were often in pairs, the first showing the lifeboat going out, the second the return to the shore with shipwrecked mariners on board. Women were often prominent amongst the onlookers, and viewers would have been aware that these were probably the wives of the lifeboat crew, all of whom were volunteers risking their lives to save others.[36] The Royal National Lifeboat Institution had recently been reorganized and given its current name, and had launched a successful publicity campaign, including a magazine. Artists were directly involved in the fundraising activities of the RNLI, which became a very successful charity. Edward William Cooke, for example, painted a picture of a lifeboat rescue in 1857 and collected funds for the Lifeboat Institution in his studio, subsequently using the money to buy a lifeboat named after him. When this lifeboat, the *Van Kook*, was involved in a successful rescue on the Goodwin Sands, he was able to paint another picture recording the event, which he exhibited in 1866.[37] The watercolourist, Edward Duncan, showed 'The Lifeboat' at the Old Watercolour Society in 1859, followed by 'The Last Man from the Wreck' in 1860; both were much admired.[38] In Lister's *Catalogue Raisonné* there are three paintings of this kind by Palmer: 'The Shipwreck' (c.1859), 'After the Storm' (1861) and 'Wrecked at Home – a Husband and a Brother Saved' (1862).[39] 'Wrecked at Home' is untraced; 'The Shipwreck' is in a private collection, illustrated in Lister's catalogue only by a tiny black and white photograph. 'After the Storm' (Figure 4.4) was on the art market in the 1970s, so there are better photographs of it available, but these are still only in black and white.[40]

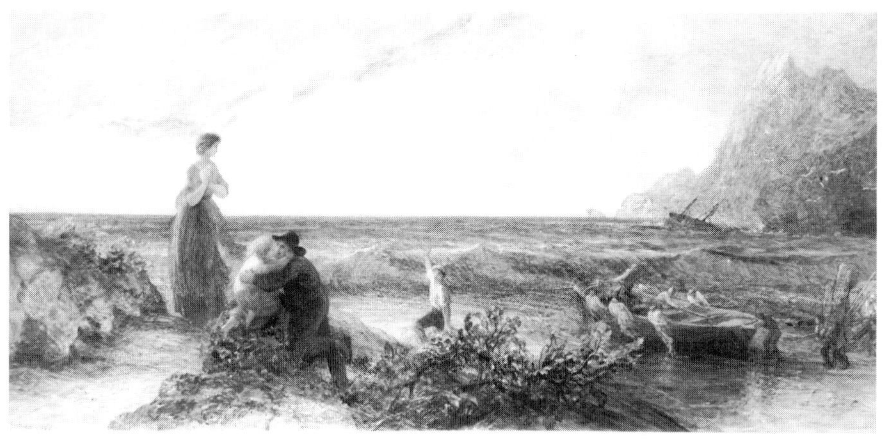

4.4   Samuel Palmer, 'After the Storm', 1861. Pencil and watercolour, 32.4 × 69.9 cm. Current whereabouts unknown. Photo: Witt Library, Courtauld Institute of Art.

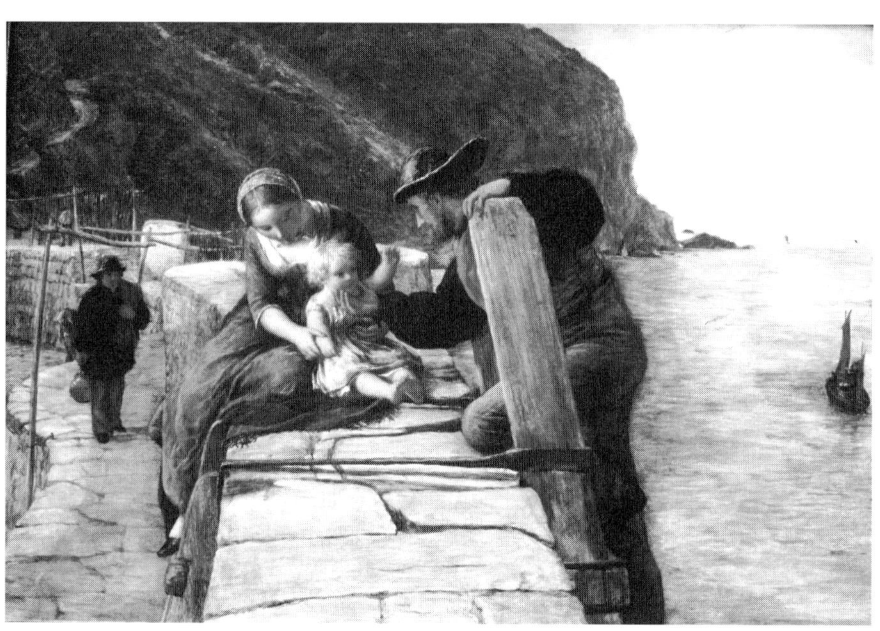

4.5   James Clarke Hook, 'The Fisherman's Goodnight', 1856. Oil on canvas, 48.3 × 76.2 cm. Private collection.

'After the Storm' was shown in 1861, and was possibly prompted by the tragic lifeboat accident at Whitby in February of that year, when all but one of the crew of twenty-four were drowned. Palmer's watercolour shows a lifeboat being launched, and there is evidence of his detailed knowledge of the operation, including the line which was cast into the waves to enable the lifeboat to pull out through a heavy surf, and a figure approaching from the right, holding oars for the lifeboatmen. The fisherman in the foreground is presumably about to go off and join the lifeboat crew with his son, while his wife looks on, her hands clasped in silent prayer.

The figure of the fisherman hugging his child is a tribute to Palmer's friend, James Clarke Hook: the figure almost exactly repeats the pose of the fisherman in Hook's oil painting, which he reproduced as an etching, of 'The Fisherman's Goodnight' 1856 (Figure 4.5).

Palmer first met Hook in 1850 when the two men became members of the Etching Club, and they soon became close friends. Palmer used to stay with Hook to escape Hannah's spring cleaning, and referred to Hook's house as Elysium.[41] There are affectionate letters to Hook, to his wife Rosalie, and to his son Bryan in the Palmer correspondence.[42] A.H. Palmer wrote a series of appreciative articles on Hook and even named his two sons after Hook's sons, Allan and Bryan.[43] It is evident that Hook and Palmer greatly respected each other's work. Hook owned at least one watercolour by Palmer, and Palmer had a complete set of early signed proofs of Hook's etchings, unfortunately destroyed in a fire in a warehouse in Canada.[44]

Hook, like Palmer, admired the simple life of those parts of the country untouched by urbanization and tourism. From the mid-1850s he chose to concentrate on life in the fishing villages, starting with Clovelly. It was in Clovelly that he posed the models for 'The Fisherman's Goodnight', right on the pier. A number of watercolours exhibited by Palmer in the late 1850s and early 1860s have titles which suggest they were similar to Hook's paintings: 'The Fisherman's Wife – Squally Weather Passing Over' (1857), 'The Fishing Boats going out' (1859), 'The Fisherman's Wife' (1862). These are all lost, but there is a description of 'The Fisherman's Wife' in the *Athenaeum*: 'a rocky coast in a wild evening, under purple and dun orange clouds, the sea tumbling wildly: a forcible and beautiful work'.[45] This suggests that the watercolour made good use of Palmer's studies of waves and sunsets. The lines of verse Palmer inserted in the exhibition catalogue drew the viewer's attention to the dangers of the fisherman's life: 'The storm and anxious night are passed,/The wished for sail appears at last'. This was a common approach to the depiction of fisherfolk in the mid-nineteenth century, when small fishing boats were often lost at sea, leaving families bereft of husbands, fathers and sons.

Several oil paintings by James Clarke Hook depict young boys going to sea, emphasizing the effect of their departure on the families they leave behind.

In 1857, for example, he exhibited 'A Widow's Son going to Sea' (now known only from a photograph), also set on the pier at Clovelly, which shows a distraught mother reluctant to let her son face the dangers of the element which has, presumably, already claimed her husband.[46] These dangers might involve shipwreck close to home (Bideford Bay was notorious for sudden storms), or, if a son joined the Navy, they might involve war overseas. This was the decade of the Crimean War (1854-56) and the Indian mutiny (1857-58). In the same year, 1857, Hook exhibited a work entitled 'The Shipboy's Letter', which was described by a reviewer in 1859 as showing 'a hard-working man and his wife … [who] suspend for a moment their daily labour to read a scrawl just received from their eldest boy, who is far away on the broad ocean, a poor cabin-boy in some government transport sailing to the Crimea or India'.[47] Two years later, Palmer's watercolour, 'A Letter from India' (1859, Johannesburg Art Gallery) took a similar theme, showing a letter being delivered to a family group in the countryside near to the sea, with rocks in the background that are reminiscent of the Valley of Rocks near Lynton in Devon.

In the late 1850s and early 1860s, Palmer painted at least four exhibition watercolours which show young boys going to, or returning from, a long sea voyage. In each case the centre of the composition is taken up by a wide expanse of open sea, bounded by rather fanciful rocks to the right, and on the left a Shoreham-like vision of a rustic cottage nestling under trees. The series began with 'Going to India or Going to Sea – The Father's Blessing and the Mother's Prayer' (Victoria and Albert Museum), which Palmer followed up with three watercolours showing a boy returning to his family. 'Returned from India' was exhibited in the International Exhibition of 1862. Like 'Going to India', this showed a father and mother and small children standing on the shore, with their son standing up waving in a rowing boat while his large sea-going ship waits in the background.[48] Two variations on the theme, 'Returned from India' or 'The Sailor's Return' (1859, Whitworth Art Gallery, Manchester) and 'The Brother Come Home from Sea' (Figure 4.6) were further scenes of homecoming, with only women and children waiting to welcome the boy home – perhaps implying that, like the boy in Hook's well-known painting, he is also a widow's son.

This choice of subject has been seen as an attempt by Palmer to make his works more saleable by adopting topical and sentimental subject matter. It is certainly true that he was very successful in selling such works.[49] What has not always been appreciated is that these subjects would also have had strong personal significance for him. His close friend, Edward Calvert, had been in the Navy and Palmer himself expressed admiration for the British warships, the 'hearts of oak'.[50] In 1857 he exhibited a watercolour (now lost) with the title 'Two Years Ago on the Southern Coast – The British Fleet in Sight', which was presumably a patriotic reference to the part played by the Navy in the Crimean War. Living in coastal villages for extended periods, and lodging

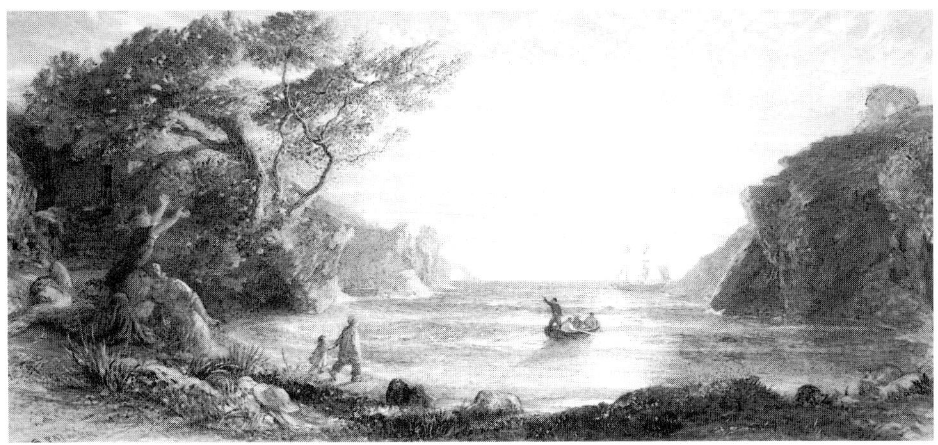

4.6   Samuel Palmer, 'The Brother come Home from Sea', 1863. Watercolour, 20 ×
43 cm. Current whereabouts unknown. Photo: Witt Library, Courtauld Institute of
Art. Private collection, courtesy of Lowell Libson Ltd.

with the villagers, he would have come across stories, or witnessed scenes, of
departures and homecomings, danger and loss. In 1856, apparently, Thomas
More himself expressed a desire to go to sea.[51]

Palmer had made a huge emotional investment in Thomas More, and he
was devastated when the boy died, at the age of nineteen, on 11 July 1861.
Nevertheless, he continued to paint the theme of a boy returning from sea
after this time, when the subject must have been very painful for him. Perhaps,
like his later watercolour and etching, 'The Lonely Tower', it provided a kind
of therapy for his grief.[52] 'The Brother Come Home from Sea' was exhibited
in 1863, with a cheerful verse about a cottage merrymaking.[53] Like the other
watercolours in the series, this draws on Palmer's studies of waves and sunsets,
with particularly effective depictions of the prismatic hues on the waves
rolling in to the shore, and of the bright cirrus clouds above the sunset.

The sea has traditionally been seen as a symbolic boundary, as well as a
purely geographical one, and this would have been a familiar idea to any
reader of poetry in the mid-nineteenth century.[54] Just as, in his earlier life,
Dulwich had been the gateway into the valley of vision, so the coast could
represent, for Palmer, the boundary between life and death, its sunlit waves
and distant islands a vision of 'prospects brightening in futurity', a glimpse
of the heavenly world to come.[55] If this was the case, then the brother coming
home from sea would be a vision of the longed-for reunion with his dead son,
a subject foreshadowed in his note in an early sketchbook, amongst themes he
intended to paint, of 'a family met in Heaven'.[56] A hint of the meaning Palmer
may have found in these visions of the open sea is provided in a note he made
about aerial perspective in 1844: 'To get vast space, what a world of power

does aerial perspective open! From the dock-leaf at our feet, far, far away to the isles of the ocean – And thence – far thence, into the abyss of boundless light.'[57]

Shipwrecks also had personal and symbolic significance for Palmer. In the 1860s, he often uses the imagery of shipwrecks and anchors to refer to his emotional distress and his spiritual state. To Alexander Gilchrist he writes, in July 1861, that he and Hannah are 'like two wrecked creatures drifting upon a plank'.[58] In March 1862, in a letter to Mrs George, he says his gallant barque has foundered, and he must drift on in an eggshell, but '*Then* comes the voice from Heaven, bidding us open our eyes and see, and stretch out our hands and *grasp* the ANCHOR OF THE SOUL'.[59] Much later, in a letter to F.G. Stephens in 1872, he writes of finding anchorage where Pascal, Bacon, Newton and Milton have lowered their cables: 'From this spiritual harbour of refuge we may look forth on the material element without terror albeit perhaps with the deepest grief …'[60] It seems likely that these later seascapes, therefore, had for Palmer a spiritual meaning, representing a safe haven at a time when the ideas of Darwin were threatening religious belief, as well as a boundary between life and death, beyond which he might hope to see his loved ones again. He had begun painting these themes in the 1850s, when Thomas More was still alive. When he continued to exhibit them in 1862 and 1863, it is likely that their meaning was intensified by his own bitter experience.

Palmer never went back to Devon or Cornwall, as far as we know, after 1861. He wrote to Edwin Wilkins Field in 1864 of his experiences in Cornwall, adding that he 'could never bear' to go again 'as Cornwall was my last tour with my dear Son'.[61] The main series of coastal scenes came to an end in 1863, the year in which he wrote the letter to James Clarke Hook which is quoted at the beginning of this chapter.[62] However, in two later works he looked back to the happy times he had spent on the North Devon and Cornish coasts. In 1874, when he exhibited 'Old England's Sunday Evening', he seems to have combined his memories of Shoreham with reminiscences of Clovelly. As in his Shoreham pictures, villagers walk through a cornfield to reach the church; but the church is set in a fertile valley leading down to a rocky coast. The open sea lies beyond. It is not a topographically accurate depiction of Clovelly Church (which is set above the village) but it is strongly suggestive of the area. To use the terms employed by William Vaughan and Elizabeth Barker in their recent article on 'The Lonely Tower', it is a 'reclamation' of both Shoreham and Devon, 'an ultimate transformation into imaginative art of deep-rooted experience'.[63] This watercolour was bought by J.W. Overbury, who was obviously receptive to imaginative art as he went on to buy the Oxford sepias from Palmer.[64]

Five years later, in 1879, he exhibited a small, exquisitely detailed watercolour entitled 'Western Shores' (Victoria and Albert Museum). This is closely based on a topographically accurate sketch of the coast to the west of

Boscastle, probably made in 1848 or 1857, with figures added.[65] A shepherd in a pink robe, probably intended to represent Christ as the Good Shepherd, steers his sheep away from a dangerous rocky headland, towards a road that leads to a sunlit village around the corner. There is a single sailing ship on the sea, suggesting, like Tennyson's poetry, the coming of death.[66] In this case, it may represent Palmer's consciousness that his own death was not far away, while the sunlit village and distant islands indicate his faith in the afterlife.

In his surviving coastal landscapes, Palmer combines sharply-observed details and effects – especially of sunsets and wave movements – with an interest in themes from modern life that were popular amongst his contemporaries. Yet, for him as for his contemporaries, these subjects – shipwrecks and rescues, the departure and return of cherished sons – had a deeper significance as well as a topical interest. Much of the pictorial evidence of Palmer's engagement with the coast, whether in his studies from nature or in his exhibition watercolours, is lost to us. Nevertheless, the fragments that remain are sufficient to show that it was an area of his work that was close to his heart, resonant both of his idyllic experiences in Shoreham and of his close relationship with Thomas More.

Notes

1. Martin Hardie and James Laver, with notes and introduction by A.H. Palmer, *Catalogue of an Exhibition of Drawings, Etchings & Woodcuts by Samuel Palmer and other Disciples of William Blake*, London: Victoria and Albert Museum, 1926, p. 43. This is illustrated as plate XII.

2. Timothy Wilcox, *Samuel Palmer*, London: Tate Publishing, 2005, p. 8.

3. Letter to Edward Calvert, July 25 1848, in Raymond Lister (ed.), *The Letters of Samuel Palmer*, Oxford: Clarendon Press, 1974, p. 460.

4. Letter to Thomas More Palmer, June 25 1849. Ibid., p. 466; letter to George Richmond, 17 July 1849; ibid., p. 472.

5. Letter to Thomas More Palmer, August 1859. Ibid., p. 562.

6. He says there are two comfortable rooms to be had opposite his lodging, 'very clean, I have no doubt, from the kind of people – and the appearance of the house generally' (letter of 17 July 1849. Ibid., p. 471).

7. For example, in a letter to John Linnell, 17 May 1829, he writes: 'Tho' living in the country I really did not think there were those splendours in visible creation which I have lately seen.' Ibid., p. 53.

8. Like other landscape painters, Palmer took advantage of the summer and autumn – the 'sketching season' – to make studies from nature, which he would later use when constructing narrative landscapes in his studio. He had done this at Shoreham too: the popular idea of Palmer as a painter who painted purely from his imagination is not borne out by the evidence.

9. For example, he dates 'View of Clovelly' (New York, Metropolitan Museum of Art) 'between 1848 & 1858'. This work is illustrated in William Vaughan, Elizabeth E. Barker, Colin Harrison et al., *Samuel Palmer (1805-1881): Vision and Landscape* (London: British Museum Press, 2005), p. 197, where it is erroneously identified as a view of Ilfracombe. A.H. Palmer assigns other coastal landscapes to the 'Kensington period', i.e. 1849-62.

10. 'I would not have been without the Devonshire reminiscences on any account – I hardly ever try to invent landscape without thinking of them.' Letter to George Richmond, 16 and 20 October 1834, Lister, *Letters*, p. 66. Raymond Lister, *Samuel Palmer: His Life and Art*, Cambridge: Cambridge University Press, 1987, chronological table, pp. xiv-xx.

11.   Vaughan, Barker, Harrison et al., *Vision and Landscape*, nos 91 and 97.

12.   A.H. Palmer, in *Catalogue of an Exhibition*, p. 44. The views of Harlech are in Raymond Lister, *Catalogue Raisonné of the Works of Samuel Palmer*, Cambridge: Cambridge University Press, 1988, nos 229, 267, 382 and 391.

13.   Letter of 3 June 1838, Lister, *Letters*, pp. 138-9.

14.   Letter to Mr and Mrs Linnell, 9 October 1838, Lister, *Letters*, p. 208.

15.   For example, Lister, *Catalogue Raisonné*, nos 292, 295, 298. 'The Prospect' (1881), a watercolour acquired by the Ashmolean Museum, Oxford, in 2005, combines a Shoreham-like foreground with a panoramic view over a bay, which is similar to the Bay of Naples.

16.   A.H. Palmer, *The Life and Letters of Samuel Palmer, Painter and Etcher*, London: Seeley, 1892, p. 106.

17.   Letters to Thomas More (July 1848, Lister *Letters*, p. 458) and Edward Calvert (25 July 1848. Ibid., pp. 459-60) show that he was in Trebarrow (Trebarwith) and Tintagel in 1848. In 1859 we find him writing letters to Thomas More from Clovelly (25 June 1849, 15 July 1849. Ibid., pp. 466-70) and also to George Richmond (17 July 1849. Ibid, pp. 471-2). In 1859 he was in Berrynarbor, to the east of Ilfracombe (letter to Thomas More, August 1859. Ibid., p. 562). In the 1840s and 1850s Palmer also went to coastal resorts closer to home, such as Hastings and Margate.

18.   This painting is discussed in Roberta J.M. Olsen, 'A watercolour by Samuel Palmer of Donati's Comet', *Burlington Magazine*, November 1990, pp. 795-6.

19.   Palmer mentions 'Kynance Cove he so strongly loved' in 'The 1861 Life's Balance Sheet'. Lister, *Samuel Palmer*, p. 197.

20.   In 1864 he writes that he had used Murray's Handbook 'for the Lizard and Land's End' (letter to Edwin Wilkins Field, 10 June 1864, Lister, *Letters*, p. 692).

21.   In 1864 he wrote to Edwin Wilkins Field: 'Were I to go again which I could never bear, as Cornwall was my last tour with my dear Son …' (Letter of 10 June 1864, Lister, *Letters*, p. 693.) A letter to Thomas More, dated August 1860, shows that he was thinking of going to Devon that summer, but there is no evidence that he ever got there: 'I am *thinking* of North Devon with light luggage in travelling bag but the weather is not tempting – so perhaps it will not transpire'. Ibid., p. 578.

22.   Letter to Thomas More, ?May 1861. Ibid., p. 602.

23.   Vaughan, Barker, Harrison et al.,*Vision and Landscape*, no. 119.

24.   Letter to Edwin Wilkins Field, 10 June 1864, Lister, *Letters,* p. 693.

25.   Letter to Miss Julia Richmond, September 1866. Ibid., p. 746; letter to James Clarke Hook, 13 August 1880, Ibid., p. 1025. A.H. Palmer (*Life and Letters*, p. 87) states that Palmer spent the greater part of July in Cornwall in 1848: 'Here, on this and other occasions, he accumulated a large number of pencil, chalk and water-colour sketches of the coast, including a three weeks' series of sunsets painted each day with precisely the same foreground of sea and rock … the sunsets were boldly and very rapidly executed, some on white, and some on tinted paper.' He adds 'The knowledge gained by this especial attention to sunsets over the sea was afterwards utilized in many works; among others, in *Robinson Crusoe, St Paul Landing in Italy*; and *The Brother Come Home from Sea.*' 'Robinson Crusoe Guiding his Raft into the Creek' (City Museum and Art Gallery, Stoke-on-Trent) was shown at the Old Water Colour Society in 1850 (Lister, no. 495).

26.   Vaughan, Barker, Harrison et al., *Vision and Landscape*, nos 121 and 122.

27.   Letter to Edwin Wilkins Field, October 1864 (Lister, *Letters*, pp. 709-10).

28.   Lister, *Catalogue Raisonné*, nos 474, 563, 455-7.

29.   For example, 'Brambles' (Yale Center for British Art). Ibid., no. 534.

30.   Sylvie Aubenas (ed.), *Gustave Le Gray 1820-1884*, Paris: Bibliothèque Nationale de France/ Gallimard, 2002, p. 332.

31.   Richard Morris, *John Dillwyn Llewelyn, 1810-1882: the First Photographer in Wales*, Cardiff: Welsh Arts Council, 1980, pp. 8-9.

32.   Vaughan, Barker, Harrison et al., *Vision and Landscape*, p. 213.

33.   F. Maclean, *Henry Moore, R. A.,* London: the Walter Scott Publishing Co. Ltd, 1905, p. 33.

34.   *Murray's Handbook for Devon and Cornwall (1859)*, Newton Abbot: David and Charles Reprints, 1971, p. 223.

35.   See note 24 above.

36.   For paintings of lifeboat rescues, see Christiana Payne, *Where the Sea Meets the Land: Artists on the Coast in Nineteenth-century Britain*, Bristol: Sansom and Company, 2007, pp. 157-62.

37.   J. Mundy, *Edward William Cooke 1811-1880: A Man of his Time*, Woodbridge: Antique Collectors' Club, 1996, pp. 237-9.

38.   Randall Davies, 'Edward Duncan (1803-1882)', *Old Water-Colour Society's Club*, 6th annual volume, 1928-29, p. 35.

39.   Lister, *Catalogue Raisonné*, nos 564, 592, 598.

40.   'Wrecked at Home' is known only from the entry in the catalogue for the Old Water Colour Society exhibition of 1862, where its full title is given as '291. *Wrecked at Home – a Husband and a Brother Saved*. 'Th'occasion met, the peril braved;/A brother and a husband saved.' It is possible that this is not a third painting, but the painting catalogued by Lister as 'The Shipwreck', which is not linked by him to any exhibition record. However, A.H. Palmer says 'Wrecked at Home' was in Palmer's 'Large Long' size, and Raymond Lister gives its measurements as 191 x 425 mm. (Lister, *Catalogue Raisonné*, no. 598). 'The Shipwreck' (311 x 672 mm) and 'After the Storm' (324 x 699 mm) are larger, and could almost be a pair. Perhaps the buyer of 'After the Storm' commissioned 'The Shipwreck' as a pendant.

41.   Palmer, *Life and Letters*, p. 137.

42.   To J.C. Hook: May 1861, Lister, *Letters*, p. 601; May 1863, p. 679; May 1863, p. 680; 13 August 1880, p. 1025. To Rosalie Hook: March 1869, pp. 801-2. To Bryan Hook: June 1871, pp. 816-18; 26 March 1881, pp. 1073-5. For a recent discussion of the Hook family, see Juliet McMaster, *Woman Behind the Painter: The Diaries of Rosalie, Mrs James Clarke Hook*, Alberta: The University of Alberta Press, 2006.

43.   A.H. Palmer, 'James Clarke Hook, R. A.', *The Portfolio*, 1888, pp. 1-9, 35-43, 74-82, 105-111, 165-70.

44.   A.H. Palmer, cited in Lister, *Letters*, p. xiii. The watercolour owned by J.C. Hook was the 'View at Tintagel', Lister, *Catalogue Raisonné*, no. 452, now in the British Museum.

45.   *The Athenaeum*, 1862, p. 567.

46.   Illustrated in Payne, *Where the Sea Meets the Land*, p. 186.

47.   *Illustrated London News*, 8 January 1859, p. 43.

48.   Photograph in Witt Library, which gives the most recent owner as the Fine Art Society. Unlike the others in the series, this shows the boy returning through a cave – perhaps inspired by the caves at Kynance Cove.

49.   'Going to India' was bought by Richard Ellison, and thus formed part of the Ellison Bequest to the Victoria and Albert Museum in 1860. 'The Brother Home from Sea' was probably bought by William Fothergill Robinson (*Samuel Palmer: an exhibition of Palmer's works with a Leger provenance to celebrate a century of art dealing* (London: the Leger Galleries, 1992), p. 27). In 1857 Palmer reported to John Linnell that, of his seven watercolours in that year's exhibition, three were sold before the exhibition opened and the remaining four were sold three minutes after the private view opened. These seven included 'The Fisherman's Wife' and 'Two Years ago on the Southern Coast – The British Fleet in Sight'. Letter to John Linnell and Hannah Palmer, ?June 1857, Lister, *Letters*, p. 532.

50.   When he was in Italy in 1838 he wrote that he had been on board HMS Pembroke, 'one of our own *fine* hearts of oak … the band struck up Rule Britannia making my heart throb with anxious fondness for our poor old country'. Letter to Miss Lizzy Linnell, 14 July 1838. Ibid., p. 156.

51.   Lister, *Samuel Palmer*, p. 190.

52.   See William Vaughan and Elizabeth E. Barker, '"Mysterious wisdom won by toil": new light on Samuel Palmer's "Lonely Tower"', *Burlington Magazine*, 147, September 2005, pp. 590-97.

53.   'Awake! Awake! Our Robin is come home;/Just landing by the bay, no more to roam!/Brothers and sisters answer to his cheer/And 'twill be merry in the cottage there;/Pullet and junket, and the old brown ale,/And all agape to hear the traveller's tale.'

54.   For the symbolic meaning of the sea in poetry, see Payne, *Where the Sea meets the Land*, pp. 21-40.

55.   In June 1838 he wrote to George Richmond: 'Landscape should be the symbol of prospects brightening in futurity' (letter of 3 June 1838, Lister, *Letters*, p. 137).

56.   Palmer, *Life and Letters*, p. 13.

57.   Ibid., p. 79.

58.   26 July 1861, Lister, *Letters*, p. 612.

59.   10 March 1862. Ibid., p. 643.

60.   4 May 1872. Ibid., p. 842.

61.   10 June 1864. Ibid., p. 693.

62.   May 1863. Ibid., p. 680.

63.   Vaughan and Barker, 'Mysterious wisdom', p. 597.

64.   Lister, *Catalogue Raisonné*, no. 669.

65.   Ibid., no. 561. It is in the Fogg Art Museum, Harvard University.

66.   As in Tennyson's *Crossing the Bar*. This use of symbolism is also to be found in the paintings of Caspar David Friedrich and William Bell Scott. See Payne, *Where the Sea Meets the Land*, pp. 26-7 and 130-32.

5

Samuel Palmer: Poetry, printmaking and illustration

Paul Goldman

Samuel Palmer was above all a literary artist. His love of the written word permeates almost everything he did, whether painted or etched, and he lived in an age when imaginative illustration in both books and periodicals attained remarkable peaks of achievement and intensity. The intention here is to discuss his work as a printmaker, briefly to look at what he did as an illustrator and attempt to assess where to place Palmer within the illustrative maelstrom that was mid-Victorian illustration.

Yet, as a printmaker he produced so little – he completed just thirteen plates and began work on a further five. How can it be, then, that with so small an oeuvre to his credit, his prints remain today highly regarded both by print specialists and art lovers alike? When major printmakers are considered critically, most viewers instinctively think of artists who produced original prints in significant numbers – for example, Rembrandt, Goya, Dürer or Toulouse-Lautrec, to name but four. In complete contrast there are comparatively few practitioners like Palmer, who produced so limited a group of single sheet prints, yet whose impressions are recognized today as being of the highest order. To stand alongside him, one could mention Mantegna, who has some 25 plates attributed to his hand, though he is unlikely to have in truth engraved more than ten himself, and Jacob van Ruisdael, whose remarkable landscape etchings run to only about a dozen plates.

So why did etching, as a technique, mean quite so much to Palmer? It appears that he saw in it several distinct advantages over painting in oils or in watercolours. It is apparent from what he wrote that it was the mechanics of the process itself, with its very slowness and laboriousness, which entirely suited his artistic temperament. This was because through it he was able to express his vision, by turning completely to works which he could cull from his imagination. He would spend lengthy periods revelling in the equipment, the acid, the feathers, the retroussage and so on and, by immersing himself so completely in the activity itself, could work at a pitch of intensity which he did not reach so naturally in the practice of painting.[1] Palmer remarked,

Oh the joy! Colours and brushes pitched out of the window ; plates the
Liber Studiorum size got out of the dear, little etching-cupboard where
they have long reposed ; great needles sharpened three-corner-wise
like bayonets ; opodeldoc rubbed into the forehead to wake the brain
up; and a Great Gorge of old poetry to get up the dreaming.[2]

The reference here has invariably been assumed to refer to Turner's great project, issued in fourteen parts between 1807 and 1819, yet one should note also that in 1838 John Sell Cotman had published a major series of landscape prints also titled *Liber Studiorum*. 'It was named by H.G. Bohn, purchaser and publisher under this title of the plates of soft-ground etchings that Cotman had made between 1810 and c.1815, prints that had not been conceived as a corpus or as related to Turner's epitome of his landscape art.'[3] It must be admitted, though, that Cotman's plates are of various dimensions, while Turner's are relatively uniform. Nevertheless, it is fair to assume that Palmer was well acquainted with both these significant publications, which are devoted entirely to landscape.

Much is made of the complexities of etching, yet in truth, the difficulties lie far more in the biting, wiping and printing of the plate than in the actual drawing on the tallow ground, which offers virtually no resistance to the etching needle. In this it differs from, for example, copper-engraving or wood-engraving, where a certain amount of physical strength to push the graver or burin across the surface is required.[4] Palmer found in etching an art form that was the closest to writing, because it seems that he felt that the marks he made on the plate were not dissimilar from those made by an author drafting ideas in pencil on paper.

Etching seems to stand quite alone among the complete arts in its compatibility with
authorship. You are spared the dreadful death-grapple with colour which makes
every earnest artist's liver a pathological curiosity … its difficulties are not such
to excite the mind to 'restless ecstasy', but are an elegant mixture of the manual,
chemical and calculative, so that its very mishaps and blunders (usually remediable)
are a constant amusement. The tickling sometimes amounts to torture, but on the
whole, it raises and keeps alive a speculative curiosity – it has something of the
excitement of gambling, without its guilt and its ruin. For these and other reasons
I am inclined to think it the best *comptu* exponent of the artist-author's thoughts.[5]

Not only does this celebrated passage display Palmer's elegant and self-deprecatory writing skills, but we also gain a glimpse into exactly how he felt that writing and etching were inextricably one and the same thing. Not for nothing does he hyphenate 'artist-author's thoughts'. Three other themes are also apparent here: 'amusement', 'curiosity' and 'excitement', which all point to an artist who not only loves what he is doing but who is also concerned to explore and to push back boundaries which are technical, intellectual and creative.

It is useful perhaps to see the etchings as falling into three distinct periods: the first covers 1850-58, the second or middle about 1860-61, and then a final late flowering during 1879-80. Palmer's first etching is 'The Willow' and it was made as his probationary plate for membership of the 'Old' Etching Club in 1850. Although there is evidence of a close observation of nature and the etching is not without its charms, it is frankly somewhat conventional in its approach. Palmer's lack of confidence at this period with the technique is clear from some of the lines in the sky which he ruled, rather than drawing them freehand. He was taken to task for this shortcoming by Thomas Creswick (1811-69), himself a fine etcher of some refreshingly naturalistic landscapes, who was a significant early influence on Palmer.[6] This influence is continued, refined and enlarged in his next etching, 'The Skylark', which was also made in 1850 (Figure 5.1) The hatching in the sky closely emulates that to be seen in Creswick's own 'The Village Church', datable to about 1840, though not issued until 1844, when it appeared in the Etching Club's second published portfolio. Palmer's now freely drawn cross-hatching and a similar interest in effects of light reveals a close study of the older artist's work.

Yet even here, in this early essay, Palmer outstrips his competent teacher with a work of extraordinary power. Already there are several quintessential Palmerian characteristics visible: the figure in the landscape, part of it but never dominant, gazing upward in rapt and respectful attention; the distant light as if emanating not just from the horizon but beyond, even from heaven itself; the dog and the bird also in complete harmony with the scene; the densely worked foreground and the Claudian view framed by trees. Palmer had honeymooned in Italy during 1837-39 and saw many of Claude's works on his travels; he described the French artist as 'the greatest landscape-painter who ever lived'.[7] Yet it is also a mark of his own inherent originality that he never became merely a slavish adherent of all Claude's themes, for he took just what he wanted from him and rejected almost as many of them as he accepted.

A.H. Palmer noted his father's trepidation over this plate, remarking '... what I so admire in it – the delicate upward flush of early dawn over thin vaporous cloud, was the result of the day's elbow grease directed not by knowledge of any etching technicality, but by knowledge of one of the most beautiful effects in nature'.[8] From this we can discern and isolate another constant preoccupation of Palmer's; the time of day or night is always uppermost in his mind in his prints, as are equally the effects of light when they occur either early or late in the day. Here one should note that it was Blake who so inspired Palmer as a printmaker. He had been entranced by Blake's intense wood-engravings for Dr Robert John Thornton's publication of the Eclogues called *The Pastorals of Virgil*.[9] Thornton (1768?-1837) was a botanical and medical writer who was responsible for one of the most sumptuous of English flower books,

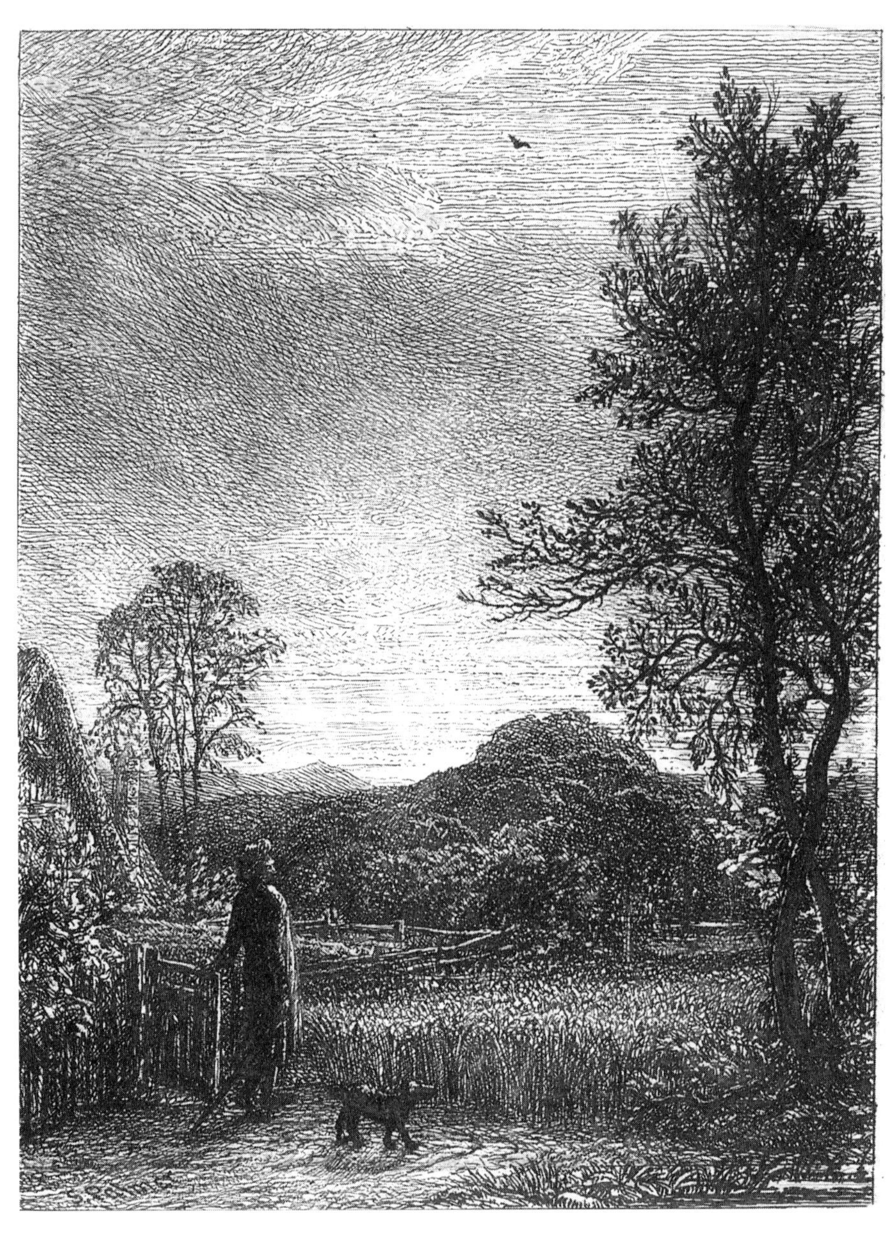

5.1   Samuel Palmer, 'The Skylark', 1850. Etching, 6th state, 11 × 8.8cm. BM 1872-5-11-983.
© The Trustees of the British Museum.

The Temple of Flora (1807), and he had commissioned Blake to illustrate Ambrose Phillips' *Imitation* of the First Eclogue in a school edition.[10] It must have been the child-like, though not childish, nature of these apparently artless images that prompted Palmer to exclaim 'They are visions of little dells, and nooks, and corners of Paradise … There is in all such a mystic and dreamy glimmer as penetrates and kindles the innermost soul, and gives complete and unreserved delight, unlike the gaudy daylight of this world.'[11] The deliberate stress on 'gaudy daylight' seems to encapsulate both the relentless glare of full sunlight, as well as the dazzling shine reflected on harsh modern machinery such as railways, the development of which Palmer so feared and dreaded.

The subject of the skylark was not a new one for Palmer, since he had made a first study (now lost) which was datable 1831-32. An ink drawing, now in the Cleveland Museum of Art, probably made in the same year as the etching, is the same size as the plate with the image reversed, so that when printed it would be in the original sense.[12] An impression exhibited at the Cotswold Gallery in London in 1927 bore Palmer's pencilled inscription 'To hear the lark begin his flight', and, with this knowledge, one can perceive a transparent link to literature, in this case to Milton's *L'Allegro* (II, lines 41-4)

To hear the Lark begin his flight
And singing startle the dull night,
From his-towre in the skies,
Till the dappled dawn doth rise …

While it is correct to be aware of Palmer's deep spirituality and religious faith, and his desire to combine a love of God with a passion for nature, it is also worth pointing out that, in his prints at least, his inspiration is regularly not verse which might be termed overtly ecclesiastical in nature. After all, the poem ends on a note of triumphant joy (lines 151-2)

These delights, if thou canst give,
Mirth with thee I mean to live.

'The Herdsman's Cottage' or 'Sunset', also of 1850, was not published until 1872 when it appeared in *The Portfolio* with a spurious title 'Sunrise'. There are already some developments from what has gone before; the intensity of the light has been heightened, the herdsman himself with his dog and other animals are harmoniously part of the scene and do nothing to damage, intrude or upset it. The sense of peace and calm is all pervading. The figure is significant but only as far as he fits within the natural world. The trees are more intensely worked, the lines increasingly deeply bitten and, unsurprisingly, the print exists in several impressions where Palmer has inked and wiped the plate differently. The manner in which an etched plate is wiped before printing can make for palpable variations between individual impressions, and Palmer evidently relished such freedom to experiment again and again.

'Christmas', or 'Folding the Last Sheep', completes the initial group of prints made in 1850. It is based on lines from a sonnet entitled 'Sonnet on Christmas' (1778) by John Codrington Bampfylde (1754-96).[13]

Old Christmas comes, to close the waned year;
And ay the Shepherd's heart to make right glad;
Who, when his teeming flocks are homeward had,
To blazing hearth repairs, and nut-brown beer,
And views, well pleas'd, the ruddy prattlers dear
Hug the grey mongrel ...

Although now largely forgotten Bampfylde's poems were well regarded in the nineteenth century; Southey considered him 'truly a man of genius' whose sonnets were 'some of the most original in our language'.[14] Palmer's print endows the sonnet with a superior poetry of his own. There are no tentative lines here but present instead is a full mastery of light and shade that is breathtaking. Details tell us more, especially about children, warmth and the solace of home. The poem's expressive limitations are transcended by Palmer's more intense vision.

In 1852 Palmer etched 'The Vine', or 'Plumpy Bacchus', which comprises two images on one plate. In the fourth state the plate is lettered with lines from *Antony and Cleopatra*, Act 2, Scene 7.

Come, thou monarch of the vine,
Plumpy Bacchus with pink eyne!
In thy fats our cares be drown'd,
With thy grapes our hairs be crown'd
Cup us till the world go round,
Cup us till the world go round!

One might have thought such sentiments extraordinary ones to inspire Palmer, with their shameless resonances of drunkenness and total abandon to the pleasures of taste and corporeal sensation. Yet he makes of them something far distant from the words of the song, producing instead an entirely secular vision, but one where he can employ his imagination to the full. Once again the play of light is deftly handled and the lines are drawn with ever more intense depth in order to accent the contrasts between darkness and sunlight more strongly. Examining the sheet in close detail, we can see even more of these contrasts – the two forms both exquisitely modelled, with the one in the foreground seemingly sleeping off the excess, while the bacchic dancer beyond is the very embodiment of drama and excitement. Yet the sleeping figure is posed in such a way as to look forward to future images. Sleep is a central motif for Palmer; he finds in it a sense of the other-worldly, and indeed the mystic communion with

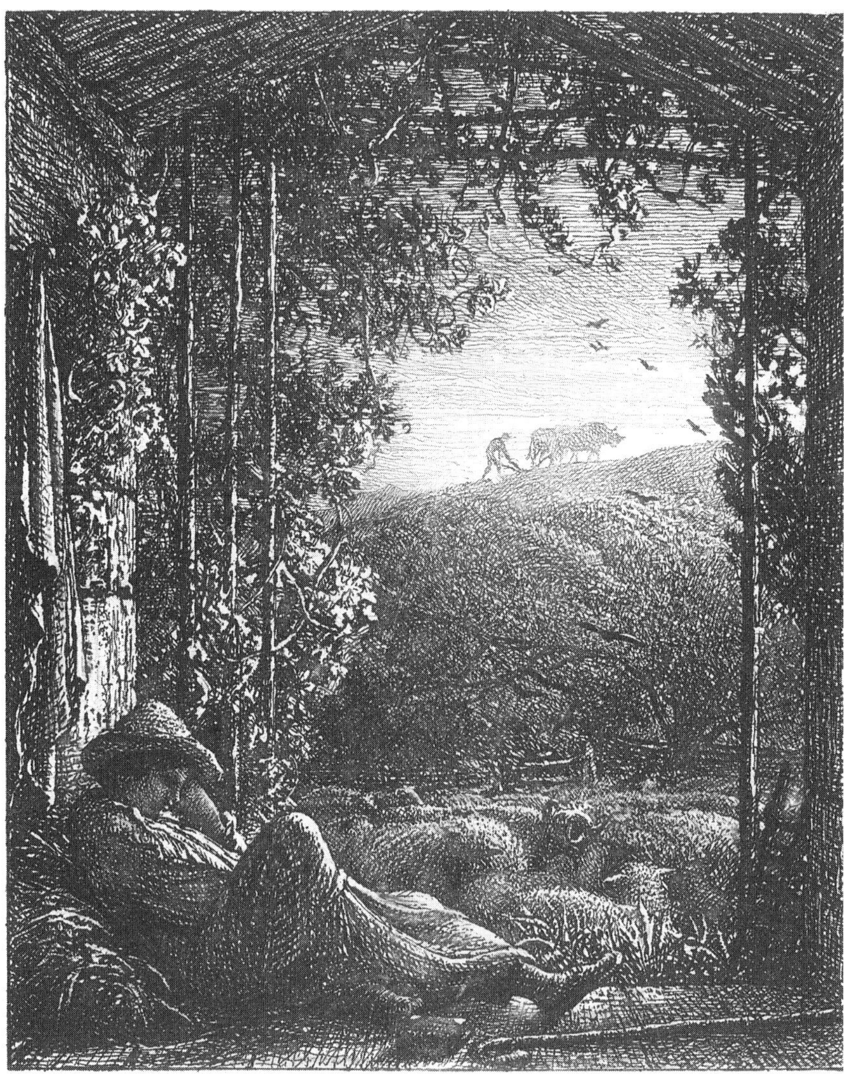

5.2   Samuel Palmer, 'The Sleeping Shepherd – Early Morning', 1854-57. Etching on chine collé, 3rd state, 12.4 × 10.3 cm. BM 1872-5-11-984. © The Trustees of the British Museum.

God that he himself was so habitually seeking in his own spiritual life. The lower of the two subjects is of four naked putti energetically collecting grapes and piling them into baskets with unrestrained delight. To the impression in the British Museum Palmer has added a pencilled title, 'Children Grape gathering', suggesting that he sees them as real infants rather than mythological constructs.[15]

In 1857 Palmer produced 'The Sleeping Shepherd; Early Morning' (Figure 5.2), but it is known that he had been working on the composition from as early as about 1854.[16] The subject of the sleeping shepherd greatly appealed to Palmer, and while it is true that he knew and admired a late second-century statue of 'Endymion the Shepherd Boy Asleep on Mount Latmos' (British Museum), it is likely to have been a general rather than a specific inspiration.[17] As in the previous plate, there is a sleeping figure in the foreground and an active one ploughing in the distance framed in a Claudian arbour. The entire scene is suffused with light rendered so intensely as almost to obscure the figure working, but in contrast to bathe the sleeper in a supernatural glow. His crook lies next to him ready for the day in the fields to come, but Palmer's interest is wholly with the position and the *action*, as it were, of sleep itself. The shepherd possesses a grandeur and a monumentality which render him something far above the mundane. This is not simply a resting worker but an idealized and an idyllic conception – man in the image of God. However, despite being so prominent in the composition he still remains part and parcel of the landscape – an earth which he will inhabit for a short period and then return to the soil – an idea echoed by the labour of turning and ploughing the land. Birth, death, resurrection, a love of God and of his creation, the belief in Jesus Christ as the Shepherd of Mankind, are all spiritual themes which may be sensed here. With one or two exceptions Palmer's prints bear such scrutiny and analysis without falling short – another reason why they remain so firmly established in the canon. On an impression of the first state, shown at the Cotswold Gallery in London in 1927, Palmer had inscribed 'Peace and Quiet'.[18]

With 'The Rising Moon', or 'An English Pastoral', or 'Evening Pastures' of about 1855-57 (Figure 5.3), we come to the first of Palmer's large plates and in it can be seen elements distilled from his years in Shoreham and his visits to Devon and to Italy. The new horizontal format allows Palmer the space to expand his vision and especially to extend his skies, a device which he continues in his next print, 'The Weary Ploughman' or 'Tardus Bubulcus', which he began in 1858. In 1865 when the eighth and final state was published in *A Selection of Etchings by the Etching Club*, Palmer exhibited an impression entitled 'The Ploughman Homeward Plods his Weary Way', making transparently clear his debt to Gray's poem of 1751, *Elegy Written in a Country Churchyard*, Lines 1-4

The curfew tolls the knell of parting day,
The lowing herd wind slowly o'er the lea,
The ploughman homeward plods his weary way
And leaves the world to darkness, and to me.[19]

Here Palmer's printmaking becomes even more concentrated on the depth of the bitten lines and ever greater contrasts, not just between light and dark but also between minute gradations in the blacks which mass monumentally, especially in the hills.

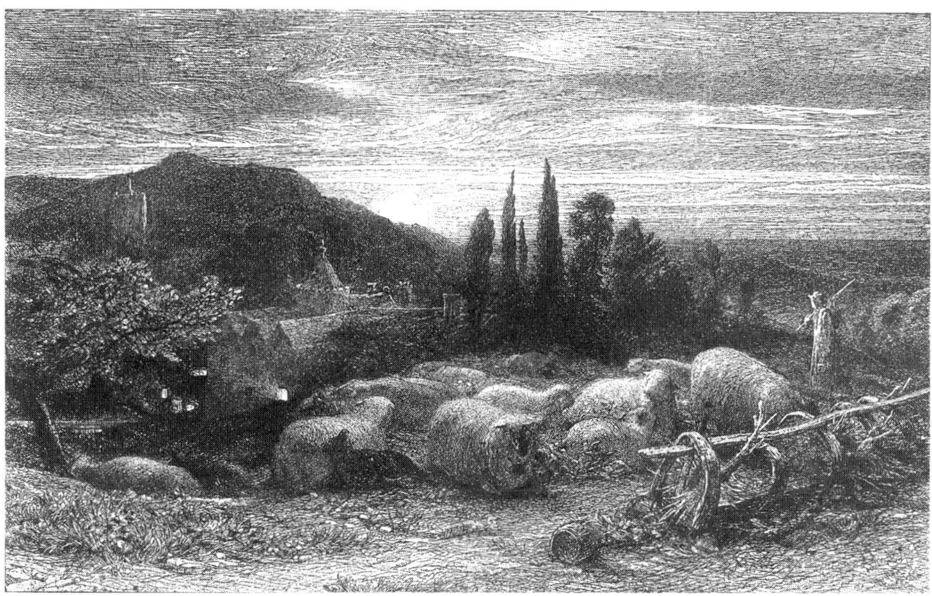

5.3   Samuel Palmer, 'The Rising Moon or An English Pastoral', c.1855-57. Etching, proof of 2nd state, 14.5 × 22.4 cm. BM 1872-5-11-977. © The Trustees of the British Museum.

With 'The Early Ploughman' or 'The Morning Spread upon the Mountains', which was begun before 1861, we reach the second or middle period of Palmer's etchings, and once again the process of increasing the scale of the composition continues. If anything, the mountains, trees, ruins and the bridge seem more determinedly Italianate and Claudian, but the figures and the animals, while central to the action, still do not dominate. Indeed one might assume that the cypress-like trees would genuinely suggest an Italian setting. Again, the time of day is significant for Palmer. In the first state the ploughman is bare-headed, but by the third he is wearing a hat. Palmer worked on the plate from time to time until the end of his life, even rebiting the plate to produce an eighth and final lifetime state.[20]

This constant reworking and revising reflects Palmer's pleasure in the medium, which allowed so many changes of mind, but it also suggests a dogged determination not to rest until satisfied with his efforts. Palmer's titles, which so regularly appear as variants, are also worth noting, because in them he frequently hints at what he really wants to express. The alternatives in themselves suggest a dissatisfaction with the written word's ability to encapsulate his vision. This plate might easily be entitled 'Ploughman in a Landscape', but 'The Early Ploughman' is not only far more atmospheric, it is also more subject specific. One can surmise that Palmer is aiming here to signify a profound view of the nature of physical work, and again of the place of mankind within creation. Yet in Palmer's prints he refrains from emphasizing the roughness and pain of farm work performed almost entirely by hand. The weather too is invariably kind to Palmer's people; rain, wind and snow are absent, and the labour depicted is rarely excessively demanding or back-breaking. There is always an element of softness and languor that is characteristically Palmerian.

'The Morning of Life', or 'A Leafy Dell', or 'Work and Gossip' (formerly 'Hercules and Cacus') was begun before 1861. It shows Palmer at the height of his powers as an etcher, now more confident in organizing both the composition and the balance between light and dark. Palmer altered the figure of Hercules into the kneeling woman and wrote to the critic Hamerton on 26 January 1872 '… it was begun years ago to illustrate a classical subject; but finding that I could no-how clip my poodle into lion-shape, I even let the hair grow, and christened him for the Art Union, *The Morning of Life*. I must try to be a better boy next time.'[21] Apart from the characteristic self-deprecating humour, Palmer shows just how long he pondered over his prints and repeatedly sought for a satisfactory title. Perhaps here he is thinking about the morning of creation, the Garden of Eden, the beginnings of humanity with an Eve-like figure in a wondrous sylvan setting.[22]

'The Bellman', of which six lifetime states are recorded, bears on the third the lettering *S. PALMER.INV.ET.FEC/MEAD.VALE/RED HILL/1879*, and with it we reach the final stage of Palmer's life and also the last phase of his activity as an etcher.[23] The inspiration here is once again from Milton, but now Palmer has turned to a more sombre and reflective text than *L'Allegro*, which had appealed to him some years earlier. The lines in the artist's mind are nos 83-4 of *Il Penseroso*.

Or the Belman's drousie charm,
To bless the dores from nightly harm

The night-watchman takes his regular walk around the bounds of the slumbering village with a measured pace, ringing his bell to signify the time and that all is well. The scene is strongly reminiscent of the Shoreham years, where Palmer had experienced his greatest inspiration. His friend and fellow artist Edward Calvert once remarked that Shoreham looked as if the Devil had not yet found it.[24]

The deeply etched lines both in the landscape and in the sky, together with the pockets of light and the smoke from the chimneys, all combine to produce a scene of timeless serenity.

Also embodied in the repeated actions of the figure of the night-watchman are the sense of both regularity and guardianship, qualities which to Palmer meant so much. The bellman himself may be viewed quite clearly as

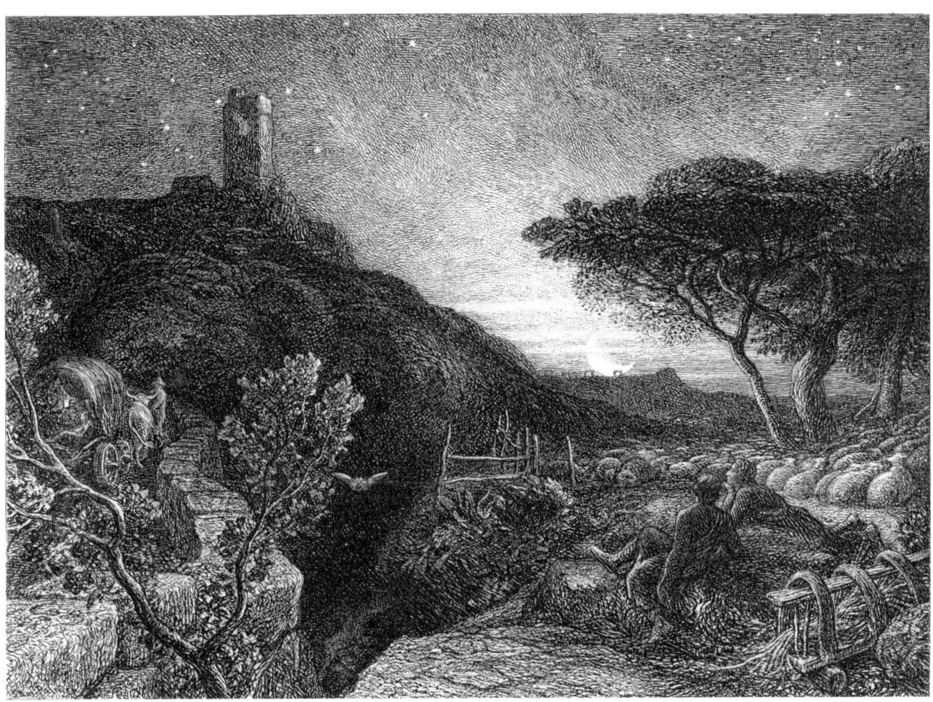

5.4 Samuel Palmer, 'The Lonely Tower', 1879. Etching, 4th state, 18.8 × 25.1 cm. BM 1910-7-16-20. © The Trustees of the British Museum.

another kind of shepherd – a worldly yet also a spiritual guide – perhaps as an earthly resonance of Jesus Christ himself.

Although the figures are enfolded by the darkness they are typically not overwhelmed by it, indeed they are safe and cherished. On 4 August 1879 Palmer wrote to Hamerton, 'I am very glad that you like my *Bellman* … It is a breaking out of village-fever long after contact – a dream of that genuine village where I mused away some of my best years, designing what nobody would care for, and contracting, among good books, a fastidious and unpopular taste.'[25]

'The Lonely Tower' (Figure 5.4) was made in the same year as 'The Bellman', 1879. Like its predecessor, it is based on *Il Penseroso*, the lines from which it is derived (85-8) following directly after those which lie at the heart of 'The Bellman'.

Or let my Lamp at midnight hour,
Be seen in som high lonely Tower
Where I may oft out-watch the *Bear*
With thrice great *Hermes* …

In complete contrast with the conclusion of *L'Allegro* Milton ends the poem thus (lines 175-6)

These pleasures *Melancholy* give,
And I with thee will choose to live.

The wistful atmosphere in both these late prints was acutely crystallized by David Cecil when he wrote, 'The Milton etchings are, after the Shoreham pictures, Palmer's finest achievements. In them he did achieve his true aims and unite earthy reality and poetic remoteness, as he had not done since the days of his youth…. [They] represent rather the memory of a vision: in them we see it, as it were, at second remove – as a reflection, an echo. But that echo, that reflection, have their own fainter and elegiac beauty.'[26]

'Opening the Fold', or 'Early Morning', was completed in 1880, just months before the artist's death on 24 May 1881. It is one of a projected set of fourteen etchings intended for an edition of *An English Version of the Eclogues of Virgil*, with Palmer's own translation. Only five plates were begun, four of which were completed by A.H. Palmer after his father's death.[27] Palmer's lines at this point in the Eighth Eclogue read,

Scarce with her rosy fingers had the dawn
From glimmering heaven the veil of night withdrawn,
And folded flocks were loose to browse anew
O'er mountain thyme or trefoil wet with dew,
When leaning sad an olive stem beside,
These, his last numbers, hapless Damon plied.[28]

Hamerton wrote of this plate that, it was 'the most completely beautiful of all Samuel Palmer's etchings … It is full of air and space, the eye wanders over it for miles, and yet at the same time there is a sweet solemnity in it … The plate is the perfect consummation of Palmer's experience, knowledge, and manual power.'[29]

By looking at the single-sheet etchings it is possible to see Palmer as primarily an illustrator of literature, and especially of poetry, but this would be to overlook his other work, which included genuine book illustration, such as the first book edition of Dickens' *Pictures from Italy*.[30] The novelist approached Palmer to provide designs for a collection of articles inspired by his recent travels in the country. There are five scenes, wood-engraved by an unidentified engraver after Palmer, entitled 'The Street of Tombs', 'Pompeii', 'The Villa d'Este at Tivoli from the Cypress Avenue', 'The Colosseum of Rome' and a vineyard view, usually known as 'The Vintage', although it is untitled in the book. Palmer seems not to have been Dickens' first choice, since he initially considered his friend Clarkson Stanfield for the project, but the latter appears to have withdrawn when he discovered (from the serial publication of the chapters) the book's clear anti-Catholic sentiments.[31]

The designs are charming enough to be sure, but of no especial distinction, and are not helped by being indifferently engraved. However, they do possess an undoubted feeling for the text. The fastidious artist complained in his voluminous notes for the engraver on two preliminary proofs of the engravings, 'In both proofs the top of the cypress is very indistinct, which greatly injures the design…. Second proof …. The thick outline on this leaf unfinishes everything about it.'[32] Palmer evidently did not get his way to his satisfaction, but perhaps of more interest is the style of these drawings. They reveal the artist much influenced by a *mise-en-page* created by artists of the German Renaissance, who had developed a device of encircling text with designs rather than encasing them within the letterpress. Many British illustrators at the time were affected by this device, notably Tenniel, and the main spur to this was the publication of a series of lithographs in 1817, by Rudolph Ackermann, of Dürer's designs for the *Prayer Book* of Maximilian of Bavaria.[33] Never again was Palmer to be given the task of illustrating any text single-handed and this is to be regretted.

It was to be ten years before Palmer was to illustrate again, and this time he did not return to the Germanic style he had employed for Dickens. In 1856 he provided nine small designs for the Rev. William Adams' *Sacred Allegories,* which was published by Rivingtons, with a second edition following in 1859. Palmer's work was better engraved by W.T. Green, W. Measom and Horace Harral. One of the first critics of this rich period of illustration remarked, 'In this year (1856) appeared the famous edition of Adams' *Sacred Allegories*…. The amazing quality of the landscapes by Samuel Palmer stood even the test of enormous enlargement in lantern slides, when Mr Pennell showed them at his lectures on the men of the sixties; had W.T. Green engraved no other blocks, he might be ranked as a great craftsman on the evidence of these alone.'[34] The images are undoubtedly memorable, but are outshone in terms of intensity by the two drawings he contributed to *A Book of Favourite Modern Ballads illustrated by Modern English Artists* (London: William Kent, 1860). These accompanied Thomas Hood's 'I remember' and James Beattie's 'The Hermit'. These seem to be arguably the finest and most obviously Palmerian of all his illustrations, aided by sensitive engraving by Edmund Evans, which allows some of the contrasts between light and dark, so characteristic of the etchings, to become clear. They are printed on slightly toned paper surrounded by floral designs in gilt.

Other artists represented include J.C. Horsley, George Elgar Hicks and Myles Birket Foster. A year later Kent published a compilation of poems entitled *Household Song* in which the 'I remember' design was reprised.

In 1866 Palmer contributed one important design to Adelaide Anne Prockter's *Legends and Lyrics* (Bell and Daldy) which was a 'New Edition, with Additions' and contained an introduction by Dickens. Entitled 'Sowing and Reaping' and engraved by Horace Harral, it is significant because it is a full-page image, in contrast to so many of his other designs for books, which are almost invariably small vignettes. The theme is one reminiscent of the etchings, with a man in the foreground sowing and another ploughing in the distance.[35] Palmer is joined in the volume by other artists including Tenniel, George du Maurier, John Dawson Watson, Mary Ellen Edwards and Thomas Morten.

Two other books deserve mention. First is an edition of Samuel Rogers' *The Pleasures of Memory* published by Sampson Low in 1865. The single design by Palmer, 'Mark yon old Mansion', is relatively undistinguished, but the book as a whole is of interest because all the images were reproduced by a new and short-lived technique called hyalography, which dispensed with the need for an engraver.[36]

More rewarding, however, is a book of exceptional rarity – *A Poetry Book for Children* published by George Bell in 1854. The four touching images of children in bucolic surroundings are some of his most tenderly felt illustrations.[37]

How then does Palmer fit in the milieu of Victorian printmaking and illustration? All his work in this area was done during Victoria's reign, yet it is tempting to view him as rightly belonging more with Blake and an earlier period. In his illustration he seems entirely untouched by the stylistic developments pioneered by the Pre-Raphaelite illustrators, notably Rossetti, Millais and Holman Hunt, who brought a high intellectualism to the literature they worked on. The dominant figures and contorted bodies and facial expressions, which they frequently employed, are singularly absent in his designs. Examples abound in the celebrated *Poems* of Tennyson published by Edward Moxon in 1857, often known simply as the *Moxon Tennyson*.

However, it is surely more correct to judge Palmer as a man of his time, and though he followed his own lonely and individualistic course, he relates naturally to some of his artist contemporaries. He knew and liked several of the etchers, notably Creswick, but also Charles West Cope. It was Cope (1811-90) who produced a posthumous portrait etching of Palmer in 1884, showing him as calm but also stoical and resolute. Stylistically it may be compared with the earnest but rather ponderous manner of artists such as William Strang (1859-1921), who rose to prominence following the revival of interest in etching in the 1880s.[38] The image is of a nobility that would have appealed to its subject, although it seems not to have been published in a formal edition and is extremely rare today.[39]

Palmer made a small but significant contribution to illustration and it is a matter of conjecture why, for example, he was not commissioned to produce a wood-engraved edition of Milton and took no part in the Dalziel Brothers' project, begun in the 1860s, to publish an enormous illustrated Bible. This finally appeared in 1881, comprising just the Old Testament and entitled

The Bible Gallery, with contributions by many of the leading artists of the day. There is a distinguished edition of Milton's *Ode on the Morning of Christ's Nativity,* with fine wood-engraved designs by William Small and Albert Moore of 1868 (published by James Nisbet), and it is somewhat curious that Palmer is not there with them. If Palmer was aware of the great etchings by the contemporary Barbizon masters such as Millet and Charles Jacque, he seems untouched by their view of humanity as a monumental protagonist battling against the elements in a harsh and brooding landscape. Some impressions of their prints were acquired by the British Museum within a few years of their creation, at about the same time as Palmer was engaged on his own prints.[40] It is also worth noting that Palmer himself presented impressions of several of his prints to the British Museum in 1872.[41]

It is difficult to place Palmer within Victorian printmaking as a genre, and indeed, it is easier to say that he is unlike most of his contemporaries in terms of style and even in subject matter. Compared with Barbizon prints, his appear nostalgic and elegaic; the world he created was one which was unrealistic even in his own time. When one thinks of some printmakers in Britain of the time, and specifically etchers, such as Seymour-Haden, Tissot, Whistler, Legros and Keene, it is taxing to try to situate Palmer within their milieu. Haden's laboured grittiness and Whistler's essential modernity, for example, are both at odds with Palmer's internalized and almost private visionary scene. Palmer can be seen as close to Claude in some ways, especially compositionally, but the intensity of his prints, particularly in terms of his figures, defines him as an artist almost alone in his dream-like visions. It is possible too to view his heirs in intaglio as Joseph Webb, Paul Drury, Robin Tanner, F.L. Griggs and Stanley Badmin, yet it is only with the etchings of Graham Sutherland that one can discern a printmaker of similar stature. Examples such as 'The Village' (1925) and 'St. Mary's Hatch' (1926) are close to Palmer both in feeling and in atmosphere.

Palmer was himself a poet in his printmaking and in his illustration. His etched landscapes are created out of a sophisticated and refined imagination which provides a view of humanity which is profound and essentially spiritual. His few single-sheet prints may themselves be seen as examples of illustration of the highest emotional and intellectual order. Although he was undeniably limited in his productivity, it is fair to propose that the finest of his prints can stand as equal in stature with the drawings and watercolours of the Shoreham period. It was another outstanding printmaker, Walter Sickert, who seems to encapsulate Palmer's genius most genuinely and justly: 'Palmer's etchings are rich, concentrated, indefatigable and intense. He had certain things to say, and he said them completely.'[42]

Notes

1.   Retroussage is a refinement of intaglio printing used to achieve a softening and more atmospheric effect. Fine muslin, passed lightly over the surface of an inked and wiped plate, catches a small amount of the ink in the lines and draws it slightly upwards; these traces of ink at the side of the lines cause them to lose some of their sharpness of definition when printed.

2.   Raymond Lister (ed.), *The Letters of Samuel Palmer*, 2 vols, Oxford: The Clarendon Press, 1974. *Letters*, 1872 (21), p. 866. Turner's *Liber Studiorum* plates (1807-19) measured approximately 184 × 260 mm. Opodeldoc was a type of soap liniment probably made by Paracelsus for varieties of medical plaster. It was essentially an alcoholic ointment which usually contained camphor, oils of marjoram and rosemary and occasionally laudanum.

3.   Adele M. Holcomb, *John Sell Cotman*, London: Colonnade Books, British Museum Press, 1978, p. 15.

4.   For detailed definitions of printmaking processes see Antony Griffiths, *Prints and Printmaking*, London: British Museum Press, 1980, 1996 (and subsequent editions).

5.   Lister, *Letters* , p. 865 (1872 (21)).

6.   Martin Hardie, *Samuel Palmer: A lecture*, London: Print Collectors' Club Publication, no. 7, 1928, p. 19.

7.   Lister, *Letters*, op. cit, p. 671.

8.   Alfred Herbert Palmer, *The Life and Letters of Samuel Palmer, Painter and Etcher*, London: Seeley, 1892, p. 99.

9.   British Museum, Department of Prints and Drawings register numbers 1919-5-28-1 and 3.

10.   Thornton, Robert John (ed.), *The Pastorals of Virgil…*, 3rd edition, London: F.C. and J. Rivingtons, 1821. See Gordon N. Ray, *The Illustrator and the Book in England from 1790 to 1914*, New York and London: Pierpont Morgan Library and Oxford University Press, 1976, no. 7, pp. 11-12.

11.   Palmer, *Life and Letters*, pp. 15-16.

12.   Raymond Lister, *Catalogue Raisonné of the Works of Samuel Palmer*, Cambridge: Cambridge University Press, 1988, nos 140, 497.

13.   See J.C. Bampfylde, *Sixteen Sonnets*, J. Millidge, London, 1778.

14.   Robert Southey, *Specimens of the Later English Poets*, London: Longman, Hurst, Rees and Orme, 1807, vol. 3, p. 434.

15.   Department of Prints and Drawings – 1872-5-11-981, 982.

16.   William Vaughan, Elizabeth E. Barker, Colin Harrison et al., *Samuel Palmer (1805-1881): Vision and Landscape*, London: British Museum Press, 2005, pp. 210-11, no. 133.

17.   Ibid., p. 162, no. 89.

18.   Lister, *Etchings*, p. 102.

19.   Vaughan, Barker, Harrison et al., *Vision and Landscape*, pp. 218-19, no. 139c. For information on Joseph Cundall as publisher to the Etching Club see Ruari Mclean, *Joseph Cundall – A Victorian Publisher*, Pinner: Private Libraries Association, 1976, p. 16. For Palmer and the Etching Club see Basil Gray, *The English Print*, London: Adam and Charles Black, 1937, pp. 105-8. Gray quoted from Francis Turner Palgrave (sel. and arr.) – *The Golden Treasury*, London: Oxford University Press, 1931, p. 145 , no. 147.

20.   Vaughan, Barker, Harrison et al., *Vision and Landscape*, pp. 219-20, no. 140.

21.   Lister, *Letters*, pp. 834-5.

22.   Lister, *Etchings*, p. 106, no. 10. Published in the seventh and final state as Plate 13 in *Etchings for the Art Union of London by the Etching Club*, 1872.

23.   See Lister, *Etchings*, pp. 106-8, no. 11.

24.   Raymond Lister, *Samuel Pamer His Life and Art*, Cambridge: Cambridge University Press, 1987, p. 42. From [Samuel Calvert] *A Memoir of Edward Calvert Artist by his Third Son*, London: Sampson Low and Co. 1893, p. 33.

25.   Lister, *Letters*, p. 970.

26.   David Cecil, *Visionary and Dreamer*, London: Academy Editions, 1977, pp. 53-4.

27.   See Lister, *Etchings*, pp. 110-12, nos 14-17. The final four cancelled plates for the project were presented to the Department of Prints and Drawings, British Museum by the late David Gould in 1959. 1959-3-7-1,2,3,4. For a loan exhibition (1991-92) single impressions were taken from each – 1990-11-9-162, 163, 164, 165. The plates were then lacquered to ensure that no further impressions will be printed. See Paul Goldman 'Samuel Palmer Etcher and Illustrator' in *Antiquarian Book Monthly Review*, vol. 19, no. 223, November 1992, pp. 498-501.

28.   Lister, *Etchings*, p. 88.

29.   Ibid., p. 88, n. 3, citing Hamerton in Martin Hardie, James Laver and A.H. Palmer, *Catalogue of an Exhibition of Drawings, Etchings & Woodcuts by Samuel Palmer and other Disciples of William Blake*, London: Victoria and Albert Museum, 1926, p. 85.

30.   London: Bradbury and Evans, 1846.

31.   Vaughan, Barker, Harrison et al., *Vision and Landscape*, p. 188, no. 110.

32.   Frederic G. Kitton, *Dickens and his Illustrators*, London: George Redway, 1899, pp. 186-7. Reprinted New York: AMS, 1975.

33.   Paul Goldman, *Victorian Illustrated Books 1850-1870 – The Heyday of Wood-Engraving*, London: British Museum Press, 1994, p. 97.

34.   Gleeson White, *English Illustration 'The Sixties'*, London: Constable and Co. 1887, p. 103. Reprinted Bath: Kingsmead Reprints, 1970. See also Robin de Beaumont, catalogue 12, London, 1989, p. 29, nos 158, 159 and Raymond Lister 'The Book Illustrations of Samuel Palmer', *The Book Collector*, Spring, 1979 pp. 77-80, 96-7.

35.   The design appears facing page 88. Horace Harral (fl. 1844-91) was not among the period's most sensitive engravers but he turns in a reasonable performance for Palmer on this occasion.

36.   See Geoffrey Wakeman, *Victorian Book Illustration – The Technical Revolution*, Newton Abbot: David and Charles, 1973, pp. 140-42. Palmer's drawing is reproduced.

37.   The book has a preface in verse signed J.C. (Joseph Cundall). See McLean op. cit. p. 79.

38.   Vaughan, Barker, Harrison et al., *Vision and Landscape*, p. 244, no. 164.

39.   See Campbell Fine Art, Catalogue 10, Tunbridge Wells, Kent, Spring 2003, no. 32.

40.   See Paul Goldman, *Shadow of the Forest – Prints of the Barbizon School*, London: British Museum, 1993.

41.   They are 'The Skylark', 'The Vine' or 'Plumpy Bacchus', 'The Sleeping Shepherd', 'The Rising Moon', 'The Weary Ploughman', 'The Early Ploughman 'and 'The Morning of Life'. Register numbers 1872-5-11- 977-984.

42.   Walter Sickert, 'The Future of Engraving', *Burlington Magazine*, vol. 27, no. 150 (September 1915), p. 229.

6

From the valley of vision to the M25: Samuel Palmer and modern culture

Sam Smiles

This chapter is intended to offer some thoughts about Palmer, modernism and modernity, taking as its central concern the importance Palmer had for a group of British printmakers in the early twentieth century. There is no doubt that Palmer's posthumous deployment by a variety of artists and critics is a phenomenon that raises a number of questions about the cultural value of landscape and the legitimacy of a romantic or spiritual response to nature in the modern period. To put it plainly, on what terms could Palmer's aesthetic be plausibly renewed in the machine age? What motivated those reappraisals of Palmer that considered his achievement, not simply as a significant contribution to English nineteenth-century art, but also as offering a possibility for twentieth-century artistic practice? And does the recuperation of his art, as a historical episode, prompt more general questions about the place of landscape in modern Britain?

To begin answering these questions we can consider two passing comments from the 1940s on the Palmer revival. The first comes from Wyndham Lewis, writing in the May 1949 edition of *The Listener* on the turning away from avant-garde practices he found characteristic of contemporary art. Noting that some artists had taken Palmer as their inspiration, Lewis mused on the implications of their fealty.

In England there is at present a retreat from the extremes: some artists go back to Cotman or Palmer and live in their time; others to some great French impressionist – or to Wilson Steer! So the big question of the moment is this: If you throw over all that the twentieth-century revolution in the arts has stood for ... *where are you going to*? Are you going *back*? Is that the only way you can think of going?[1]

Given Lewis' commitment to progressive art and his impatience with any complacent invocation of cultural heritage, his questioning of Palmer's relevance was, perhaps, to be expected. But others shared his feeling that Palmer's ecstatic art sat awkwardly in contemporary Britain. Kenneth Clark, in his book *Landscape into Art*, also of 1949, was pessimistic that Palmer's vision could be reconciled with modernity. For Clark, 'Palmer remains the last painter of Virgilian landscape. His flocks and sheaves of corn, his harvest moons and trees weighed down with fruit, symbolize a passionate conviction that the good life can only be lived in terms of pastoral simplicity.' But the artist's ability to work with that tradition had been severely compromised by the rational calculation of Palmer's contemporaries; the struggle for existence postulated by Malthus and Darwin had rendered such idyllic visions 'mere moonshine', as far as Clark was concerned. If developments in political economy and science signalled the death knell of the imagination's ability to invoke the pastoral perfection of a Golden Age, the logical inference to be drawn was that any modern art orientated to pastoral was effectively living beyond its imaginative means. It is no surprise, therefore, that Clark believed Palmer's example to have had 'almost too pervasive an influence on recent English painting', which, presumably, should have been attending to other matters.[2] Clark was certainly in a good position to know about Palmer's artistic influence and its effects; a few years earlier, in recognition of Graham Sutherland's admiration for Palmer, he had given Sutherland one of his Palmer drawings.

Yet for all their disapproval, Clark and Lewis were correct that a number of artists had modified their styles in the wake of the Palmer revival, using his example to re-engage with rural England.[3] For painters, the apogee of this enthusiasm coincided with the neo-Romanticism of the 1940s; for engravers, the Palmer revival was at its height in the late 1920s and the early 1930s. In both cases, there followed a swift decline in interest, for Palmer's influence on modern art was not sustained. Yet the fact that Palmer was taken up by twentieth-century painters and engravers and was, arguably, more influential on contemporary practice than any other Romantic artist, is worth exploring. This chapter is therefore designed to provide some contexts for thinking about Palmer's recuperation in the first half of the twentieth century and to suggest that a number of issues more widely associated with debates about Englishness, landscape and culture between the wars can be brought to bear on the Palmer revival of this period.

First, however, as a justification for this chapter's title, we may consider two aspects of Palmer's renewed salience in the later 1970s. There was, first of all, the mobilization of Palmer's work in and around Shoreham as part of a campaign to stop the M25 encroaching on the valley of the river Darent, or 'Samuel Palmer country' as it was sometimes called.[4] Geoffrey Grigson, one of Palmer's most important modern critics who had written significant studies on Palmer in the 1930s and 1940s, spoke eloquently, but in the end uselessly, of the need to preserve the Shoreham landscape inviolate.[5] The coming of the

M25 motorway, together with the M20 and M26, now contain the village and its hinterland within a triangle of arterial roads, triumphantly imposing late twentieth-century amenity values on a landscape described in the 1920s as a refuge from modern life.[6]

I will return to the tension between artistic vision and technological modernity below, but for now we may note simply that Palmer's association with the Shoreham landscape was recruited to preserve a traditional landscape from change. Palmer is one of only three canonical British artists, Constable and Stanley Spencer being the others, whose national reputation is founded on an identity with a particular place. Like Constable, his response to that locale is considered of such cultural significance that the landscape in question requires protection. What the campaign to reroute the M25 suggested was that Shoreham was special because Palmer's vision had sanctified it and, further, that in so doing Palmer had drawn out of the landscape something especially important about English culture. A response to the spiritual qualities vested in the landscape necessarily stood in opposition to the material and technocratic ideology of modern culture. As the President of the Shoreham Society described it, the campaign wished to preserve the 'typical understated English picturesque aura which Samuel Palmer captured perfectly' from 'the computer-minded road planners'.[7] As we shall see, this opposition between traditional England and modern technocracy can also be found in the printmakers who fell under Palmer's sway in the early twentieth century.

The other and rather better known event of the 1970s was the revelation in 1976 that for many years Tom Keating had been producing Palmer pastiches that were being passed off as authentic by unscrupulous dealers.[8] Those who knew Palmer's genuine productions were not impressed. Grigson described the Keating forgeries as 'cook-ups'; Graham Sutherland and Paul Drury, drawing on the admiration they had had for Palmer since 1924, reacted 'as if an old friend – long dead – had been impersonated with the aid of liberally and clumsily applied "make up".'[9] Yet in one sense Keating is a valuable witness insofar as his fake Palmers, with their crude bodging together of motifs, say something about the way Palmer had come to be understood; Keating's pastiche Palmers only fooled people because they were willing to think of Palmer in such clichéd terms. In a review of 1977, Grigson identified the context which linked the forger and the deceived as the Palmer 'situation', where high prices for Shoreham work fuelled the collector's desire for known but untraced paintings of that period.[10] But he could have extended this thought into something beyond the mechanics of the art market, allowing the Palmer 'situation' to encompass the early twentieth-century construction of Palmer's artistic identity. For Grigson and others, Palmer's work at Shoreham gave the key to his achievement, a visionary encounter with landscape that was recaptured to some extent in his later etchings. In evaluating his career in these terms, the mystical qualities of Palmer's art became paramount; Keating's formulaic production of pictures with shepherds, flocks and harvest moons was a response to this new critical consensus. It will be necessary to consider further the idea of pastiche when reviewing the work of those etchers inspired by Palmer working from the 1910s onwards, especially Frederick Landseer Griggs, Paul Drury, Graham Sutherland and Robin Tanner (Figures 6.1-6.4).

The facts of these engravers' response to Palmer are reasonably well known and have, in any case, been very well covered in recent publications and exhibitions.[11] In brief, Griggs (1876-1938) first came to know of Palmer's etchings of Virgil's *Eclogues* in the library of the Hitchin Mechanics Institute in about 1890.[12] Griggs began etching in 1913 and although very few of his prints tackle the same pastoral subject matter as Palmer's, the density of line and super-saturation of detail emulate what Palmer once referred to as 'matter aggregating matter'. In a retrospective letter of 1925, Griggs declared 'My love for the things Samuel Palmer loved is my first and last love, so I know no other artist who loved them so well, and whose love so showed forth in his work.'[13]

A younger generation, all students at Goldsmiths', were first introduced to Palmer's etchings in 1924, when one of their number, William Larkins (1901-74), bought an impression of Palmer's 'The Herdsman's Cottage' from a shop in Charing Cross Road. Larkins himself seems to have made no attempt to modify his style or subject matter and the prints he made up to 1930, when he stopped production, predominantly explored aspects of city life.[14] But for Graham Sutherland (1903-80) and Paul Drury (1903-87) this encounter with Palmer's vision was decisive. Their appetite for Palmer may have been partially satisfied with the exhibitions of his work mounted by the Cotswold Gallery, Frith Street, in 1924, 1926 and 1927, but the major confirmation of their enthusiasm was the important exhibition at the Victoria and Albert Museum in 1926 organized by A.H. Palmer, Martin Hardie and others.[15] The experience of seeing so much of Palmer's output brought together also keenly affected another Goldsmiths' student, Robin Tanner (1904-88). In 1926 Sutherland and Drury met Griggs for the first time, who invited them to his home in Chipping Campden, where he shared with them his expertise in printing. Tanner met Griggs three years later, on Varnishing Day at the Royal Academy in 1929, but he already knew of his work from the spring exhibitions of the Royal Society of Painter-Etchers. Tanner later recalled that he responded not to Griggs' grandeur of conception, nor to his Catholicism and nostalgia for medieval England, but to his ability to realize different textures in etching and the intensity of his feeling for the Cotswolds.[16]

Like Griggs before them, the three Goldsmiths' students found a patron in Molly Bernhard-Smith, who ran the XXI Gallery in London between the wars, specializing in printmaking and especially the work of artists associated with the etching revival. Sutherland had his first one-man show at the gallery in 1925 and his second in 1928, Drury had his first one-man show there in 1929.

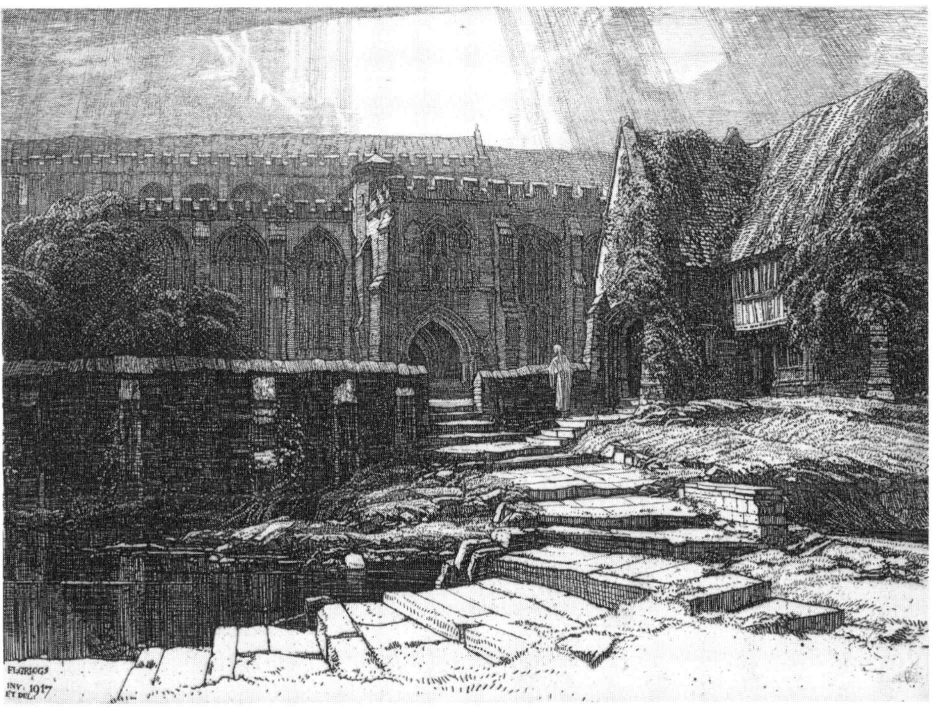

6.1   Frederick Landseer Griggs, 'Sellenger', 1917. Etching, 35.7 × 24.2 cm. BM 1923,0413.1. © The Trustees of the British Museum.

Before the 1929 recession, which saw prices for etchings virtually collapse within a couple of years, printmaking offered a reasonable living. Sutherland, for example, was earning approximately £700 per annum from his etchings, producing no more than four plates a year, each one of which yielded 75 impressions which he sold to collectors at four guineas a piece.[17]

Other etchers working in the late 1920s and 1930s were also touched by Palmer's example to some extent, among them Allan Gwynne-Jones, Edward Bouverie Hoyton and especially Stanley Roy Badmin.[18] Badmin took up printmaking in 1928 and developed a rich etching language broadly comparable to the work produced by Sutherland, Drury and Tanner. In a review of 1932 the art critic of *The Times* linked him with Griggs and Palmer as artists seeking to extract the poetical suggestion immanent in English landscape.[19] Badmin also exhibited his work at the XXI Gallery, including a one-man show in 1930, and produced upwards of six etchings a year from 1928 to 1931, selling them at two to three guineas each. Following the disintegration of the print market, in the mid-1930s he reoriented his career to illustration. Nevertheless, some of these later images bear the diluted traces of Palmer's inspiration and his illustrative work included collaborations with Griggs on the illustrations for Clifford Bax's *Highways and Byways of Essex* (1937).[20]

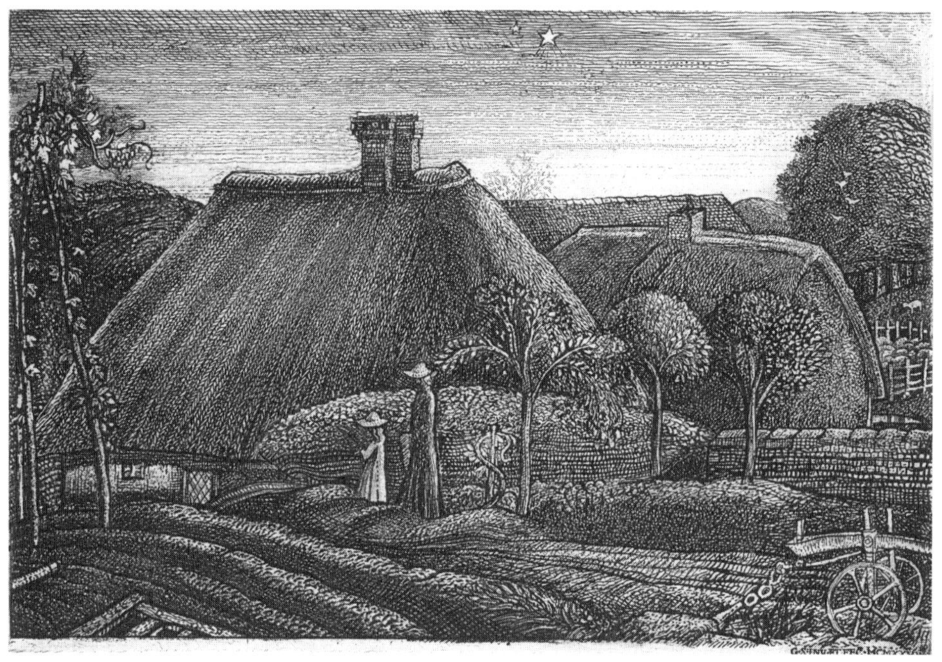

6.2   Graham Sutherland, 'Lammas', 1926. Etching, 11.0 × 16 cm. BM 1949, 0411.489.
© The Trustees of the British Museum. © Sutherland estate.

What differentiates Badmin from his older colleagues at Goldsmiths' is his willingness to work as a commercial illustrator and, more significantly, his readiness to represent not merely a Palmer-inspired countryside but also another side of England. Badmin's line engraving of 1930, 'Suburbia', is unthinkable as a print by Drury, Tanner or Sutherland; nor were any of them prepared to detail modern transport or industry, even in the anodyne treatment Badmin adopted.

Griggs died in 1938. Of the three younger artists, Sutherland, Drury and Tanner, the direct impact of Palmer can be observed in a relatively small number of prints, and only in Tanner's case was Palmer to remain influential throughout his career.

Sutherland made just under a dozen etchings influenced by Palmer's example, between 1925 and 1928. Drury produced five Palmer-inspired etchings but turned away from Palmer's influence after 1933. Tanner etched six Palmer-like designs between 1927 and 1939, but the depression in the print market slowed his output in the 1930s and he stopped printmaking altogether from 1944 until 1970. In the work of all three Goldsmiths' artists the move away from current etching practice, with its rather spare technique, to the density of line and richness of inking seen in these plates was striking, but so was the emotional investment in place. Sutherland and Drury were given the distinction of a lengthy critical appraisal in *Print Collector's Quarterly* in 1929, where the links between them, Griggs and Palmer were outlined.[21]

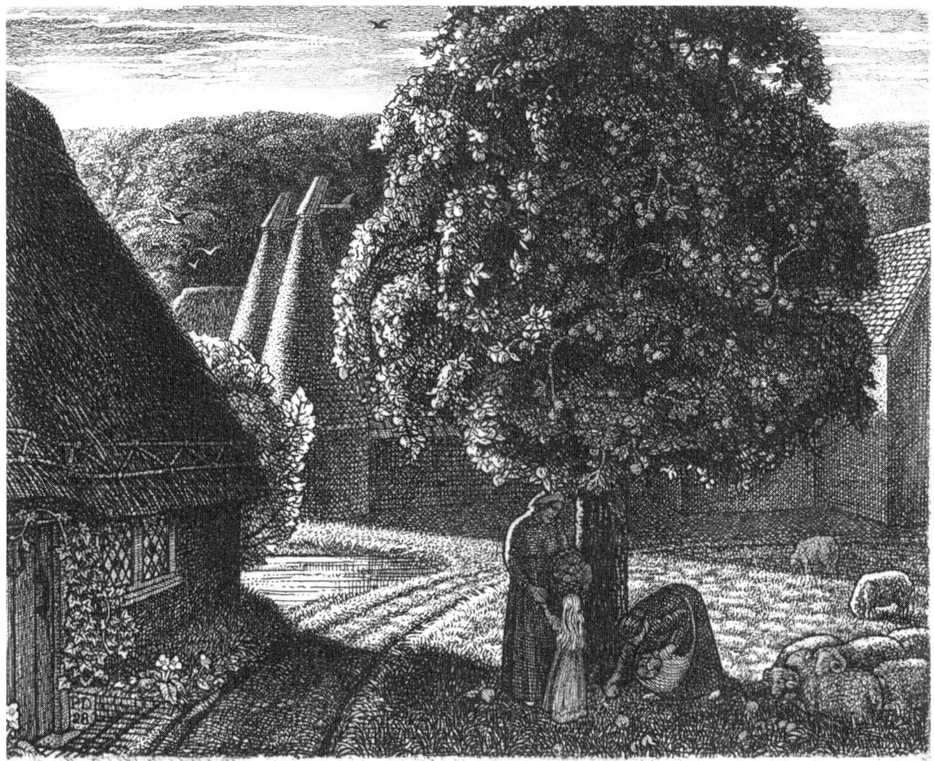

6.3   Paul Drury, 'September', 1928. etching, 10.4 × 13.3 cm. BM 1928,1110.21. © The Trustees of the British Museum. © Estate of Paul Drury.

Because the approach adopted by the Goldsmiths' etchers is so obviously indebted to Palmer's example, analysis of the prints they produced has concentrated on technique and rather overlooked the places they represented or imagined. But place was not uncontentious between the wars, especially when that place was the English countryside. At the time these prints were made, a considerable body of thought was orientated to considering how the rural way of life could be reconciled with modernity and the growth of the metropolis. Many were alarmed at the disappearance of the traditional countryside. Laurence Binyon in his book of 1925, *The Followers of William Blake*, compared the London that Blake and his friends knew, with its easy access to the countryside on both sides of the Thames, with 'the monstrous acreage of stone pavements spreading forlornly through interminable suburbs'.[22] In contrast, Drury, Sutherland and Tanner offered a return to a landscape Palmer would have understood. In the critical appreciation Sutherland received in 1929, his choice of etching as a medium was explained almost as a species of rescue archaeology for a vanishing world:

… he discovered in [etching] the best means of portraying those intimate and recondite qualities of rhythm and repose which are still to be found in many parts of the English countryside. It is true that these qualities are everyday becoming more difficult to find in our landscape, but even where they are in process of disappearing they can be pieced together by one possessing imagination and a love for the past.[23]

Sutherland's approach to representing England was summed up as 'distilling on to copper the essence of one aspect of a village life now almost completely passed away'.[24]

Necessarily, therefore, the anachronistic look of these plates jarred with many aspects of contemporary life, a world of modern transport and communication, with spreading cities and ribbon development. Which of these perceptions was the real England? A divided sense of national identity was widely shared and it is caught in a 1936 *News Chronicle* competition for photographs of Britain, divided into two categories: 'the picturesque old Britain … its traditional pastimes and toil, its ancient houses and shady lanes' and 'the new Britain embodying all that is best and worst in twentieth century work, life and social customs'.[25] Two years earlier, in 1934, J.B. Priestley's *English Journey* talked of the three Englands he encountered on his travels: Old England of the cathedrals, the colleges and the Cotswolds, nineteenth-century England of industry and urbanization and post-war England in which a more Americanized culture was appearing, typified by new technologies, filling stations and the architecture of modern leisure.[26] With respect to the Cotswolds and Old England, Priestley memorably describes a visit to Griggs and a fierce debate over his anti-modernist stance and his refusal to believe in the reconciliation of authentic English culture with the machine.[27]

Griggs for his part had recently been sounding off to *The Times* about the disturbance of noise from cars and motorbikes, which he took care to associate with the most aggressive modernism of 'Signor Marinetti and his futurist disciples, who advocate louder and louder din and sleeplessness and see the greatest art in the machine, and even aesthetic value in madness.' What particularly enraged him was that this emissary of the machine age was having a socially destructive effect on small towns like his own Chipping Campden.

A few years ago the long street of this town was as peaceful as it is beautiful, a most desirable place to live and work and rest, but now its beauty is scarred for the sake of the traffic that has shattered its peace. The same is true all over the country, and one result is that fine house property standing on streets becomes less valuable and tends to fall more and more into the hands of those to whom its decent upkeep is either unprofitable or of little concern.[28]

Griggs' own beliefs were founded on the perception that modern and especially urban lifestyles had led to spiritual impoverishment. He particularly endorsed the remarks in Palmer's 'Observations on the Country and on Rural Poetry', when Palmer talked of poetry's ability to repair the broken link between the city dweller and the cultivation of his natural earth, presenting to fancy what is lost to sight by substituting rural images for 'the foulnesses without' of the urban scene. Griggs was often to quote from this passage in his letters.[29] He was pessimistic about modern culture, the loss of religious sensibility, the heedlessness of contemporary living, the ugliness of the built environment. As Graham Sutherland remembered, Griggs 'thought real England had been damned, as one of his titles, *Ex Anglia Perdita*, suggests'.[30] If this reaction was essentially a cultural one, recoiling from the worst excesses of the modern world, it could also be explicitly political. Griggs had a strong antipathy to progressive politics, siding with the landed interest in 1910 against the Liberal Government's attempt to introduce a Land Tax to pay for the recently introduced state pension. He wrote at the time of 'this ghastly tide of Socialism and Indecency that is changing the character of England'. The December 1910 election, called to break the legislative impasse over the Land Tax, provoked Griggs to describe it as 'this degrading and thrice disgusting general election! DAMN IT! And damn these Demagogues'.[31] Griggs' angry rhetoric here calls to mind Palmer's 'Address to the Electors of West Kent' and he would no doubt have been pleased to receive A.H. Palmer's endorsement of his general opinions. Writing to Griggs in 1927, Palmer confirmed that 'all your yearnings and all your hatreds are absolutely in accord with S.P.'s own'.[32]

If the vision of England Griggs wished to perpetuate was at odds with social and economic change, so too was the countryside that Sutherland, Drury and Tanner explored. Their recourse to the seasonal round of the farmer's year, locating agriculture in traditional hamlets tucked away in narrow valleys was indeed a picture of 'village life now almost completely passed away'. Yet in reality even the residue of British village life was not isolated from change. Despite what their prints portray, a world of well-tended fields and organic rural communities, farming in Britain throughout the 1920s and early 1930s was in a parlous state, struggling to get free of the agricultural depression that had begun in the 1870s. Temporary respite had come during the First World War, when the need to respond to food shortages had seen farms expand their operations and their incomes rise. Government attempts to protect agriculture after 1918 failed, however. The Agriculture Act of 1920, which had promised stable prices for cereal crops and a four-year period of notice for the withdrawal of these guarantees, was repealed with immediate effect in 1921. The 'great betrayal' saw a collapse in farm prices and very low incomes for the rest of the 1920s, exacerbated from 1929 by the depression. Limited protection was introduced in 1932, but prices fell still further in 1933 before beginning a slow recovery. The collapse of the rural economy was made evident by neglected hedgerows, untended fields and dilapidated farm buildings.[33]

Clearly, this is not the world usually visible in the prints of the Goldsmiths' group, whose portrayal of the countryside shows a fecund and well tended landscape. Indeed, the only ruinous buildings associated with their production appeared just before the impact of their exposure to Palmer was felt. In 1924 both Sutherland and Drury took dilapidated farm buildings as subjects. Sutherland produced the etching 'Number Forty-Nine', showing a ruined cottage. Drury made drawings of decrepit rural buildings for an etching to be entitled 'Ill fares the land,' but the design he planned was too close to Sutherland's subject and Drury decided not to proceed.[34] As we have seen, Larkins purchased Palmer's 'Herdsman's Cottage' in 1924 and its influence is manifested in a very different treatment of rural subjects in the following years. When one looks over the group's etchings at their most Palmer-like, the vision of the English countryside they present is a perfected world, one in which nature gives up her bounty almost spontaneously.

In portraying the countryside in ways that Palmer would have understood, the etchings of the Goldsmiths' group can be contrasted with the contemporary imaging of the countryside in the wood engravings of Clare Leighton. Her book *The Farmer's Year: A Calendar of English Husbandry* (1933) was preoccupied with seasonal tasks and most of what she depicts is traditional, unmechanized labour, with steam-power alone making its appearance in 'March: Threshing' and 'June: Hay-making'. But her observations of rural activities are much more obviously keyed to the representation of contemporary work. Leighton's prints proved influential, not merely for the revival of wood-engraving but also because her imagery bore on the concerns of influential writers, such as G.K. Chesterton, Noel Brailsford and J.C. Squire, debating the land issue across the political spectrum. Leighton herself adopted socialist principles and her prints characteristically offer an exploration of labour, with the agricultural workers' activities dominating the compositions. As she said in the preface of her 1937 book *Country Matters*, 'If I am defiant in my defence of the countryside it is because I know it to be the last hope for sanity. Here, in the heart of the labouring man, is the strong sane humour of the earth, without which there is no health.'[35] The muscularity and vigour of her designs, heroizing work and detailing the effort involved in keeping land productive, contrasts markedly with the landscapes of Sutherland, Drury and Tanner. Although the results of husbandry are everywhere apparent in their etchings, when agricultural labourers are included their appearance is so generalized as to make of work a timeless activity, as opposed to a reflection of twentieth-century life. In their images the density of line, rich chiaroscuro and heavy inking have the effect of folding those few workers one can discern into the landscape. The result is to offer a mystical union of man and nature, but that union seems peculiarly blithe in the circumstances of the agricultural crisis.

If this suggests that Sutherland, Griggs and Drury approached the agricultural landscape somewhat heedless of its very real difficulties, they were not alone. The celebration of landscape as an ideal, irrespective of its actual circumstances, can be found in the literature of the period in which the rural landscape was valorized as a place of authentic experience, in contradistinction to the meretricious culture of the city. The pastoral had received a new impetus with the writings of the Georgian group of poets in the 1910s and 1920s, while the countryside as a repository for older, more traditional values had been popularized by writers like Mary Webb, whose fifth and last novel, *Precious Bane*, was published in 1924. After her death in 1927, and endorsed by Stanley Baldwin, the book became a huge popular success. Webb's fiction used Shropshire and Herefordshire locations; Constance Holme and Sheila Kaye-Smith in novels published in the 1910s and 1920s did much the same for Westmorland and Sussex respectively. In all of them, the life of country people, bound to the rhythm of the seasons and in touch with natural emotions, suggests a telluric relationship to place.

Stella Gibbons' satirical riposte in *Cold Comfort Farm* (1932) is itself a good indicator of the popularity of these interpretations of country life between the wars. Gibbons' heroine Flora Poste is an agent of modernity who descends on the eponymous farm with a mission to drag it into the twentieth century, but Gibbons' stark polarization of two ways of life was but a comic exaggeration of a serious debate about the contribution of the countryside to modern Britain. There was a growing sense that the rural component of the nation's identity was vulnerable to the worst excesses of modern culture and the Council for the Preservation of Rural England was founded in 1926 to protect it. As David Matless has shown, the inter-war period saw numerous debates on the impact of modernity on the rural community. Positions taken over the future of the countryside were complex and many-sided, but together they constituted a spectrum of approaches from what Matless styles the reactionary modernism of the Preservationists, advocating planned rural development and sympathetic to the Council for the Preservation of Rural England, to the more obviously backward-looking pastoralism of the Organicists, opposed to most aspects of modern farming practice and planning. Both sides were united, however, in recommending a return to self-sufficient small communities, seeing the nucleated English village as a perfected social unit. As might be expected, the Organicists laid more stress on the retention of craft skills so that work, life and spirit were indissoluble, thereby healing the divisions created by mechanization and the alienation of labour.[36] It is, of course, the nucleated English village that the Goldsmiths' group tended to portray and, as with the debates over the future of the countryside, we can assume that the popularity of their etchings was not only derived from their technical achievement, but also because they tapped into a deeply-felt agreement about what constituted the essence of the English countryside. The Palmer revivalists might therefore be understood as condensing in their images an England-as-wished-for, during a period of great usncertainty about the future of the countryside.

The tension between the forces of modernization, all dynamism and aggression, if its detractors were to be believed, and the conservative pastoralism of the defenders of the traditional English countryside, can best be observed by contrasting different approaches to the same landscape. In May 1927,

Stanley Roy Badmin published an illustration in *The Graphic* entitled 'A Scar on the Kent landscape – the new Maidstone road above Wrotham'. Wrotham is a few miles east of Shoreham, and thus close to the heart of Palmer country, and in many ways this image, with its concentration on the cultural impact of the new roads required by the motorcar, anticipates the agitation against the M25 fifty years later. But irrespective of any dismay about the coming in of modernity, the area around Shoreham was not a pristine pre-modern environment; even small villages were developing. Indeed, in 1933 'The Hopfield', a house built in nearby St Mary's Platt and designed by the modernist architect Colin Lucas, was included in *Unit One* as part of that group's bid to establish the avant-garde credentials of British art and architecture and to outline the possibility of cultural renewal on those lines. Yet neither Badmin's protest against change, nor Lucas' embrace of it, seem to inhabit the world portrayed by the Goldsmiths' group. Sutherland, who based himself in Sussex during these years, offered a very different view of the countryside, one from which all signs of modernity have been banished. His print 'Lammas' (Figure 6.2) of 1926, for example, finds cultural value not in modernity but in a spiritually-conceived seasonal round of sowing and harvest. It was prints like this that caused the critic Edward Sackville-West to declare in 1943 that Sutherland, inspired by Blake and Palmer, possessed 'the receptive eyes which alone can reflect the fast changing idyll of contemporary England'.[37] But by fast changing he in fact meant fast disappearing; Sutherland's vision in these years is not at all dynamic and clings instead to an idea of the rural that never alters.

When it came to describing these etchers' attitudes to English landscape, the most vocal and the most passionate was Robin Tanner. He deprecated the violation of the countryside by new technologies, speaking in later years of 'a world of pastoral beauty that could be ours if we did but desire it passionately enough, instead of littering it with poles and wires, corrugated iron, pylons, and barbed wire'. Tanner was clear that the vision offered by his plates was a deliberate evasion of this ugly reality: '... it is an escape into what Blake called "the real and eternal world"'. Tanner evoked Thomas Traherne's mystical understanding of the countryside, whose 'corn is orient and immortal wheat' and where 'everything is at rest, free and immortal'.[38] His aesthetic was based on a deliberate eschewal of the everyday and a determination to condense the experience of nature into elaborately worked etchings.

Tanner lived in north-west Wiltshire, at Kington Langley, about fifty miles south of Griggs in Chipping Campden. He identified himself strongly with the local scene, finding all his subjects within a few miles of his home. Just over ten miles to the east Geoffrey Grigson had put down roots in Broad Town, likewise finding in the Wiltshire landscape a sounding board for his deepest concerns. It is a nice coincidence, in that respect, that Wessex and the Cotswolds activated some of the most enthusiastic contemporary appreciation of landscape by the ruralist writer H.J. Massingham.

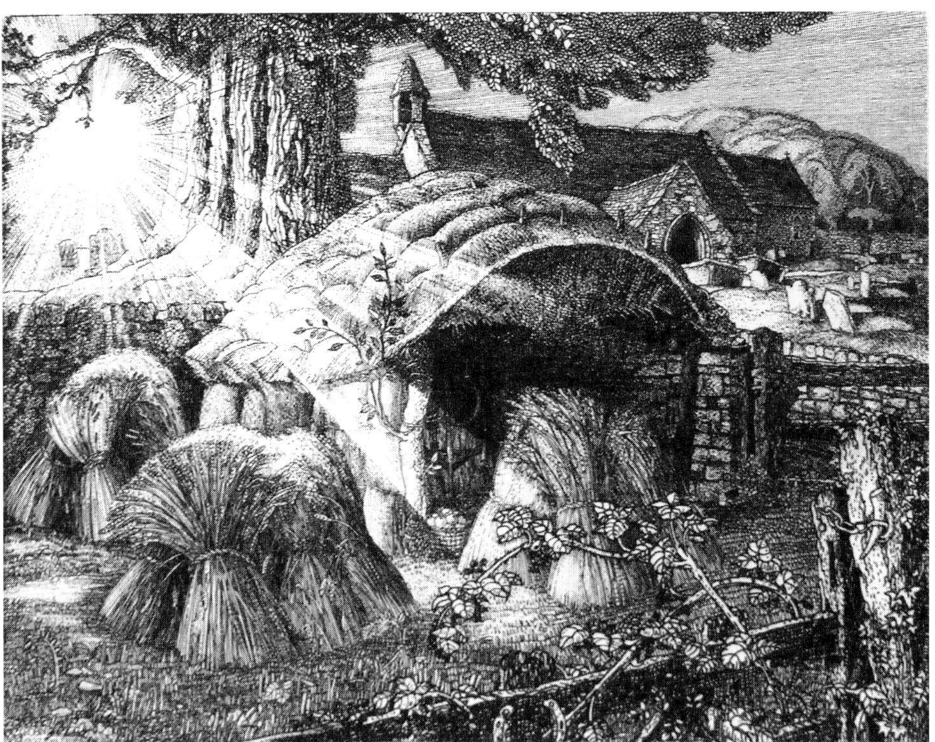

6.4   Robin Tanner, 'Martin's Hovel', 1927. Etching, 16.7 × 21.5 cm. Devon Learning Resources collection. © Crafts Study Centre, University for the Creative Arts, Farnham.

With Massingham, too, the land, the spirit, the very identity of England as a historical palimpsest, were contested by the forces of modernity. Massingham shared with Griggs a belief in the importance of traditional craft values, not simply for the dignity and authenticity of the objects produced by those means, but also for their role in maintaining or restoring an ethos that opposed the dehumanization of labour within systems of mass production. Like Griggs, he too found spiritual nourishment in Catholicism and saw the countryside, with its alternative to the ersatz pleasures of the big city, as offering the prospect for a better life. Organic farming and craft skills both honoured the material to be worked and the means of working it, so placing man in harmony with the divine creation. In this connection, it is telling that when Massingham wrote an enthusiastic account of war-time flax production in Wiltshire, although he illustrated his account with photographs by Bill Brandt, it was the spirit of Edward Calvert he evoked to sum up what he witnessed in the fields as the steepled flax was laid out to dry. For Massingham the purposeful activity of the workers, combining craft knowledge with repetitive movement, was almost ritualistic. 'So little more was there to do – a slight formalizing of the scene, a closer pattern and I might have been looking at a complete picture by Calvert, *The Cider Feast* or *Sheep Shearing*. In these the workers are celebrants and the task is a form of worship. I could not have believed that I should in this age have witnessed a scene of timeless social husbandry like this.'[39]

Clearly, etching as practised by Griggs and the Goldsmiths' group is also a craft skill of a very high order. Some of Tanner's prints, for example, required upward of 1,000 hours of work.[40] And the laboriousness of the task of etching and printing a plate was understood by these Palmer followers to be a mark of integrity when capturing a spiritualized vision. Both the subject and the effort involved in realizing it could be seen as bastions against a more superficial modern world. Shortly after his conversion to Catholicism in 1912, Griggs offered a working definition of what mattered to him: 'Think of dear old Samuel Palmer (who ought to have been a Catholic, and wasn't so far away) think of the Country, the Sky, and the Seasons. Pastoral imagery, and how it's derived mainly from the Scriptures, and what is there more beautiful?'[41] Sutherland converted to Catholicism in 1926. On the margin of his etching of that year, 'St Mary Hatch,' Sutherland inscribed in pencil an extract from Psalm 14: Domine Quis habitabit in tabernaculo tuo quis requiescet in monte sancto tuo qui ingreditur sine macula et operata justitiam ('Lord who shall abide in thy tabernacle? Who shall dwell in thy holy hill? He that walketh uprightly and worketh righteousness'). Beyond its more obvious meaning it is possible that Sutherland also had in mind the 'righteousness' of honest craft work. Tanner, too, was moved by a spiritual attitude to etching. Unlike the Catholics, Griggs and Sutherland, he was a Quaker, but the intensity of his religious beliefs was, if anything, greater than theirs. As he declared towards the close of his life: 'Every plate I etch is a sort of religious declaration ... I want to celebrate my adoration of my creator and the wonder of the earth by trying, on sheets of copper, to create a heaven that is this very earth.'[42]

We know from Sutherland's reminiscences that the emotional impact of Palmer's work was decisive. 'I was amazed at its completeness, both emotional and technical ... It seemed to me so wonderful that a strong emotion, such as was Palmer's, could change and transform the appearance of things.'[43] Sutherland also recalled that he and fellow students at Goldsmiths' made pilgrimages to Shoreham and that 'some of us on our own expeditions (I am almost ashamed to say), even wore cloaks in imitation of the "Ancients"'.[44] But for all this enthusiasm, the question that requires an answer is whether Palmer's new acolytes had reinvigorated or traduced his original vision. Are we are looking at emulation or pastiche? Writing to *The Times* on 7 August 1976 in the wake of the Keating forgery revelations, Grigson summed up the differences between Keating's fakes and genuine Palmers as follows: 'Each is made up of Palmerrish elements, it is true. Yet in these, severally and in conjunction, everything is wrong; every stroke exhibits weakness, instead of that peculiar fullness and "realness" maintained by Palmer in his Shoreham years, in which he felt himself to be a kind of religious alchemist transmuting the base (wonderful as it might be by itself) into a simulacrum of divinity.'[45]

When we look closely at the prints made in deliberate echo of Palmer's vision, what is immediately striking is the extent to which they are so unlike his. Griggs, arguably the finest technician of all these printmakers, rarely followed Palmer into a pastoral mode and was at his most successful in producing grandiose images of real or imagined mediaeval buildings. As the oldest artist and already developed as a mature engraver at the time of the Victoria and Albert Museum's exhibition, his response to Palmer can be distinguished from the Goldsmiths' group, who both in technique and subject matter owe a much closer allegiance to Palmer's version of pastoral. Here, however, it is important not to overstate the case, as though these printmakers were completely in thrall to Palmer's vision. As student printmakers they could draw on techniques associated with other engravers, Whistler, Meryon, even Rembrandt, and outside the core group of Sutherland, Drury and Tanner, the admixture of stylistic influences supplementing Palmer's approach to engraving is notable. Close examination of the work produced by Sutherland, Drury and Tanner reveals that their approach to Palmer, while not slavish, was most notably faithful in the heavy working of the plate and the use of the white paper, even in shadow, to produce the 'thousand little eyes' that Palmer valued. Yet while their prints take inspiration from Palmer's technique as an etcher, they produce very different results. To compare Palmer's 'Weary Ploughman' with their work is to be made aware of a palpable loss of intensity, even grandeur from Palmer's achievement.

By the late 1940s the Palmer revival had run its course. In 1947 Geoffrey Grigson published *Samuel Palmer, the Visionary Years*. His acknowledgements of those who had assisted him in getting up this study shows the extent to which Palmer's earlier work had become of interest to the intelligentsia over the previous twenty years. As well as collectors and curators, the list included poets, artists and critics, among them Gordon Bottomley, Thomas Lowinsky, Sir Frank Short, Graham Sutherland, John Piper, John Craxton, Martin Hardie, Herbert Read, Kenneth Clark and Nicholas Pevsner. Yet, towards the end of the book, bidding farewell to Palmer once the Shoreham years were over, Grigson included some comments that were addressed to Palmer but may also stand as something of a rebuke to those artists and printmakers who followed Palmer in the twentieth century: 'Pastoral without passion becomes vacant and soft – a sheep is either a paradisiacal creature or a woolly object; and by sticking to pastoral, Palmer missed the fullness of life, shut, or limited, it would be fairer to say, both his eyes and his mind, turned his old powerful bias into a weaker prejudice, and prejudice into dogma.'[46] If we apply these remarks to Griggs, Sutherland, Tanner and Drury they make for uncomfortable reading, and the reason they do so is summed up by Grigson's final musings on the question of Palmer's followers. Thinking of the development of English art up to the 1940s, Grigson observes that: '… the successors of Sickert and Gilman and his friends have asked themselves whether naturalism cannot be enlivened with some of the richness and roundness (though not the aerial subtlety) of Palmer. But they may ask themselves, how much did the richness and roundness, how much did Palmer's vision and its discoveries depend upon his belief?'[47] Grigson's observation offered a caution for artists simply titivating English landscapes with a smattering of Palmer's devices.

Looking back at the work of Sutherland, Tanner and Drury, and their commitment to a vision of English pastoral between the wars, can they be exempted from the kinds of strictures Grigson advances about Palmer's post-Shoreham work? Was the intensity of their belief, Catholic or Quaker, sufficient to avoid the fate that had overtaken their idol? In a slightly earlier essay on Palmer, published in 1941, Grigson investigated Palmer's politics and concluded that the close connection between Palmer's art, religiosity and conservative politics had been its undoing. As his politics were outflanked and his religious ardour cooled, his art began to lose its purpose. Grigson's conclusion was that, despite Palmer's protestations to the contrary, he should have engaged more fully with his own time: 'He did not yield to the century. No, but he did not grasp it, use it and overcome it. He did not gain the deep, necessary worldliness of a Delacroix.' And where Palmer had failed, those who followed his retreat from the world had allowed the vigour of romanticism to degenerate into an art of sentimentality and prettiness', from which all mystery had been squashed and squeezed'. For Grigson, the creative bankruptcy of that tradition had been exposed by the uncompromising truth and worldliness of Whistler, Degas and Sickert.[48] When this essay was published the Palmer revival was already acknowledged in printmaking and was becoming increasingly significant in painting. Grigson makes no mention of it, and one suspects that his silence was due to the revivalists' failure to grasp the twentieth century with the worldliness he thought appropriate to modern consciousness.

This chapter has proposed that the Palmer revival can be usefully considered not only 'vertically', as an inheritance from romanticism, but also 'horizontally', as a moment of artistic production whose contemporary context is worth recuperating. Once we accept that possibility, it is clear that Palmer's ability to fuse artistic vision with religious conviction was not easily emulated in the twentieth century. Not because the spiritual beliefs that Griggs, Sutherland and Tanner held were shallow, for they were all sincerely religious artists, but because the context in which a subject could be invested with spiritual meaning had altered so radically. Not only were the circumstances of the British art world very different from those of a hundred years earlier, but, more significantly, attitudes to landscape itself had changed. Like Palmer before them, their engagement with nature was deeply personal, but equally it needs to be understood in the circumstances of its time.

When Palmer was working at Shoreham new farming practices were transforming both the face of the land (with the enclosure acts) and the employment pattern of agricultural labour (with low wages and the introduction of threshing machines). The Swing riots of 1830, which affected south-east England, were a response to these worsening conditions. Shoreham was not isolated from these changes and one of the local farmers whom Palmer knew personally had his barn and cornstack burnt in September 1830.[49] Palmer's art, however, in its deliberate avoidance of naturalism was concerned to transfigure the landscape, to lift it out of any political and economic reckoning and to articulate instead its spiritual resonance. It was a deliberate retreat from the world, which he wrote about nostalgically from Italy in 1838.

For a long time after our return, we hope that there will be no occasion to leave our native country, but should enjoy to sojourn some day with you in our beautiful vales, to hide ourselves from an impertinent world in tangled orchards; to go sitting on our thyme hills, and in our magic Northern twilight to hear the village clock ticking in his grey tower …[50]

Although Palmer's Shoreham paintings were idiosyncratic in their intensity of vision, even the more attenuated vision of his later career maintained his determination to make a poetic response to landscape.[51] His mature work sustained him because the Victorian art world itself had increasingly endowed landscape with qualities of sentiment and nostalgia.

But Palmer's vision was not something that could be transported wholesale as a source of inspiration once that Victorian vision had faded. For all their commitment to the rural and the spiritual, those etchers who followed Palmer were working at a time when the possibility of investing the countryside with spiritual values was made peculiarly difficult by the advances of modern culture. Although they, too, were working at a time when the agricultural landscape was in crisis and they were therefore, on the face of it at least, confronting a similar situation, the Palmer revivalists worked in very different cultural circumstances. As we have seen, in a secular age the agricultural landscape was brought firmly into rational understandings of planning and development. Likewise, nature as a possibility for the artist was conditioned by developments in art practice. An artist working with landscape subjects between the wars was conscious that the whole Romantic tradition had been thrown into question, following Impressionism's embrace of modernity. More recent developments, associated especially with Cézanne and the Cubists, had further problematized the nature of representation itself. To work consciously in emulation of a nineteenth-century visionary artist was clearly to dissent from the new paradigm.

It is unnecessary, however, to polarize this debate, suggesting that the nostalgia implicit in these prints is automatically to be deprecated in contrast to scenes of industrial Britain between the wars; as though, say, Edward Wadsworth's investigations of the heavy industries of the Black Country were more authentic images of this period. Nor, for that matter, should we crudely ascribe stylistic traits to cultural orientations, as if modernism in the visual arts (when modernism is defined in formal terms, as a set of stylistic attributes) is inevitably attuned to the contemporary world, whereas other artistic developments (i.e. those styles seemingly at odds with modernism) owe their allegiances elsewhere. Even the most cursory examination of the period reveals that explorations of modernity, which is to say social and technological modernity, need not deploy stylistic modernism, nor for that matter did stylistic modernism inevitably engage with modernity so defined. Instead, what we find is a complex matrix of artistic effort, with artists and critics attempting to stake out positions within the art world of the time. In the case of Palmer's modern followers, some might argue that their aesthetic, in its deliberate refusal of much contemporary art practice, is not only in tune with Palmer's own rejection of the dominant practices of the early nineteenth century, but is also broadly analogous to those 'primitivistic' strategies so often encountered in the modern movement, from Gauguin to the early Jackson Pollock; or, less contentiously, that Griggs, Sutherland, Drury and Tanner's investment in place and in Englishness is only finitely removed from their contemporary Paul Nash's understanding of the 'genius loci' as the mainspring for his art.

Yet for all the possibility of placing the Palmer revival within broader currents in British twentieth-century art, we also have to recognize that it occupied a very particular position: it seemed to valorize the rural landscape as a retreat from or an alternative to modernity. At a time of profound cultural transformation, this vision of the English countryside signalled that other, older, social and spiritual possibilities should be invoked. In the last analysis, the subject matter of these prints, whether medieval (Griggs) or rural (Sutherland, Drury, Tanner) is indicative. What it manifests is the same suspicion of modernity found in numerous commentaries appearing in the 1920s and 1930s: that modern culture, orientated primarily to urban experience and technological innovation, carried with it a mechanistic, inhumane and over-rationalized understanding of the world whose domination posed very real threats to a more compassionate way of life. To that extent the phenomenon of the Palmer revival may be understood to have hypostasized a cultural perception specific to the peculiar circumstances of the early twentieth century.

Notes

1. *The Listener*, 12 May 1949, cited in Walter Michel and C.J. Fox (eds), *Wyndham Lewis on Art*, London: Thames and Hudson, 1969, p. 397. My thanks to Alan Munton for bringing this to my attention.

2. Kenneth Clark, *Landscape into Art*, London: John Murray, 1949, pp. 71-2.

3.   Including Sutherland, Tanner, Drury, Griggs, Ravilious, Laurence Whistler, Craxton, Minton, Badmin and Hoyton among others.

4.   See, for example, Michael Baily, 'Why the M25 is Britain's No 1 priority road,' *The Times*, 29 August 1978, p. 6.

5.   See his letter to *The Times*, 26 March 1976.

6.   Arthur Mee, *Little Treasure Island: Her story and her glory*, London: Hodder and Stoughton, 1920, p. 19.

7.   Raymond Plummer, letter to *The Times*, 27 March 1976.

8.   The story was broken by Geraldine Norman in *The Times* of 16 July 1976, although dealers such as David Gould had sounded the alarm six years earlier in a letter to *The Times* of 13 March 1970, and the Palmer scholar Raymond Lister was equally sceptical.

9.   Geoffrey Grigson, letter to *The Times*, 7 August 1976. Graham Sutherland and Paul Drury joint letter to *The Times*, 3 August 1976.

10.   Geoffrey Grigson, 'The Samuel Palmer Situation,' *Times Literary Supplement*, 15 July 1977, p. 852.

11.   See Colin Harrison, 'Palmer and the Neo-Romantics', in William Vaughan, Elizabeth E. Barker, Colin Harrison et al., *Samuel Palmer: (1805-1881): Vision and Landscape*, London: British Museum Press, 2005; Jolyon Drury, *Revelation to Revolution: The Legacy of Samuel Palmer. The Revival and Evolution of Pastoral Printmaking by Paul Drury and the Goldsmiths' School in the 20th Century*, Ashford: Jolyon Drury, 2006; Jerrold Northrop Moore, *The Green Fuse: Pastoral Vision in English Art 1820-2000*, Woodbridge: Antique Collectors' Club Ltd, 2007. Recent exhibitions include *The Legacy of Samuel Palmer: Paul Drury, Graham Sutherland and the Pastoral Print*, Ashmolean Museum, 2004; *Visions of Landscape: Samuel Palmer and Robin Tanner*, Fine Art Society, London, 2004; Simon Martin, Martin Butlin and Robert Meyrick, *Poets in the Landscape: The Romantic Spirit in British Art*, Chichester: Pallant House Gallery, 2007; Anne Anderson, Robert Meyrick and Peter Nahum, *Ancient Landscapes, Pastoral Visions: Samuel Palmer to the Ruralists*, Southampton City Art Gallery, 2008.

12.   Jerrold Northrop Moore, *F.L. Griggs (1876-1938): The Architecture of Dreams*, Oxford: Clarendon Press, 1999, p. 14.

13.   Letter to R.A. Walker dated 26 March 1925 in ibid., p. 15.

14.   In 1932 he joined the advertising agency J. Walter Thompson as its art director and ceased etching. See Gordon Cooke, *William Larkins. Etchings of the East End in the 1920s and other scenes*, London: Robin Garton Gallery, 1979.

15.   Martin Hardie, James Laver and A.H. Palmer, *Catalogue of an Exhibition of Drawings, Etchings & Woodcuts by Samuel Palmer and other disciples of William Blake*, London: Victoria and Albert Museum, 1926. Hardie, for his part, drew attention to Griggs, Sutherland and Drury's inheritance of Palmer's mantle in lectures he gave to the Art Workers' Guild and the Print Collectors' club in 1927. See Drury, *Revelation to Revolution*, pp. 57-8.

16.   Robin Tanner, *The Etcher's Craft*, Ilkley: Scolar Press/Friends of Bristol Art Gallery, 1980, pp. 14 and 52.

17.   See Roger Berthoud, *Graham Sutherland: A Biography*, London: Faber, 1982, pp. 47-57.

18.   Bouverie Hoyton won the Rome Prize for etching in 1926 and travelled widely in Europe from 1926-29. Consequently, his plates lack the association with the English scene characteristic of Sutherland, Drury and Tanner in this period. Gwynne-Jones produced eleven etchings in total, some of which owed a debt to Palmer, but they lack the intensity of response seen in the work of Sutherland, Drury and Tanner.

19.   Cited in Chris Beetles, *S.R. Badmin and the English Landscape*, London: William Collins Sons & Co, 1985, p. 47.

20.   He also illustrated Grigson's *Shell Guide to Trees and Shrubs* (1958).

21.   David Ogg, 'The Etchings of Graham Sutherland and Paul Drury,' *Print Collector's Quarterly*, 16, January 1929, pp. 76-100. Ogg was a Fellow of New College Oxford and was commissioned to write the article by Campbell Dodgson after he had heard Martin Hardie's lecture at the Print Collectors' Club in November 1927. See Drury, *Revelation to Revolution*, p. 69.

22.   Laurence Binyon, *The Followers of William Blake – Edward Calvert, Samuel Palmer, George Richmond and their circle*, [1925] London and New York: Benjamin Blom, 1968, p. 4.

23.   Ogg, 'The Etchings', p. 79.

24.   Ibid., p. 81.

25.   As reported in *Photography*, July 1935, p. 36. Cited in David Mellor, 'British Art in the 1930s' in Frank Gloversmith, *Class, Culture and Social Change: A New View of the 1930s*, Brighton: Harvester Press, 1980.

26.   J.B. Priestley, *English Journey: being a rambling but truthful account of what one man saw and heard and felt and thought during a journey through England during the autumn of the year 1933*, London: W. Heinemann, 1934, pp. 398-403.

27.   Ibid., pp. 63-5.

28.   *The Times*, 23 September 1933. Griggs' letter was a contribution to a discussion about the need to control car noise initiated in the letters pages of 4 August and continued on 16 September.

29.   Moore, *F.L. Griggs*, p. 15.

30.   Quoted in Roger Berthoud, *Graham Sutherland: A Biography*, London: Faber, 1982, p. 54.

31.   Moore, *F.L. Griggs*, pp. 67-8.

32.   Letter dated 18 January 1927, in ibid., p. 191.

33.   From the turn of the century to the 1930s arable land declined from 54.7 per cent to 35.4 per cent, and in its place pasture rose from 41.5 per cent to 54.9 per cent and rough grass from 11.6 per cent to 18.2 per cent. For information on farming and the countryside see Paul Brassley, Jeremy Burchardt and Lynne Thompson (eds), *The English Countryside Between the Wars: Regeneration or Decline?* London: Boydell Press, 2006; also J.K. Bowers and P. Cheshire, *Agriculture, the Countryside and Land Use: An Economic Critique*, London: Methuen, 1983.

34.   See Robin Garton, *Catalogue Raisonné of the Prints of Paul Drury, 1903-1987*, London: Garton & Co, 1992, p. 58.

35.   Clare Leighton, *Country Matters*, London: Victor Gollancz, 1937, p. xv.

36.   See David Matless, *Landscape and Englishness*, London: Reaktion, 1998.

37.   Edward Sackville-West, *Graham Sutherland*, London: Penguin Books, 1943, p. 12.

38.   Tanner, *Etcher's Craft*, 1980, p. 18. Traherne was also a modern rediscovery. His work had remained in manuscript until published as *Poems* (1903) and *Centuries of Meditations* (1908).

39.   H.J. Massingham, 'The Wiltshire Flax-Mill, An Example of True Husbandry', *Geographical Magazine*, 1943-44, vol. 16, pp. 369-79. p. 376. Massingham knew the organicist Rolf Gardiner and would surely have approved his attempt to revive the Wessex flax industry, taking over a derelict flax mill at Slape in West Dorset and using it as a base to coordinate West Country flax production. Gardiner wanted to reintroduce flax feasts and harvest festivals, continuing what he was doing at Springhead, but wartime production was too urgent to incorporate these older rituals and Gardiner left the business in 1942, ceding it to the Home Flax Directorate.

40.   Tanner, *Etchers Craft*, p. 33.

41.   Letter to Russell Alexander dated 13 February 1912 in Moore, *F.L. Griggs*, p. 74.

42.   Letter to Nicolas McDowell dated 14 June 1976 in Robin Tanner, *The More Angels Shall I Paint*, Monmouth: The Old Stile Press, 1991, pp. 27-8. Tanner and his wife, Heather, did not call themselves Christians: 'The Jesus we conceive from our reading, is a much stronger and more magnificently dangerous revolutionary than even most Quakers will acknowledge.' Ibid., p. 27.

43.   Quoted in *The English Vision*, catalogue 10, William Weston Gallery, London, 1973, n.p.

44.   Simon Martin, Martin Butlin and Robert Meyrick, *Poets in the Landscape: The Romantic Spirit in British Art*, Chichester: Pallant House Gallery, 2007.

45.   *The Times*, 7 August 1976.

46.   Geoffrey Grigson, *Samuel Palmer: The Visionary Years*, London: Kegan Paul, 1947, p. 138.

47.   Ibid., p. 140.

48.   Geoffrey Grigson, 'Samuel Palmer: the Politics of an Artist,' *Horizon*, vol. 4, no. 19, 1941, pp. 327-8.

49.   Raymond Lister, *The Letters of Samuel Palmer*, Oxford: Clarendon Press, 1974, vol. 1, p. 14.

50.   Ibid., p. 155.

51.   I have touched on this before in 'Samuel Palmer and the Pastoral Inheritance,' *Landscape Research*, vol. 11, no. 3, Winter 1986, pp. 11-15.

7

Palmer and the dark pastoral in English music of the twentieth century

Simon Shaw-Miller

The pastoral has proved to be a vital and flexible genre, which, throughout western history, has served a variety of audiences and artistic purposes. In one dominant guise it has been equated with Arcadia, that magical place where shepherds dwelt, concerned less with sheep or foot rot than with poetry or the melodies of their flute: a simple landscape which offers a retreat from reality and the present.[1] In Schiller's *On Naïve and Sentimental Poetry* (1795-1800) such an idyll becomes defined as an *Empfindungsweise* (mode of experience), a psychological and expressive state, rather than a subject or place. The Romantics found in the pastoral's Arcadian guise a degenerate form of verse and revolted against its decorative and nostalgic elements. George Crabbe, for example, in his poem *The Village* (1783), writes 'I grant indeed that fields and flocks have charms/For him that grazes or for him that farms/But when amid such pleasing scenes I trace/The poor laborious Natives of the place', ending the stanza, 'Then shall I dare these real ills to hide/In tinsel trappings of poetic pride?' (Book 1, lines 39-48). This is an open attack on the conventions of the classical pastoral. In 1800, as Schiller was conceptualizing the psychological mode of the pastoral, the poet William Wordsworth was promoting realism (albeit somewhat tempered) rather than escapism as the emphatic coin of the pastoral – he writes of his long and tragic narrative in *Michael*, bearing the subtitle 'A Pastoral Poem':

> … Beside the brook
> Appears a straggling heap of unhewn stones!
> And to that simple object appertains
> A story – unenriched with strange events,
> Yet not unfit, I deem, for the fireside,
> Or for the summer shade. It was the first
> Of those domestic tales that spake to me

Of shepherds, dwellers in the valleys, men
Whom I already loved; not verily
For their own sakes, but for the fields and hills
Where was their occupation and abode.
And hence this Tale, while I was yet a Boy
Careless of books, yet having felt the power
Of Nature, by the gentle agency
Of natural objects, led me on to feel
For passions that were not my own, and think
(At random and imperfectly indeed)
On man, the heart of man, and human life.
    … Upon the forest-side in Grasmere Vale
There dwelt a Shepherd, Michael was his name;
An old man, stout of heart, and strong of limb.
His bodily frame had been from youth to age
Of an unusual strength: his mind was keen,
Intense, and frugal, apt for all affairs,
And in his shepherd's calling he was prompt
And watchful more than ordinary men.[2]

A story unenriched, not out of books, but set in a specific place (Grasmere Vale, Cumbria) and a time (the recent past), about the life and death of a particular shepherd – not a Corin (a generic shepherd) but an old man named Michael.

As this suggests, the pastoral is not a simple concept, nor is all classical pastoral as decadent or as far from the 'dignities of plain occurrence' (as Wordsworth puts it) as the Romantics might make it appear in their modulation of the form. But the move from a universalizing myth of simplicity to a psychological and individualized narrative is characteristic of late eighteenth- and early nineteenth-century pastoral poetry. The humblest of poetic forms grows ever more complex and hybrid in both form and content, growing from a sense of loss considered in reflection, as poems of the past become poems of history.

Pastoral depends on dialectic relationships, between art and nature, or city and country, for example. These are threads running through all the arts in relation to the pastoral, especially their employment of landscape as a counter to the developing townscape. The pastoral was revivified as the industrial revolution developed through this period and the tension between town and country became more pronounced.[3] John Barrell explored the loosening of constraints on the pastoral tradition in art in the period leading up to the focus of this chapter, in his book *The Dark Side of the Landscape*.[4] Although Palmer is nowhere mentioned in Barrell's book, he is a key artist in the process of thinking through the complexities of the pastoral.

I want to use Palmer as an entry point for a discussion of the pastoral in English music in the twentieth century, where the concept is not bucolic and Arcadian, but of a darker hue. I shall argue that a critical, dark pastoral, one that was not simply a rejection of modernity, but rather a substantial and critical dialogue with it, dominated English music. And this is the position English music's leading figure, Vaughan Williams, occupies; his music is not, as is often believed, a denial of modernism, but rather a critical discussion and exchange with it. Modernism's relationship with Romanticism in a British context is more one of incorporation than opposition, as many examples show. Neo-Romanticism in art absorbed many modernist influences, but played them out in relation to ideas of landscape as a site of resolution. The concomitant revival of interest in Samuel Palmer helps to fill this landscape with pathos. This 'dark pastoral' continues to the present, and may possess an even keener edge in the context of our growing awareness of the imperatives of eco-politics in the early twenty-first century.

This chapter will seek to identify some of the formal and technical characteristics that are deployed in linking the pastoral and music. The associative element in this process is taken as given; this chapter explores instead the notions of space and distance, which, in addition to having a technical manifestation, are also indicative of nostalgia, for pastoral involves a relationship with the past; it is the 'art of the backward glance',[5] but a dialectical one. In music, the pastoral is closely linked, not to the image of the shepherd and his flute (first mentioned in Homer's *Iliad* (18, ll.525-6)), but rather to the sound and tunes he played upon it.[6] But the music of the folk is (as we shall see) a complex phenomenon, and some music that calls itself pastoral declines to call upon 'folk music'. An example of this can be found in the mid-twentieth century in the music of Alan Rawsthorne (1905-1971), which I'll briefly consider before turning to the principal focus of this chapter, Vaughan Williams, in whose music the folk tradition is a more conspicuous feature.

The City of Birmingham Symphony Orchestra, under Meredith Davis, first performed Rawsthorne's second symphony, sub-titled 'Pastoral', on 29 September 1959. Rawsthorne is not generally considered a pastoralist, for his musical language does not draw on folk song and modal harmony. It can best be described as an extended diatonic syntax of competing minor and major tonalities: modes built by conflicting (augmented) triadic structures. For example, A-C-C♯ can be used to generate the F major triad ([F]-A-C) and A major (A-C♯-[E]) or minor triad (A-C-[E]). If the A then moves down a semi-tone to G♯, then F minor ([F]-G♯/A♭-C) and C♯ minor (C♯-[E]-G♯) or major (C♯-[E♯]-G♯) can be generated, and so on. These chords create a symmetrical division of the octave that is ambiguous in relation to its root, because an augmented chord in equal temperament will generate the same chord from any of its constituent notes. This produces a sense of harmonic space as the chord unfolds infinitely. An example occurs at the very opening of the symphony (*Allegro piacevole*) as the following chord unfolds through the orchestra: E-B-G-D♯-A♭-C. This chord can be derived from the augmented triads of G major (G-B-D♯) and C major (C-E-G♯ [A♭]), or non-augmented chords of E minor

(E-G-B) and A♭ major (A♭-C-E♭ [D♯]).[7] So tightly ordered a structure produces a harmonic ambiguity (bi-tonality), which is by its nature ambivalent, producing a sense of tonal greyness (more straightforward tonality tends to be employed by Rawsthorne in order to lift the mood). The movement is in sonata form, but with a second subject that is more an extension of the first subject than an independent contrast. This is a tendency in much of Rawsthorne's music, and is particularly apposite here, as a grey mood of melancholy pervades the symphony, and is made explicit through the use of text in the vocal line of the finale.

The slow second movement is ternary (*poco lento e liberamenta*), and opens with a melody on solo horn, an archetypical pastoral instrument, but not the natural, open horn we shall see used by Vaughan Williams. Rather, we have a more confined, constricted one, uttering not a modal but a chromatic melody (between A minor and major), marked at the close of the tune by a cadence approached by semi-tones. A rather gloomy march forms the middle section of this movement, a rhythmic contrast still marked by chromatic constrictions, which is soon locked into a three-part canon, before the horn lament returns to close the movement.

The third movement (*allegro giocoso*) is a species of country dance in 6/8 time that is not so much a jig as a mix between a jig and a tarantella (a dance of death), and does not derive from original vernacular material. The violin tune of the middle section pulls against the jig in its duple dotted quavers. The movement could be described as in loose rondo form, or more simply as ternary.

An abrupt end leads to the fourth movement (*andante*), which has the same harmonic basis as the opening movement. This soundscape supports a solo trumpet which gives way to the soprano solo, another unusual feature of the symphony which it nevertheless shares with Vaughan Williams' third. Unlike Vaughan Williams' solo voice, however, Rawsthorne uses a text, a sonnet by the Tudor poet Henry Howard, Earl of Surrey (1516-47):

The soote season, that bud and bloom forth brings
With green hath clad the hill and eke the vale
The nightingale with feathers new she sings;
The turtle to her make hath told her tale.

Summer is come, for every spray now springs:
The hart hath hung his old head on the pale;
The buck in brake his winter coat he flings;
The fishes flete with new repaired scale.

The adder all her slogh away she slings;
The swift swallow pursueth the flyes smale;
The busy bee her honey now she mings;
Winter is worn that was the flowers bale.

And thus I see among these pleasant things
Each care decays, and yet my sorrow springs.[8]

This text underlines the ambiguity already mentioned in Rawsthorne's harmonic language, disquiet at the heart of the dark pastoral. At the end of the first stanza, the strings take up a rhythmic variation of the country-dance from the previous movement, but this temporary up-beat mood soon evaporates. The text's final twist depresses any naïve hope; 'yet my sorrow springs', the voice echoing the horn lament from the second movement on the word sorrow. We conclude, as at the opening of the movement and indeed the symphony, on the same augmented triads, with a solo violin replacing Howard's words with an ascending passage. The presence of a text in this last movement makes the pastoral content explicit, and allows us to relate musical passages (and their twinned text) back to their earlier appearances in the piece. John McCabe writes that this movement would have been an ideal choice for Rawsthorne's own funeral service: 'The song, almost more than any other piece, was perhaps the purest expression of the most personal of all his musical visions, the awareness of time future (autumn) contained within time present (spring)'.[9] I shall return to this evocation of T.S. Eliot in my coda on David Matthews's *In the Dark Time*.

In what follows I want to consider the pastoral as purely instrumental music. The spirit of pastoral touched many twentieth-century British composers. Pastoral is various, and to do justice to this variety each case deserves separate consideration. For this reason, I shall focus on one composer, Ralph Vaughan Williams, and one work, the *Pastoral Symphony*, his third. This work lays the ground for my theme both explicitly and implicitly and will act as an exemplum. I shall, however, bring the analysis up to date by considering the work of one of our most distinguished contemporary composers, David Matthews. In consideration of his orchestral work *In the Dark Time* I shall argue that the pastoral tradition extends into the twenty-first century. As Matthews has put it himself, 'if that pastoral tradition can no longer be sustained in its innocence, perhaps another might replace it, which reconciles our romanticized sense of a picturesque past with the brutal facts of history'.[10] This dark pastoral is an artery filled with the blood spilt in the First World War, and which flows from the music of Vaughan Williams, whose music, for those with ears, is far from the 'cow-pat pastoralism' of which he is often accused.

I should like to continue with a story, some of which is factual, some conjecture. On 9 February 1875, the vicar of Christ Church in Down Ampney in Gloucestershire died. He left behind a wife, two sons and a daughter. On the death of her husband, Margaret, the wife, left the vicarage in Gloucestershire to live with her sister, Sophie, at their family home close to the village of Coldharbour in Surrey. The home was Leith Hill Place, which had been built in the late seventeenth century and which her father had bought in 1845, living there until his death in 1880. The father's name was Josiah Wedgwood III, grandson of the founder of the Staffordshire pottery company, whose wife Caroline, Margaret's mother, was the eldest sister of Charles Darwin.

Margaret's youngest child, a son, had been born on 12 October 1872, just two years before his father's death and the subsequent move to Leith Hill Place. The boy's name was Ralph Vaughan Williams, and he spent his childhood in a house surrounded by trees, rhododendrons and azaleas, overlooking the Surrey Downs and the Sussex Weald. He spent much of his time, when he wasn't exploring the grounds, practising on an organ that his mother had erected for him in the hall of Leith Hill Place, and having music and violin lessons from his Aunt Sophie. At the age of eight he followed a correspondence course run by the University of Edinburgh. He passed both the preliminary and advanced examinations, before going on to a preparatory school at Rottingdean and then to Charterhouse. Later he attended the recently established Royal College of Music before going up to Trinity College, Cambridge, as his grandfather Josiah had done some 70 years before him.

Abutting the grounds of Leith Hill Place is Leith Hill Tower, a fortified folly built in 1765 by Richard Hull on what is the highest point in the south of England. Hull, then the owner of Leith Hill Place, had obtained the permission of his neighbour, Mr Evelyn of Wotton, to build what was described as a 'Prospect House'. Its construction was based on a typical fourteenth-century Wealden Tower.

I had the Tower built and completed by October 1765 using local stone
and local labour. It then consisted of two rooms 'neatly furnished'
with prospect glasses [telescopes] in order to enjoy the view. Living
locally at Leith Hill Place, the hill was my great joy. I requested that,
after my death, my body would be laid to rest under the Tower.

The National Trust discovered his bones in 1980, following excavation and restoration work. On a plaque on the side of the tower he placed this inscription (which is still visible):

Traveller! In order that thou mayest see in all directions the beauty of
the earth, this tower, visible from afar, was erected by Richard Hull,
Esq., of Leith Hill Place, in the reign of George III, 1765, as a delight
not only to myself, but also to my neighbours and to all.

And you really can see in all directions – on a clear day to the English Channel in one direction and to St Paul's Cathedral in the other.

With the advent of the railways, Leith Hill Tower became a popular site for day trips. Visitors would be taken by horse and carriage from Dorking station to Leith Hill Hotel, on the Abinger Road in Coldharbour, and then on to picnics around the Tower.

Eight miles north-east of the Tower is Furze Hill House, Mead Vale, Redhill. In 1862 Samuel Palmer moved to Furze Hill. There he had a studio, and from its window he could see Leith Hill Tower. In the year in which Vaughan Williams was born, 1872, Palmer wrote, explaining the significance of the location:

In 1861, after the loss of our elder son, who
'died in harness', full of noble purpose,
we came hither, and from the window at
which I am writing, I can see the slopes
of the Leith Hill, a woodland ridge,
behind which, in Abinger churchyard,
the hope and ornament of my life lies
alone under his simple monument till it
is opened to place me by his side.[11]

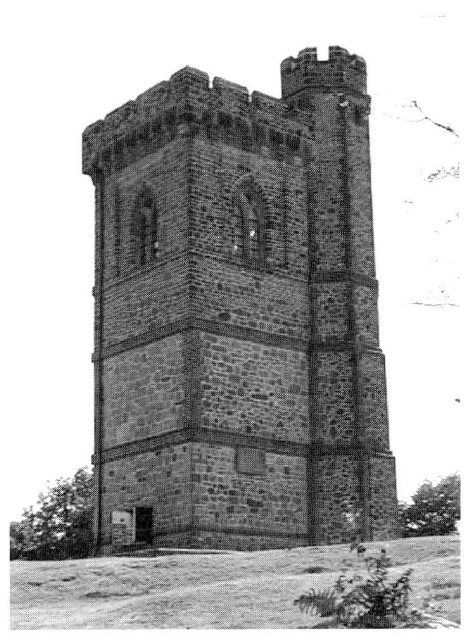

7.1   Leith Hill Tower, Surrey. Constructed 1765. Photograph by Dr Elizabeth Stanway (Astrologist).

Since Helen Irwin's article in 1981, most scholars agree that Leith Hill is the tower represented in Palmer's depictions of 'The Lonely Tower', a subject taken from Milton's early poem, *Il Penseroso*. Its best known manifestation is as an etching of 1879.[12] Within the pastoral there is often a conflation between a lost Eden and the loss of childhood's innocence. We might remember that pastoral begins in the *Idylls* of Theocritus, with the recollection of his own Sicilian boyhood, and is developed in the *Eclogues* of Virgil – the very text for which Palmer was devising a series of etchings at the time of his own death.

As William Vaughan and Elizabeth Barker have argued, there is a specific connection between the landscape depicted in these tower images and this most tragic event in Palmer's life, the death of his son.[13] Indeed, this connection is strengthened in the later versions of the work. The cloudless sky of the 1879 etching reveals a constellation that fixes the time of his son's death. They write, 'it can be shown that the position of the Great Bear and the Heavenly Twins, viewed from Leith Hill looking north-north-east at the moment of the death of Thomas More Palmer (5.54 a.m. 11 July [1861]) was almost an exact match with the stars as they appear in Palmer's later versions of *The Lonely Tower*'. In addition, the etching of 1879 appears to incorporate the new additions to Leith Hill Tower undertaken by W.J. Wotton in 1864 (two years after Palmer moved to Furze Hill), an upper room and battlement, and, most distinctively, a high octagonal external stair turret.[14]

Now for the conjecture. In 1879, when Palmer looked out of his studio window to Leith Hill tower and in the direction of his son's tomb, Vaughan Williams was seven years old, and was playing on Leith Hill in the company of his older brother and sister. Perhaps, having had a picnic at the foot of the tower, he climbed with his siblings to the top, and in looking north east, he returned Palmer's gaze across the distance of only eight miles. Vaughan Williams and Palmer are connected by a landscape, and a concern for what that landscape signifies.[15] Apocryphal though the conceit may be, it allows an introduction to ideas central to both the notion of landscape and, specifically, the pastoral in art and music: look and distance, space and time.

In his study of the critical idiom of the pastoral, Peter Marinelli makes the elegant argument that, 'if pastoral lives for us at all at the present time, it lives by a capacity to move out of its old haunts in the Arcadian pastures and to inhabit the ordinary country landscape of the modern world, daily contracted by the encroachment of civilization and as a consequence daily more precious as a projection of our desires for simplicity'.[16] Within the tradition of the pastoral, the countryside has its meaning as an antidote to the city and its environs. Landscape requires specific sites of vision (which Hull's tower consciously provided), and the concept of distance is of defining importance: landscape is a gaze across a space.

Let us consider this in relation to the Palmer we have already seen. The distance between the couple in the foreground of Palmer's image 'The Lonely Tower' and the object of the gaze (the tower) is made more dramatic by the chasm that lies between them. This chasm is exaggerated in the later etching, becoming a fissure, a rupture in the landscape itself. Its depth is sharpened through the medium of line and the stark tonal contrast of black and white. But distance is not solely signified by space, it is also present in time.

The solace of the past is perhaps an inevitable consequence of modernity, as we are overwhelmed by a present that is ironically 'melting into air.' For Palmer, on the cusp of this modernity, his project was less general and his solace more specific. His unreachable past was that manifested in the tragic loss of his son. In 'The Lonely Tower' it is pictorially represented by a look back across time and space, the chasm between 1861 and 1879. The mood here is what we might call 'dark pastoral', a foretaste of what was to become more common in the modern pastoral of the late nineteenth century and the early twentieth century; the pastoral of Thomas Hardy's *Far from the Madding Crowd* (1874), *The Return of the Native* (1880) or *Tess of the D'Urbervilles* (1891); or the William Morris of *Under An Elm Tree* (1889), or Mary Webb's *Gone to Earth* (1917); also in much of the poetry of Edward Thomas, A.E. Housman, and, of course, the First World War poets, whose landscapes form a counterpoint to the picturesque sites of the so-called Georgian poets.

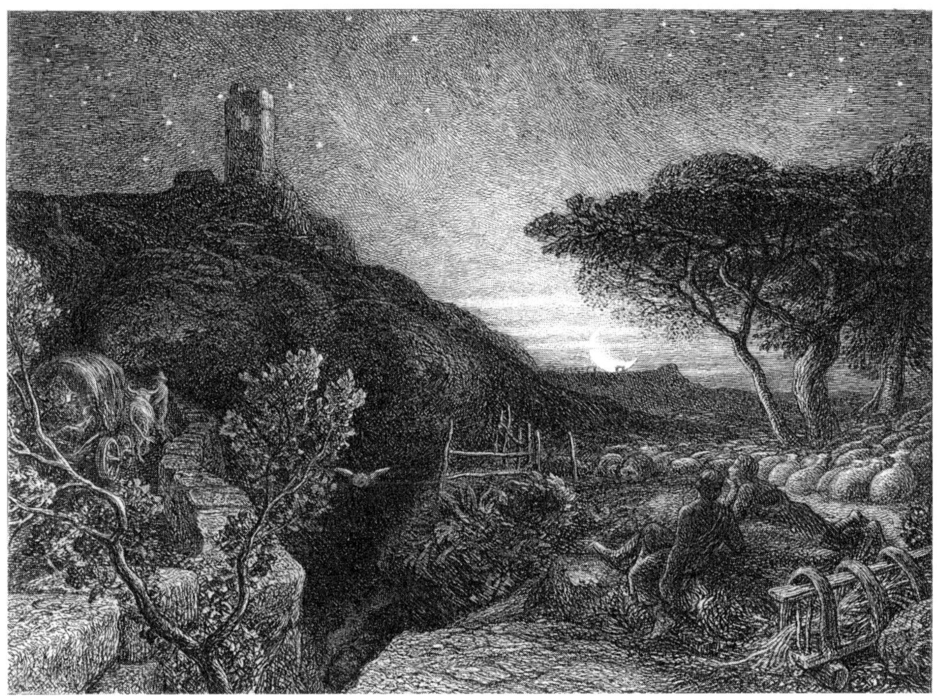

7.2   Samuel Palmer *The Lonely Tower*, 1879. Etching, 18.8 × 25.1 cm. Yale Center for British Art, Paul Mellon Collection, USA/The Bridgeman Art Library.

This space does not have to be represented solely horizontally, as in 'The Lonely Tower', but might also signify vertically. In Palmer's 1843 oil painting 'The Rising of the Skylark', there are again interesting differences between the etching and the oil. In the etching, the man observing and listening to the bird wears a smock (see Figure 5.1), while in the oil he is less of the country, more an observer, a visitor (see Figure 7.4). The distance from the country necessary for the pastoral has shifted from outside the frame, from viewers of an holistic country scene, to an observer now within the frame. It has been suggested by Timothy Wilcox that this new figure is, in fact, the poet Shelley, as the figure resembles a portrait of the poet by Palmer's friend Joseph Severn.[17] For Shelley, in his 1820 poem 'To a Skylark', the bird is distant, it is a symbol, a 'blithe spirit', distant in space as it climbs to heaven. The first two stanzas:

Hail to thee, blithe Spirit!
Bird thou never wert,
That from Heaven, or near it,
Pourest thy full heart
In profuse strains of unpremeditated art.
Higher still and higher

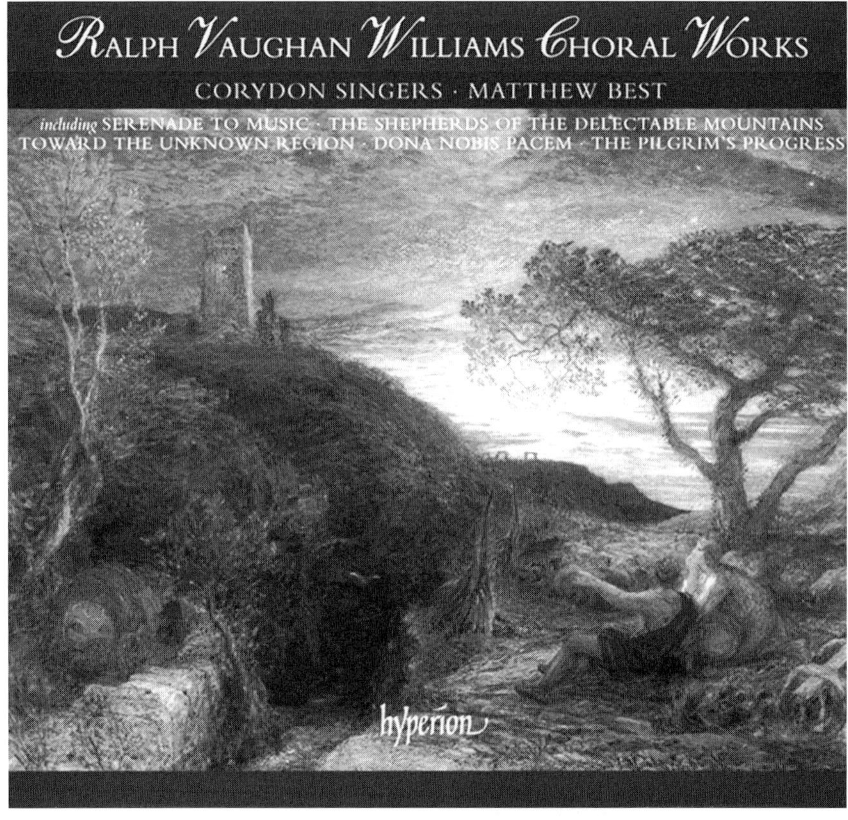

7.3   *Ralph Vaughan Williams Choral Works*, CD, Hyperion Records, 2008. (Cover: Samuel Palmer, 'The Lonely Tower', 1868. Watercolour and bodycolour and gum arabic on London board, Yale Centre for British Art, Paul Mellon Collection, USA/The Bridgeman Art Library).

From the earth thou springest
Like a cloud of fire;
The blue deep thou wingest,
And singing still dost soar, and soaring singest.[18]

In 1866 Palmer wrote to Mrs Richmond saying 'Shelley, if I remember, assures the bird that after all he is no lark at all but a spirit! A spirit! "I say – none of that!" the bird might have replied.' An additional distance is thus exposed between real bird and symbol. But, whichever signifies, the distance between the space of the poet and the space of the bird is bridged by song. Sound, like a look, is also connected to space and time and can connect us across a distance. In turning to Vaughan Williams we see concerns on a similar theme, as Wilfrid Mellers put it 'If there is a soundscape that offers an

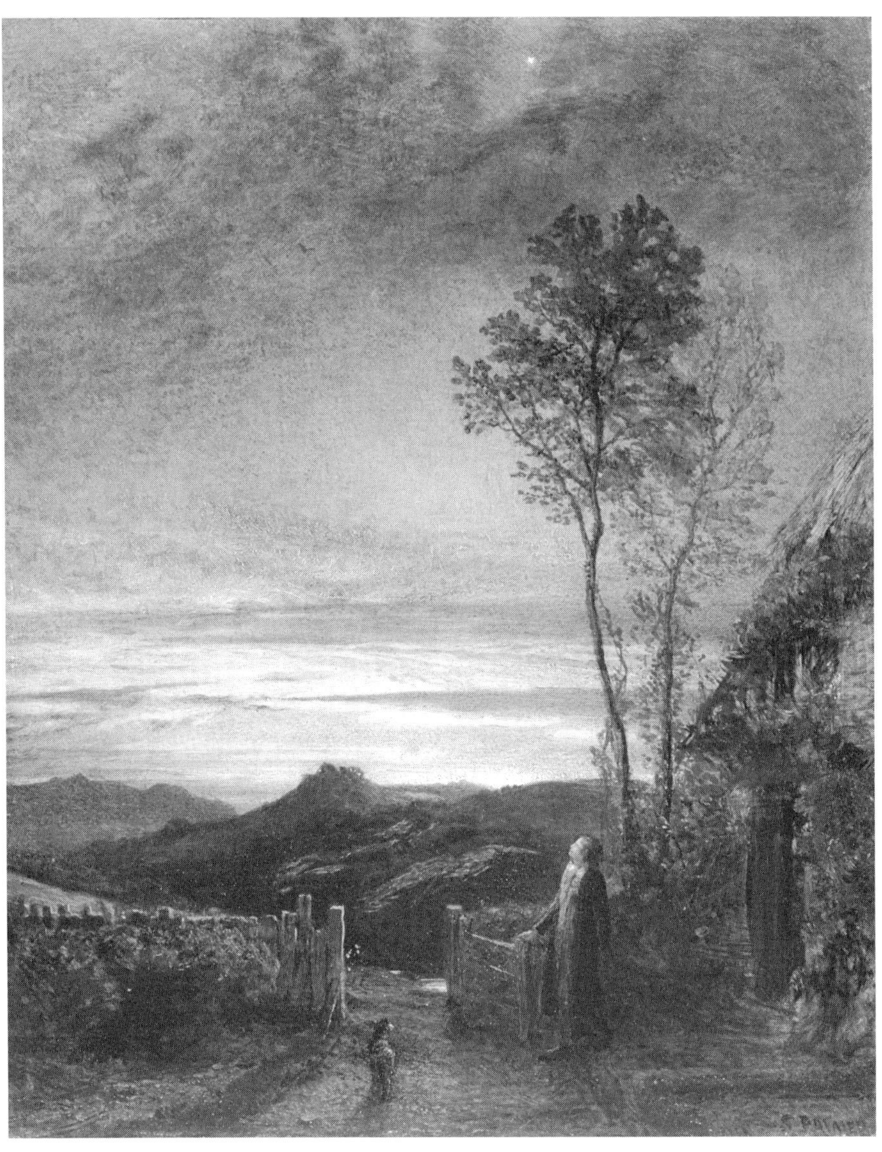

7.4   Samuel Palmer, 'The Rising of the Skylark'. Oil on board.
© National Museum Wales/The Bridgeman Art Library.

aural complement to Palmer's landscapes, it is Vaughan Williams's *The Lark Ascending*.'[19] But this is not a simple site, not a plain Arcadian pastoral space, for Vaughan Williams' work is dated 1914, 'the year of the war that was to silence English larks of most breeds'.[20]

The Lark Ascending for violin and small orchestra is not based on Shelley's poem, but quotes a simpler, more direct poem by George Meredith. This extract is inscribed in the score:

He rises and begins to round,
He drops the silver chain of sound,
Of many links without a break,
In chirrup, whistle, slur and shake …
For singing till his heaven fills,
'Tis love of earth that he instils,
And ever winging up and up,
Our valley is his golden cup
And he the wine which overflows
To lift us with him as he goes …

Till lost on his aerial rings
In light, and then the fancy sings.[21]

It was composed and revised by Vaughan Williams without performance between 1914 and 1920, and might fairly be said to represent a key moment in the development of Vaughan Williams' aesthetic. Its first full performance was given in the old Queen's Hall, London, on 14 June 1921, played by the dedicatee, Marie Hall, with the British Symphony Orchestra under Adrian Boult.

The issue of folk music is an important, if often misunderstood, aspect of Vaughan Williams' work. As he himself makes the point: 'A musician who wishes to say anything worth saying must first of all express himself … English composers do not spring from the peasantry. Indeed, in England there is no true peasantry for them to spring from.'[22] Nevertheless, the folk song movement, headed by Cecil Sharp, offered Vaughan Williams a number of benefits. It was, musically, a complete contrast to the musical language of Wagner, who cast a long shadow over all late nineteenth- and early twentieth-century culture. It was necessary for all young composers to position themselves *pro* or *contra* Wagner. But folk music did more than simply offer a harmonic or melodic resource, it also represented, through William Morris, an anti-bourgeois, sentimental continuity with a neglected tradition of English cultural life; James Day has suggested that 'Vaughan Williams' nationalism was rooted … in a love for the underdog.'[23] This support for the lower classes also has a source in the radical strain of the Wedgwood–Darwin outlook, and a liberal disposition to accept things on merit rather than fashion, which was drilled into him as a child. The link between this anti-Wagnerian musical language and folk music can be detected in the promotion of melodic invention over harmonic innovation, and emotional candour over structural complexity.[24]

That is not to say that what developed as an English 'national school' was characterized by structural insecurity. Rather, it is a matter of emphasis, or of degree. Formal structuralism, as it might be seen to have developed from middle European serialism, was overlooked in favour of modal harmony and organic development. And in common with William Morris' concern for pre-industrial values, a belief in the significance of solid craftsmanship was promoted. Thus, while it might be hard for us to appreciate, the re-evaluation of folk music in the early years of the twentieth century was more radical than it might seem to us, a hundred years later.

Let us briefly consider a few of the musical elements of *The Lark Ascending*. The overall structure is a simple ternary form (A – *Andante sostenuto*, B – *Allegretto tranquillo* (quasi andante), A), a common vernacular structure. The opening violin cadenza, the rising lark figure, is based on a wandering pentatonic scale (from open d[1] to d[4]) (a), which segues into a descending pentatonic melody (b):

Ex. 7.1   Opening violin cadenza, Ralph Vaughan Williams, *The Lark Ascending*. © J. Curwen & Sons / Faber Music Ltd, London. Reproduced by kind permission of the publishers.

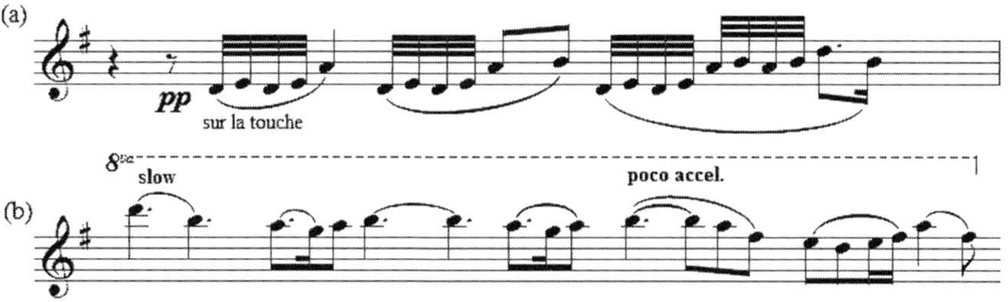

Such scales are a common feature of much folk music: they are easy to harmonize. The modal harmony refers back to the musical language of sixteenth-century English music, which Vaughan Williams first used extensively in *The Fantasia on a Theme by Thomas Tallis*, written just before *The Lark Ascending*.[25]

This modal and pentatonic material allows the use of what would be defined as dissonances in conventional tonal music, and is compounded by his employment of what conventional music considers forbidden devices, as, for example, in the use of parallel fifths in the accompaniment figure following the violin cadenza (6 before letter A). The adoption of a 6/8 meter for most of the A section, and its subdivision of 2/4 for the B middle section (letter G), again recalls the adoption by Baroque dance suites of the rustic dance of the *gigue* (see Example 7.2):

Ex. 7.2   Accompaniment figure, Ralph Vaughan Williams, *The Lark Ascending*.
© J. Curwen & Sons / Faber Music Ltd, London. Reproduced by kind
permission of the publishers.

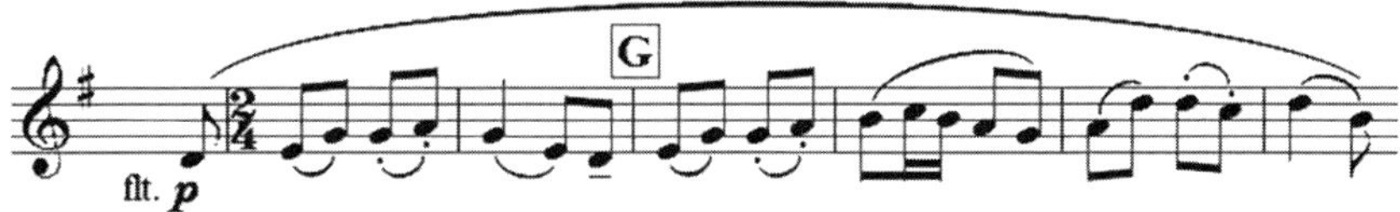

It is popular to read this work as a commentary on nature and man, or
individual and community; even becoming and being (in all cases, the violin
represents the first term, the orchestra the latter). Indeed, the recapitulation
of the violin's theme by the full orchestra (*tempo del principio* (1 before letter
U), and the thematic integration of the A and B sections, which is most
marked in the violin's adoption of the 2/4 and 6/8 themes in the middle
section (at letter J and letter R), can be viewed as a reconciliation between
such oppositions.

The work straddles the First World War. The twentieth-century pastoral
can only really be understood as a counterpoint to the two great cataclysms
of that century, the First and Second World Wars. Accordingly, Vaughan
Williams' use of folk music underwent significant changes. In such pre-
war works as *The Norfolk Rhapsody*, he incorporates and works up tunes he
had collected himself. After the war, and in *The Lark Ascending*, he develops
original themes modelled on a more generic conception of folk material,
gained through the familiarity he acquired by collecting it. This generic
approach is also true of the song of the lark. It is not an attempt to emulate
the feverish song of the lark as it attempts to distract us from the location
of its nest. This is lark as symbol; it is an analogue, not a representation.
Indeed, it is this anthropomorphism, the cultural moulding of nature
that, for Vaughan Williams, locks the interdependence of man and nature
together, and forms the synthesis and resolution of oppositions.

Like Palmer, whose lonely tower is a memorial to his lost son, so too
Vaughan Williams produced a kind of memorial. His *Pastoral Symphony*
(his third) was conceived, to use his own words, 'as an elegy for a lost
generation'; Michael Kennedy has called it 'Vaughan Williams' 1914-18 war
requiem'. The apparent serenity of this work was gestated during Vaughan
Williams' war service in France. He recalled this time in a letter to his wife,
Ursula, in 1938: 'It's really wartime music, a great deal of it incubated when
I used to get up night after night with the ambulance wagon at Ecoivres, and
we went up a steep hill and there was a wonderful, Corot-like landscape in
the sunset – it's not really lambkins frisking at all, as most people take for
granted.'[26] Up a hill to see a view, just like Leith Hill ... it is interesting that
the landscape is seen through the eyes of a painter, albeit a French painter,

but then Vaughan Williams had studied orchestration with the young Maurice Ravel before the war in 1908. The first sketches of the symphony date from 1916, but prolonged work waited until just after the war in 1919, and it was completed by the summer of 1921. The *Pastoral Symphony* was first performed at the Royal Philharmonic Society concert on 26 January 1922, and was revised in 1955.

Some have seen this work as typical of the disinterestedness of music in the face of politics and 'real' life. It was famously dismissed by the composer Philip Heseltine (aka Peter Warlock), as reminiscent of a 'cow looking over a gate'.[27] But this is to imagine that for music to be about something it needs to have some kind of onomatopoeic relationship to it. It does not have to be like a war to be about the war. To demand such a correlation is, indeed, simplistic, and diminishes the range of ways in which music connects to the world through its identity as a culturally embodied practice.

Let us look a little more closely at the *Pastoral Symphony* to see how it creates what Donald Tovey so eloquently called the 'power behind all this massive quietness'.[28] This understatement and authority is what is sometimes missed, yet it is exactly this that gives the work its dark pastoral nature. The pentatonic modal harmony (mixolydian on G in the first movement) and the alternation between duple and triple meters in the first movement create a harmonic space, or landscape, against which the opening melodies can drift. The work emerges from oscillating woodwind triads with a low string perfect fifth. The listener accustomed to classical phrasing is placed slightly off-centre (see Example 7.3).

This asymmetrical metering is also common in folk song. The harmonization follows the technique of Debussy, in that the chords trace the melody up and down the scale, instead of adopting independent melodic counterpoints. But, as Tovey has pointed out, Vaughan Williams adds another principle to this: melodic motives are often locked on to particular harmonizations, and more than one motive and its harmonization can drift about independently. Technically, this is called bi-planar or tri-planar harmony (depending on the number of independent harmonic blocks). Note the characteristic sliding modulation from A major to F♯ major via G♯ major and E major, at letter E (see Example 7.4).

This creates a subtle rhythmic and harmonic tension. The pentatonic melodies themselves recall folk music, as we discussed earlier, but in a darker, more dissonant landscape, the solo violin statement (which emerges in a number of places in this movement) early on recalls the *Lark*; we shall hear another 'lark' at the work's close. The violin later takes up a counterpoint with the cor anglais and then the clarinet and oboe, which might be described as a second subject, although the whole movement is not in strict sonata form, it weaves pentatonic motives and planer harmonies together to sustained symphonic effect.

Ex. 7.3 First movement, Ralph Vaughan Williams, *Pastoral Symphony*. © J. Curwen & Sons / Faber Music Ltd, London. Reproduced by kind permission of the publishers.

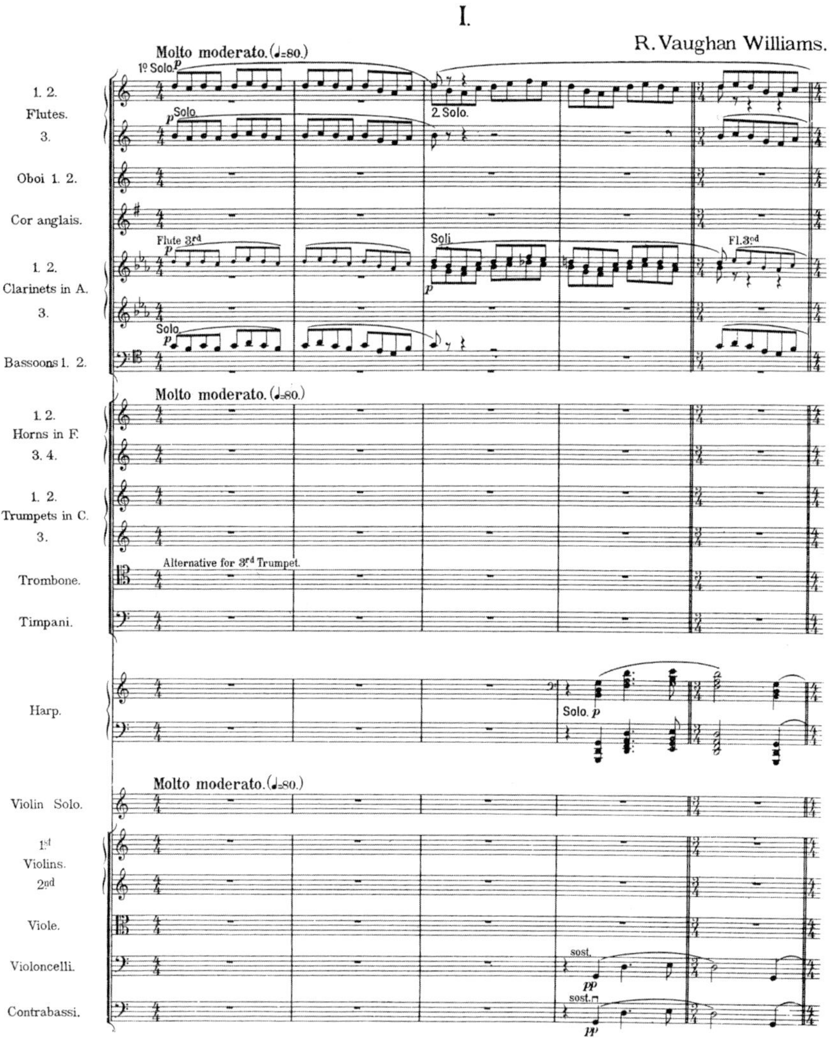

This pentatonic character is perhaps most marked in the second movement (see Example 7.5).

At the very opening, over a held chord of F minor (F, C, A♭) on muted strings, a solo horn develops a pentatonic idea separate from the accompaniment. This separation is emphasized by the prominence of the A (♮), G and E (against the F, C, A♭). This independence creates a sense of space within the musical landscape, in opposition to the more

Ex. 7.4   Second movement, Ralph Vaughan Williams, *Pastoral Symphony*. © J. Curwen & Sons / Faber Music Ltd, London. Reproduced by kind permission of the publishers.

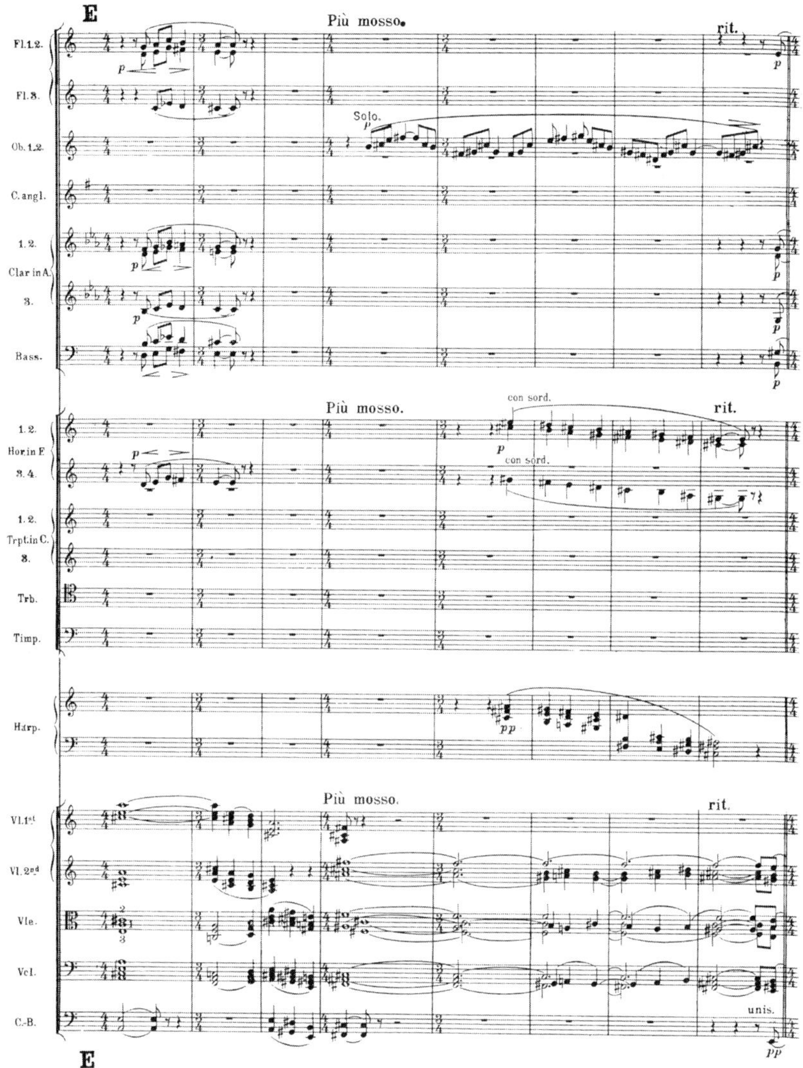

conventional, close-knitting of melody and accompaniment. This sonic landscape will be deployed again in the elemental seascape of the *Riders to the Sea* (1932) and to great effect in the *Sinfonia Antartica* (1952), where this sonority first accompanied actual images; the bleak frozen landscapes of director Charles Frend's *Scott of the Antartic* (1948).[29] It is also present in the staggering harmonic inertia of the last movement of Vaughan Williams' other 'war' symphony, the Sixth (1947). This harmonic independence

Ex. 7.5   Opening of second movement, Ralph Vaughan Williams, *Pastoral Symphony*. © J. Curwen & Sons / Faber Music Ltd, London. Reproduced by kind permission of the publishers.

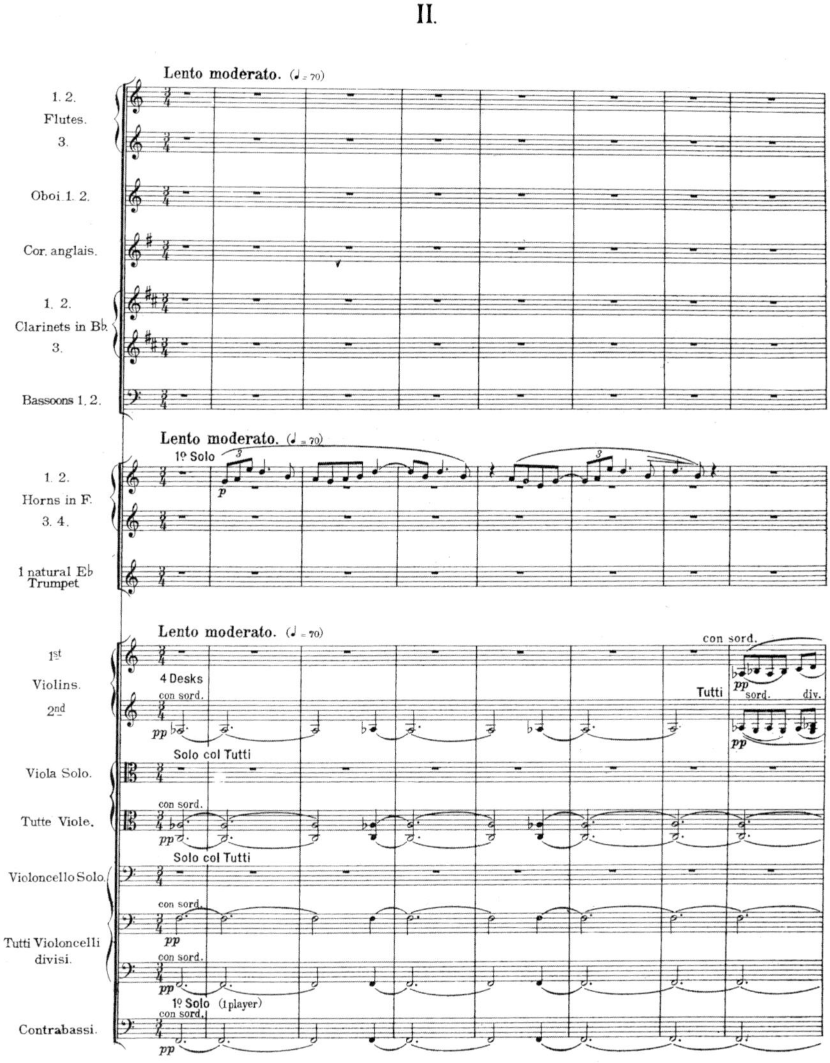

II.

Lento moderato. (♩ = 70)

1. 2.
Flutes.
3.

Oboi. 1. 2.

Cor. anglais.

1. 2.
Clarinets in B♭.
3.

Bassoons 1. 2.

Lento moderato. (♩ = 70)

1º Solo

1. 2.
Horns in F.
3. 4.

1 natural E♭ Trumpet

Lento moderato. (♩ = 70)

1st
Violins.
2nd

4 Desks
con sord.
con sord.
Tutti
con sord.
div.

Solo col Tutti

Viola Solo.

con sord.
Tutte Viole.

Solo col Tutti
Violoncello Solo.

con sord.
Tutti Violoncelli divisi.
con sord.

1º Solo (1 player)
con sord.
Contrabassi.

recurs in the second movement of the Pastoral in the solo trumpet line in E♭ (natural trumpet) played on natural harmonics, an ethereal last post whose untempered sounds appear dissonant, but are in fact a consequence of the natural overtone series (the B♭ and D – the seventh and ninth partials here sounds flatter than a tempered B♭) (see Example 7.6).

Ex. 7.6   Second movement of Ralph Vaughan Williams, *Pastoral Symphony*. © J. Curwen & Sons / Faber Music Ltd, London. Reproduced by kind permission of the publishers.

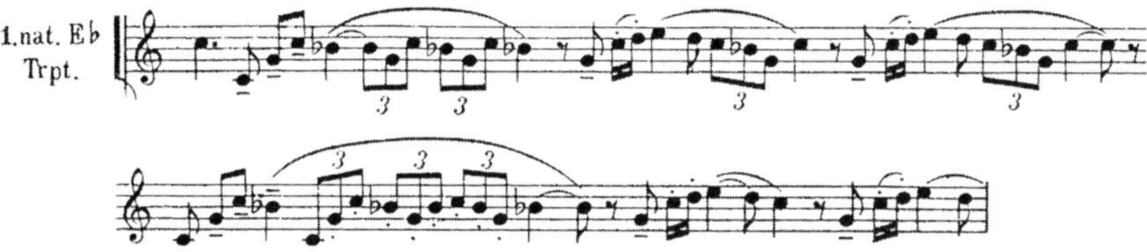

This is also heard in the natural horn solo (in F) at the close of this movement, where, again, the B♮ and D stand out as natural harmonics. This tuning links the instrument to its more primitive forebears and the natural tunings of untempered nature, but it also creates a more desolate and vulnerable melody, teetering on the edge of collapse.

This sense of collapse is relieved in the third movement, which seems to start much more emphatically, with rhythmic triplet figures in triple time (see Example 7.7). As in Rawsthorne's *Pastoral*, the slow, second movement is followed by a species of country-dance. However, feet soon trip over themselves; by the fourth bar the pulse is modified with syncopated horn chords, and seven bars after that (*poco animato*) a trumpet tune emerges in cross-rhythm with the lower strings. This is followed by a freer flute and harp episode, answered again by a solo violin. These two themes then combine, leading to a middle section (letter E). The general plan is that of a 'scherzo' with two trios (in the relative major, G). The 'trio' section has a folksong-like brass episode in a mixolydian mode. The opening section is rescored and repeated, as is the trio. The movement ends with apparently new fugal material (2 bars after letter S) marked presto, which resolves by incorporating the opening theme and coming to rest quietly on a G minor cadence. Mellers sees the peasant dance in this movement as a ghostly echo of something long dead and quotes from 'East Coker', the second of T.S. Eliot's *Four Quartets*:

> In that open field
> If you do not come too close, if you do not come too close,
> On a summer midnight, you can hear the music
> Of the weak pipe and the little drum
> And see them dancing around the bonfire.[30]

Despite being written 20 years after the symphony, Eliot's poem confronts a similar mood, one that we will revisit in David Matthews' *In the Dark Time*, whose title comes from a line in the last of the *Four Quartets*.

Ex. 7.7   Third movement of Ralph Vaughan Williams, *Pastoral Symphony*. © J. Curwen & Sons / Faber Music Ltd, London. Reproduced by kind permission of the publishers.

III.

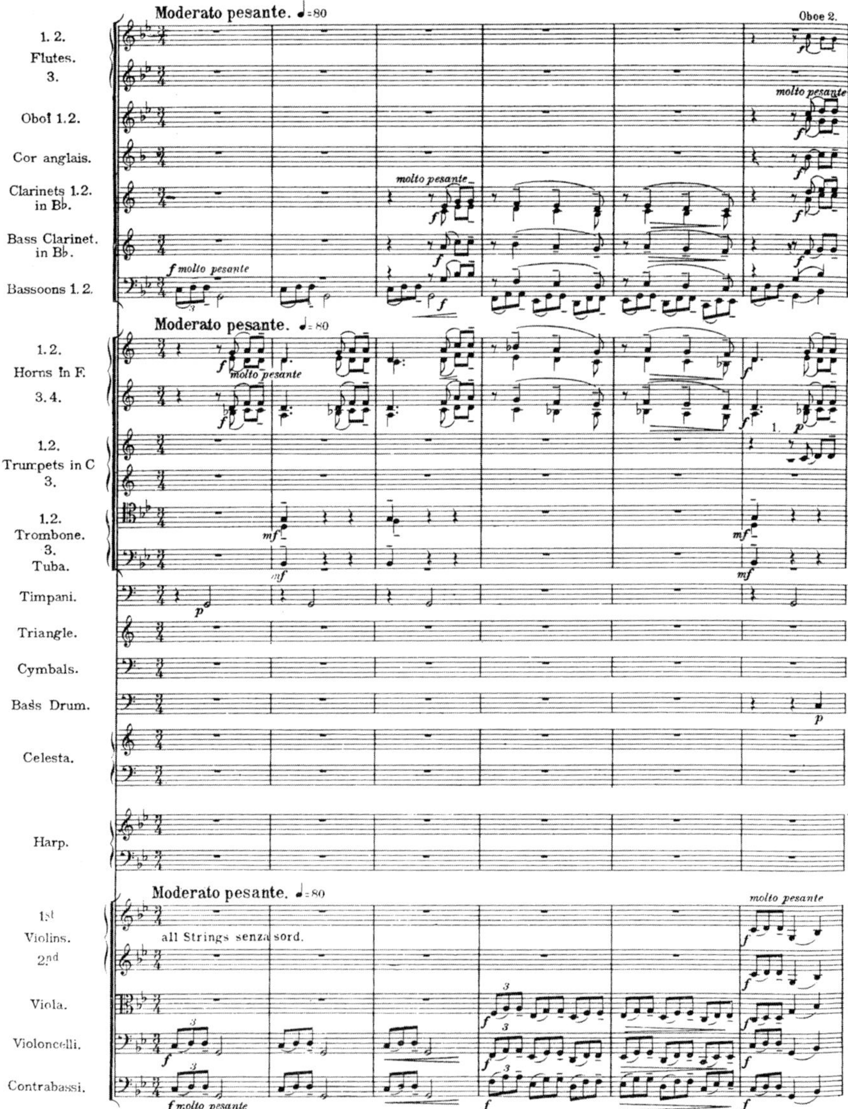

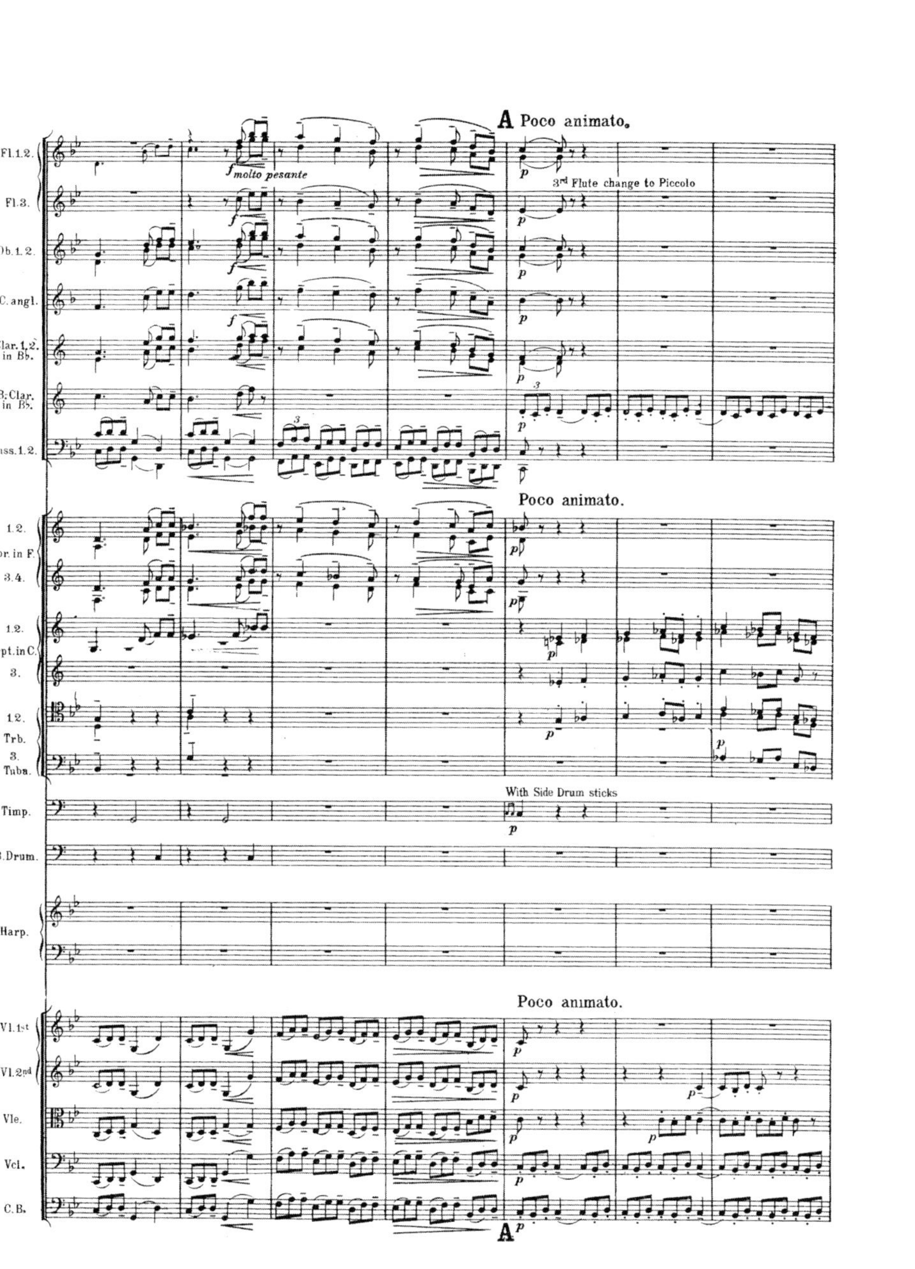
A Poco animato.
Fl.1.2.
f molto pesante
Fl.3.
3rd Flute change to Piccolo
Ob.1.2.
C. angl.
Clar.1.2. in Bb.
B.Clar. in Bb.
Bass.1.2.
Poco animato.
1.2. Hor. in F.
3.4.
1.2. Trpt. in C.
3.
1.2. Trb.
3. Tuba.
With Side Drum sticks
Timp.
B.Drum.
Harp.
Poco animato.
Vl.1st
Vl.2nd
Vle.
Vcl.
C.B.
A p

Ex. 7.8   Last movement of Ralph Vaughan Williams, *Pastoral Symphony*. © J. Curwen & Sons / Faber Music Ltd, London. Reproduced by kind permission of the publishers.

IV.

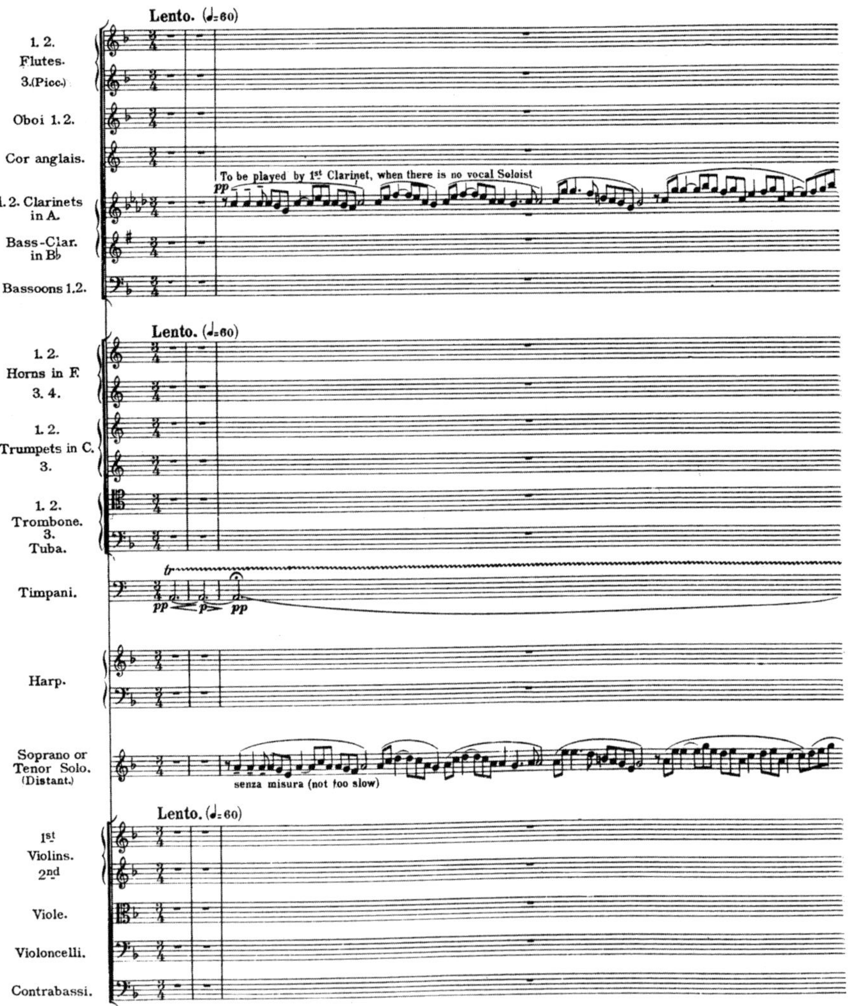

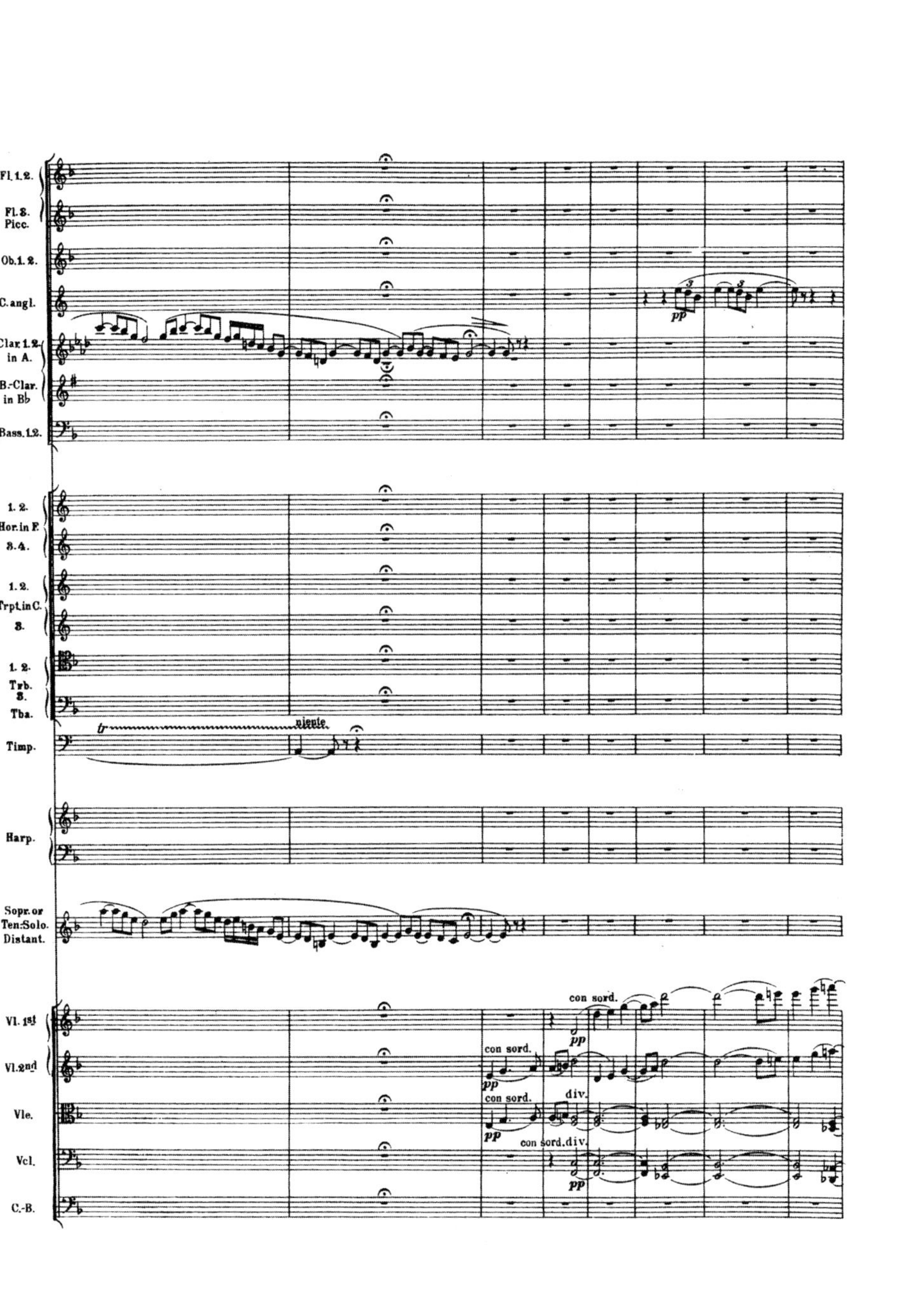

Fl. 1.2.
Fl. 3.
Picc.
Ob. 1. 2.
C. angl.
Clar. 1. 2.
in A.
B.-Clar.
in Bb
Bass. 1. 2.
1. 2.
Hor. in F.
3. 4.
1. 2.
Trpt. in C.
3.
1. 2.
Trb.
3.
Tba.
Timp.
Harp.
Sopr. or
Ten: Solo.
Distant.
Vl. 1st
Vl. 2nd
Vle.
Vcl.
C.-B.
pp
con sord.
con sord.
con sord.
div.
con sord. div.
pp
pp
pp
pp
niente

The last movement, which pulls together elements of the previous movements, opens, after the briefest of pauses (a literal breath), with a soft drum roll on A, over which an offstage human voice sings a wordless pentatonic rhapsody. Again, the voice gives a tangible sense of space as it is positioned away from the orchestra, singing across the distance, as a lark (see Example 7.8). A short bridging passage brings us to the main subject: a stately, gently unfolding, pentatonic melody in two asymmetrical phrases, first in the woodwind, and then the *pianissimo* brass and strings further the benediction. This melody, blossoming as it does throughout the whole orchestra, cannot help but stand as a communal counterpoint to the lone human voice at the opening and closing of this movement. A more agitated middle section follows in contrast, travelling through a number of modulations, until a unison passage at the climax subsides into a restatement of the benediction. The movement ends as it began, with a lone, distant, human voice over the thinnest of harmonic pedals.

It is worth noting in passing that another wartime symphony shares many of these implicit pastoral traits. Edmund Rubbra's *Symphony no. 4* was composed in 1942. Referring to the symphony he wrote: '[it] had to be scored in my Army life. I took it everywhere I went in the army, and in whatever available space I could have I finished it, and conducted it in battle dress, as far as I can remember, at the Albert Hall Prom [14 August 1942].'[31] The opening movement (which, like much of Rubbra's music, contains the germinal seeds of all that is to follow) constructs a harmonic landscape, built from a repeating backdrop of third-inversion dominant seventh chords, in a syncopated crotchet, crotchet, triplet-quaver pattern, with a sustained, smooth melodic figure of a falling fifth and a rising major third (which is later compressed to a falling fourth and a rising minor third). The contrast between the regular pulse of the unresolved dominant sevenths chords and the sweep of the melodic line provides a tangible musical space, akin to, but differently constructed from, the calm opening of Vaughan Williams's third. The organic construction from limited, germinal cells of material is, like Vaughan Williams, in contradiction to the structuralism of modernist, modular construction.

As a coda to this account, I shall discuss a work by a contemporary composer whose aesthetic is in a conscious critical relationship to this pastoral tradition. David Matthews (b. 1943) has composed a number of works that assume this lineage, to name a selected few; *Music of Evening* op. 11, *Toccatas and Pastorals*, op. 13, *September Music* op. 24, *Chaconne* op. 43, *A Cloud Sequence* Op. 45, *The Music of Dawn* op. 50, *The Sleeping Lord* op. 58, *From Sea to Sky* op. 59, *A Vision and a Journey* op. 60, *Burnham Wick* op. 73, the *Aubade* op. 83, *String Quartet No. 10* op. 84, *Movement of Autumn* op. 98 and recently in his *Symphony No. 6*, op. 100.[32] This last work makes the connection with Vaughan Williams explicit. The symphony explores variations on the hymn Vaughan Williams wrote for his own 1906 edition of *The English Hymnal*: 'Down Ampney,' named by the composer in honour of his own birth-place.

I shall focus on Matthews' large orchestral work *In the Dark Time* op. 38 (1985), a symphonic poem that emphatically brings the idea of the dark pastoral up to date. The title comes from a line in the final poem of T.S. Eliot's *Four Quartets*, 'Little Gidding' (1942):

A glare that is blindness in the early afternoon.
And glow more intense than blaze of branch or brazier,
Stirs the dumb spirit: no wind, but pentecostal fire
In the dark time of the year.

In its imagery this stanza shifts from a natural glare through blindness to the glow of the spirit in 'midwinter spring'; a temporal shift, also, from the natural world of time and the seasons to a deeper, timeless reality. But unlike Howard's more pessimistic text set by Rawsthorne, Mattthews' work ends, as does Eliot's poem, in a more optimistic mode: 'all shall be well'.

Matthews' piece, like Eliot's poetic quartet, is intimately connected to the modulations of the seasons. *In the Dark Time* emerged from an earlier work of Matthews called *September Music* (1979). In its turn, *In the Dark Time* was conceived as October to March, or winter to spring music (it was composed during the months that inspired it). Both *September Music* and *In the Dark Time* have related harmonic cores, what Matthews has appropriately called a germinal chord: it might be described as a compound of a second inversion B♭ major triad, with G and A♭, plus D and A major triads at the top: B♭-D-F-G-A♭-D-F♯-A-C♯-E (which can be heard in the introduction in several guises). This harmony, unfurled as melody, is also responsible for the principal horn theme, also heard during the introduction and again in the coda. The opening rising triplet motif (G-A♭-B♭-D) is simultaneously balanced by a descending phrase spread through the strings in contrary motion (D-[C]-B♭-A♭-G) (see Example 7.9). This sense of straining upward, but being pulled back is perhaps the dominant feature of the piece. To give a couple of instances: the viola melody at figure 7; the solo violin phrase one after figure 10 which is pulled down to a low rumbling figure in the bass register of the piano and double basses.

One of the most exhilarating climaxes comes at figure 23: the violin phrase descends through four octaves to an open G pedal against brass interjections, which are answered by muted brass as if from afar. Both the distance travelled by the strings (four octaves) and the answering of the brass by a muted echo produce a dense and active space within the musical landscape. This provides, as did Vaughan Williams by other means, a tangible sense of physical space within the orchestra, which is further enhanced by Matthews' frequent use of *divisi* string writing. The constraint on upward movement is finally released at figure 55 when the melody achieves complete lift-off, disappearing from view three bars later and ascending far beyond Vaughan Williams' lark.

Ex. 7.9 Opening of David Matthews, *In the Dark Time*. © J. Curwen & Sons / Faber Music Ltd, London. Reproduced by kind permission of the publishers.

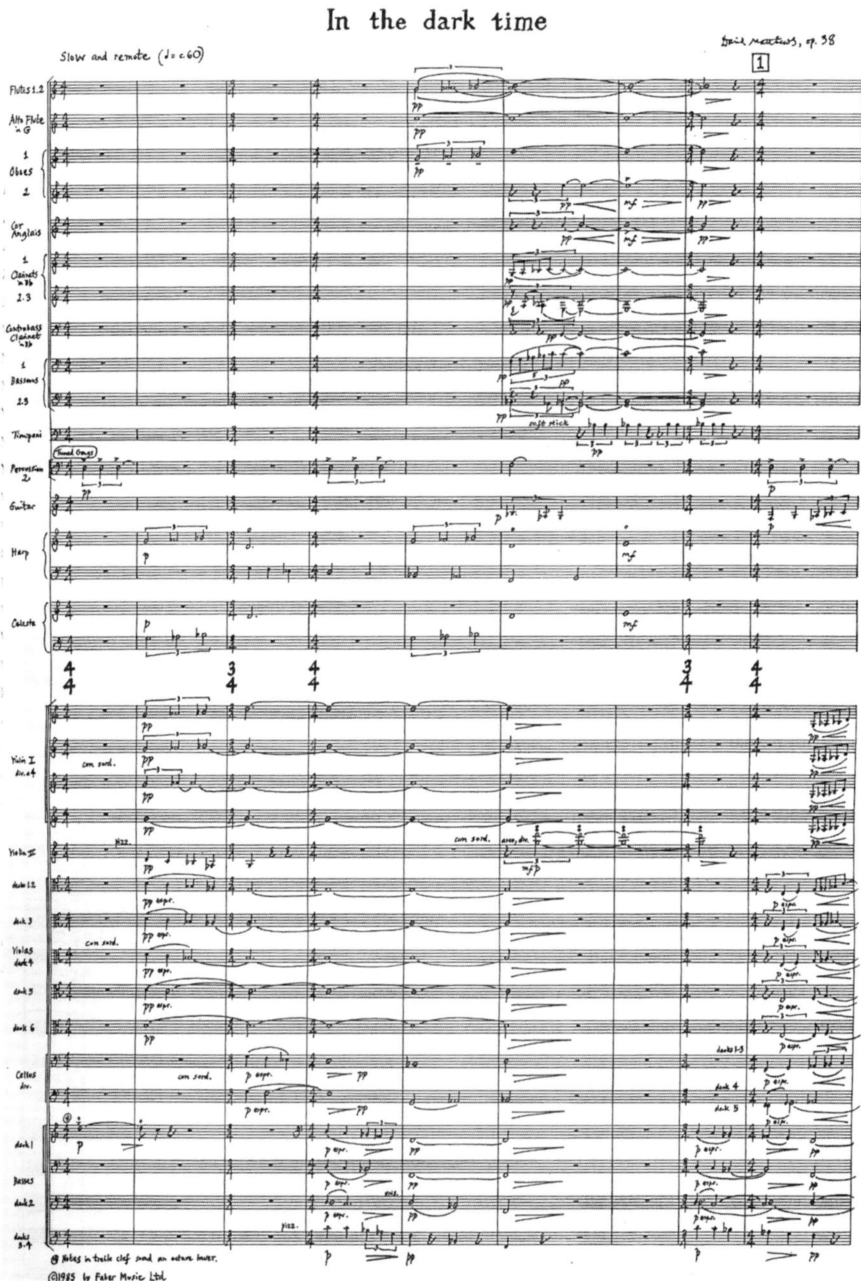

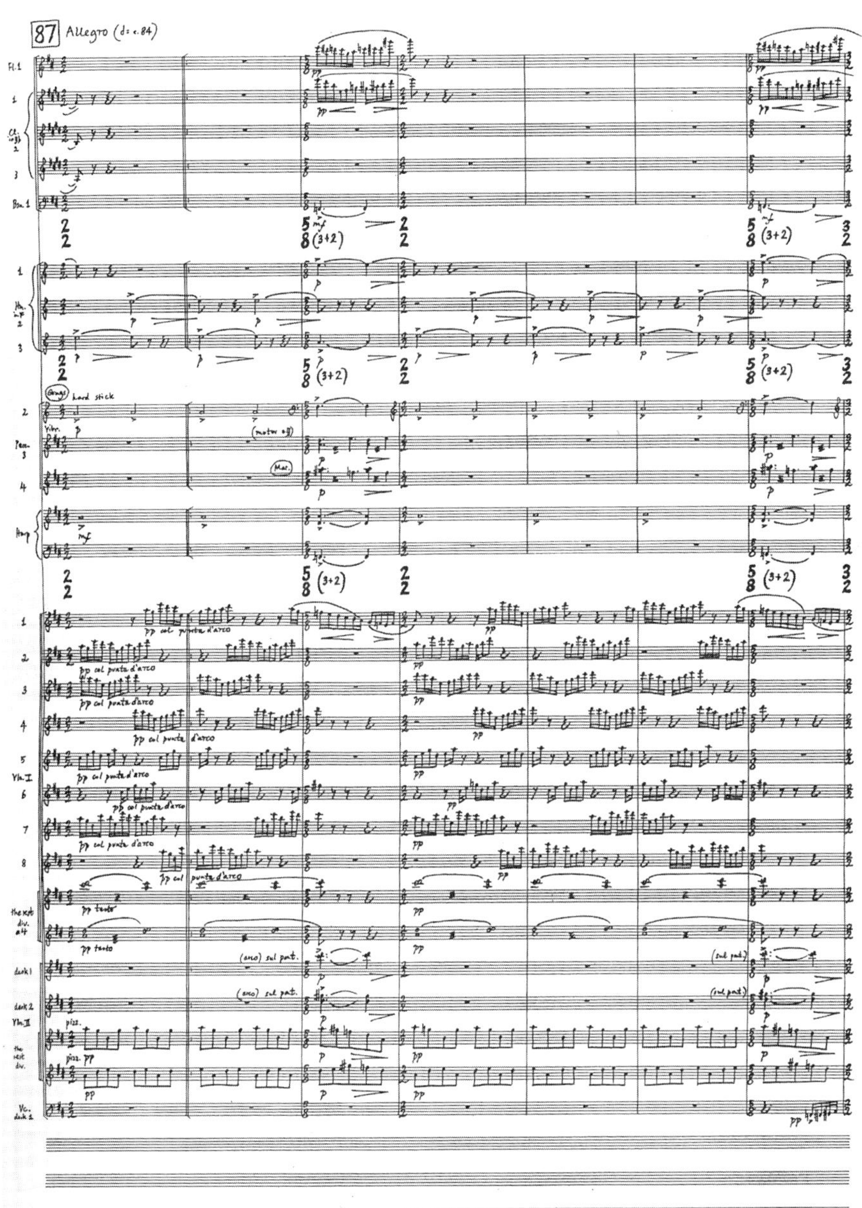

The second half of the work consists of slower harmonic explorations in dispersed harmony, in contrast to the rhythmically terse and melodically aspirational first half. The use of static chords and pedal notes here provides a rich, textured and extended sonoric landscape. Finally, in the coda, the original melodic material emerges from this wide harmonic background, with highlights provided by delicate celeste flourishes. The horn melody is re-established, which in turn ushers in a new semi-quaver passage on the violins in D major at figure 87 (see Example 7.10).

This sequence is passed around between *divisi* strings, finally bubbling up through the cellos to the violins, against a double bass restatement of the three-note, opening diminished third (F-F♯-G♯). The semi-quaver sequence finally dissolves, optimistically, on a unison e^3 harmonic held over three soft, ethereal notes on the temple bells.

The work does not attempt to mimic seasonal change in any literal way, although the seasonal cycle gives the piece its form. The seasonal metaphor is extended to the employment of small (germinal) motifs throughout the work, some of which bud and grow while others wither and come to nothing. Ultimately the work moves through the dark time, emerging in the coda with the D-major semi-quaver passage, to suggest the light and buds of spring.

Pastoralism is, as this chapter has sought to demonstrate, no mere nostalgia. I have, throughout this chapter, been concerned to stress the radical aspect of the pastoral, its identity as a site for critique, and its intimate relationship to the presence of death. Birth and death are at the very soul of rural life. The best of this pastoral art could not be further from the 'cow-pat' school accused by Constant Lambert.[33] Matthews' work is an apt conclusion, because the germinal character of the harmonic material in *In the Dark Time* manifests an optimistic renewal of the pastoral tradition. In maintaining continuities with the past, Matthews also perceives the regenerative heart of dark pastoral for the beginning of the twenty-first century.

Notes

1. Such pastoral ideals may also function as an eschatological religious symbol, as in Christ the Good Shepherd, for example.

2. William Wordsworth, 'Michael', in *English Poetry II: From Collins to Fitzgerald*, vol. 41. The Harvard Classics. New York: P.F. Collier & Son, 1909-14; (poem no. 372). [Online]. Available at: http://www.bartleby.com/41/372.html [accessed: 8 March 2010] 2010.

3. The impact of Darwin on views of the countryside and nature is also highly significant, though outside the scope of this chapter.

4. John Barrell, *The Dark Side of the English Landscape: The Rural Poor in English Painting 1730-1840*, Cambridge: Cambridge University Press, 1980.

5. Peter V. Marinelli, *Pastoral*, London: Methuen, 1971, p. 9.

6.   The earliest surviving settings of pastoral poetry are the 'Pastourelle' of medieval France. The thirteenth-century *Jeu de Robin et Marion* ascribed to Adam de la Halle, is an entire pastoral play set to music.

7.   John McCabe, *Alan Rawsthorne: Portrait of a Composer*, Oxford: Oxford University Press, 1999.

8.   *The Poems of Henry Howard, Earl of Surrey*, (London: Eilbron Classics, 2005, reprint of original 1894 edition, pp. 3-4).

9.   Ibid., p. 285. The actual music played was the slow music of his Piano Sonatina, on the organ.

10.   CD notes by the composer for a recording of his chamber orchestra work, *Burnham Wick* (1997).

11.   *The Portfolio*, 35, November 1872, pp. 163-4.

12.   Helen Irwin, 'Samuel Palmer, Poet of Light and Shade', *Apollo*, 114, August 1981, pp. 103-9.

13.   William Vaughan and Elizabeth E. Barker, '"Mysterious wisdom won by toil": new light on Samuel Palmer's "Lonely tower"', *The Burlington Magazine*,147, September 2005, pp. 590-97.

14.   Ibid., pp. 593-4.

15.   There may also have been a more tangible connection between Palmer and the Vaughan Williams family. When Palmer rented a farmhouse – High Ashes – on the slopes of Leith Hill for his dying son Thomas More, he rented it from a 'Miss Lomax' who was, the editor of Palmer's letters, Raymond Lister supposes, a relative of Roland Lomax Vaughan Williams, who subsequently lived in High Ashes himself (according to the General Post Office (GPO) directory for 1870). In a letter to John Linnell dated March 1861 Palmer refers to a 'Justice Williams' who lived in an 'old manor-like house' nearby. This might have been Leith Hill House. Lister identifies Justice Williams as Sir Edward Vaughan Williams (1797-1875). See Raymond Lister (ed.), *The Letters of Samuel Palmer*, 2 vols. Oxford: Clarendon Press, 1974 (pp. 588-9). I am indebted to William Vaughan for drawing this to my attention.

16.   Marinelli, *Pastoral*, p. 3.

17.   Timothy Wilcox, *Samuel Palmer*, London: Tate Publishing, 2005.

18.   Percy Bysshe Shelley, 'To a Skylark', in Sir Arthur Thomas Quiller-Couch, *The Oxford Book of English Verse*, Oxford: Clarendon, 1919 [c.1901]; (poem no. 608), [Online].Available at: http://www.bartleby.com/101/608.html {accessed: 8 March 2010].

19.   Wilfrid Mellers, *Vaughan Williams and the Vision of Albion*, London: Barrie and Jenkins, 1989, p. 62.

20.   Ibid., p. 62.

21.   *The Lark Ascending* (full score). Oxford: Oxford University Press, 1925, reprint 2005, p. 4.

22.   From Vaughan Williams' first published article 'A School of English Music', *The Vocalist*, vol. 1, no. 1, April 1902, p. 8.

23.   See James Day, *Vaughan Williams (Master musician)*, London: Everyman, 1975 p. 83.

24.   This should obviously not imply that there are no points of connection between Vaughan Williams and Wagner, simply that folk music offered a way of moving from the mainstream of Austro-German musical influence.

25.   Composed in 1910, revised in 1913 and 1919.

26.   Ursula Vaughan Williams, *R.V.W. a Biography of Ralph Vaughan Williams*, London: Oxford University Press, 1964, p. 121.

27.   Quoted in Michael Trend, *The Music Makers: The English Musical Renaissance from Elgar to Britten*, London: Weidenfeld & Nicolson, 1985, p. 102.

28.   Donald Francis Tovey, *Essays in Musical Analysis: Symphonies and other Orchestral Works*, [1935-39], London: Oxford University Press, 1981, reprint, p. 524.

29.   Cinematography by Osmond Borradaile, Jack Cardiff, and Geoffrey Unsworth.

30.   See Wilfrid Mellers, p. 91.

31.   Quoted after Ralph Scott Grover, *The Music of Edmund Rubbra*, Aldershot: Scolar Press, 1993, p. 87.

32.   First performed by the BBC National Orchestra of Wales under Jan van Steen, at the Royal Festival Hall, London as part of the BBC Promenade concerts, 2 August 2007.

33.   See Constant Lambert, 'Nationalism and the Modern Scene', in *Music Ho! A Study of Music in Decline* [1937] reprint London: Faber, 1966, pp. 151-62.

Bibliography

Almond, Gabriel A., Chodorow, Marvin and Pearce, Roy Harvey (eds), *Progress and its Discontents*, Berkeley: University of California Press, 1982.

Anderson, Anne, Meyrick, Robert and Nahum, Peter, *Ancient Landscapes, Pastoral Visions: Samuel Palmer to the Ruralists*, Southampton City Art Gallery, 2008.

Anon., 'Rise and Progress of Painting in Water Colours', *The Repository of Arts*, vol. 9, 1812-13.

Athenaeum, The

Aubenas, Sylvie (ed.), *Gustave Le Gray 1820-1884*, Paris: Bibliothèque Nationale de France/Gallimard, 2002.

Bampfylde, J.C., *Sixteen Sonnets*, J. Millidge, London, 1778.

Barry, James, *An Inquiry into the Real and Imaginary Obstructions to the Acquisition of the Arts in England*, London: T. Becket, 1775.

Beetles, Chris, *S.R. Badmin and the English Landscape*, London: William Collins Sons & Co, 1985.

Bell's New Weekly Messenger.

Berthoud, Roger, *Graham Sutherland: A Biography*, London: Faber, 1982.

Bignamini, Ilaria and Postle, Martin, *The Artist's Model. Its role in British Art from Lely to Etty*, Nottingham: Nottingham University Art Gallery, 1991.

Bindman, David, 'The Politics of Vision: Palmer's *Address to the Electors of West Kent'*, in William Vaughan, Elizabeth E. Barker, Colin Harrison et al., *Samuel Palmer: 1805-1881: Vision and Landscape*, London: British Museum Press, 2005.

——, *Blake as an Artist*, Oxford: Oxford University Press, 1977.

Binyon, Laurence, *The Followers of William Blake – Edward Calvert, Samuel Palmer, George Richmond and their circle*, [1925] London and New York: Benjamin Blom, 1968.

Blackman, R.J., *The Soul of the City: London's Livery Companies*, London: Sampson Low, 1931.

Boast, Mary, *The Story of Walworth*, London Borough of Southwark, 2005.

Bowers, J K. and Cheshire, P., *Agriculture, the Countryside and Land Use: An Economic Critique*, London: Methuen, 1983.

Brassley, Paul, Burchardt, Jeremy and Thompson, Lynne (eds), *The English Countryside Between the Wars: Regeneration or Decline?* London: Boydell Press, 2006.

Brown, David Blayney, *Samuel Palmer 1805-81: Catalogue Raisonné of the Paintings and Drawings, and a Selection of Prints in the Ashmolean Museum*, Oxford: Ashmolean Museum, 1983.

Butlin, Martin, *Samuel Palmer. The Sketchbook of 1824*, Clairvaux: Trianon Press, 1962; reissued by Thames and Hudson, 2005.

Calvert, Samuel, *A Memoir of Edward Calvert Artist by his Third Son*, London, Sampson Low and Co. 1893.
Cecil, David, *Visionary and Dreamer*, London: Academy Editions, 1977.
Clark, Kenneth, *Landscape into Art*, London: John Murray, 1949.
Cooke, Gordon, *William Larkins. Etchings of the East End in the 1920s and other scenes*, London: Robin Garton Gallery, 1979.
Craig, William Marshall, *A Course of Lectures on Drawing, Painting and Engraving*, London: Longman, Hurst, Rees, Orme, and Brown, 1821.
Davies, Randall, 'Edward Duncan (1803-1882)', *Old Water-Colour Society's Club*, 6th annual volume, 1928-29.
Day, James, *Vaughan Williams (Master musician)*, London: Everyman, 1975.
Dickens, Charles (ed.), *The Life of Charles James Matthews*, 2 vols, London: Macmillan 1879.
Draper, F.W.M., *Four Centuries of Merchant Taylors' School, 1561-1961*, London: Oxford University Press, 1962.
Drury, Jolyon, *Revelation to Revolution: The Legacy of Samuel Palmer. The Revival and Evolution of Pastoral Printmaking by Paul Drury and the Goldsmiths School in the 20th Century*, Ashford: Jolyon Drury, 2006.
Eaves, Morris, *The Counter-Arts Conspiracy. Art and Industry in the Age of Blake*, Ithaca and London: Cornell University Press, 1992.
——, *William Blake's Theory of Art*, Princeton: Princeton University Press, 1982.
Elmes, James, *A General and Bibliographical Dictionary of the Fine Arts*, London: Thomas Tegg, 1824.
European Magazine
Examiner, The
Exhibition of Drawings, No. 9 Soho Square, London, 1822.
Fenwick, Simon and Smith, Greg, *The Business of Watercolour: A Guide to the Archives of the Royal Watercolour Society*, Aldershot: Ashgate, 1997.
Gage, John, *Colour in Turner: Poetry and Truth*, London: Studio Vista, 1969.
Garton, Robin, *Catalogue Raisonné of the Prints of Paul Drury, 1903-1987*, London: Garton & Co, 1992.
Goldman, Paul, *Victorian Illustrated Books 1850-1870 – The Heyday of Wood-Engraving*, London: British Museum Press, 1994
——, *Shadow of the Forest – Prints of the Barbizon School*, London: British Museum, 1993.
——, 'Samuel Palmer Etcher and Illustrator', *Antiquarian Book Monthly Review*, vol. 19, no. 223, November 1992.
Gray, Basil, *The English Print*, London: Adam and Charles Black 1937.
Greathead, Alexandra, 'Samuel Palmer's Materials and Techniques: The Early Years' in William Vaughan, Elizabeth E. Barker, Colin Harrison et al., *Samuel Palmer (1805-1881): Vision and Landscape*, London: British Museum Press, 2005.
Griffiths, Antony, *Prints and Printmaking*, London, British Museum Press, 1980.
Grigson, Geoffrey, 'The Samuel Palmer Situation,' *Times Literary Supplement*, 15 July 1977.
——, *Samuel Palmer: The Visionary Years*, London: Kegan Paul, 1947.
——, 'Samuel Palmer: the Politics of an Artist,' *Horizon*, vol. 4, no. 19, 1941.
Grover, Ralph Scott, *The Music of Edmund Rubbra*, Aldershot: Scolar Press, 1993.
Hardie, Martin, *Samuel Palmer: A lecture*, London, Print Collectors' Club Publication, no. 7, 1928.
——, Laver, James and Palmer, A.H., *Catalogue of an Exhibition of Drawings, Etchings & Woodcuts by Samuel Palmer and other Disciples of William Blake*, London: Victoria and Albert Museum, 1926.

Harrison, Colin, *Samuel Palmer*, Oxford: Ashmolean Museum, 1997.

Herring, Sarah, 'Samuel Palmer's Shoreham Drawings in Indian Ink. A Matter of Light and Shade', *Apollo*, vol. 148, November 1998.

Holcomb, Adele M., *John Sell Cotman*, London: Colonnade Books, British Museum Publications, 1978.

Howe, P.P. (ed.), *The Complete Works of William Hazlitt*, London and Toronto: Dent, 1930-34.

Illustrated London News

Irwin, David, *John Flaxman 1755-1826. Sculptor, Illustrator, Designer*, London: Studio Vista/Christies, 1979.

Irwin, Helen, 'Samuel Palmer, Poet of Light and Shade', *Apollo*, 114, August 1981.

John Bull

Keating, Tom, Norman, Geraldine and Norman, Frank, *The Fake's Progress: The Tom Keating Story*, London: Hutchinson and Co., 1977.

Keynes, Geoffrey (ed.), *Blake Complete Writings*, London: Oxford University Press, 1976.

Kitton, Frederic G., *Dickens and his Illustrators*, London: George Redway, 1899 Reprinted New York: AMS, 1975.

Lambert, Constant, 'Nationalism and the Modern Scene', in *Music Ho! A Study of Music in Decline* [1937] reprint London: Faber 1966.

Lasch, Christopher, *The True and Only Heaven: Progress and its Critics*, New York: Norton, 1991.

Leger Galleries, *Samuel Palmer: an exhibition of Palmer's works with a Leger provenance to celebrate a century of art dealing*, London: the Leger Galleries, 1992.

Leighton, Clare, *Country Matters*, London: Victor Gollancz, 1937.

Lister, Raymond, *A Catalogue Raisonné of the Works of Samuel Palmer*, Cambridge: Cambridge University Press, 1988.

——, *Samuel Palmer: His Life and Art*, Cambridge: Cambridge University Press, 1987.

——, 'The Book Illustrations of Samuel Palmer', *The Book Collector*, Spring 1979.

——, *Samuel Palmer. A Biography*, London: Faber and Faber, 1974.

—— (ed.), *The Letters of Samuel Palmer*, Oxford: Clarendon Press, 2 vols, 1974.

Maclean, F., *Henry Moore, R. A.*, London: The Walter Scott Publishing Co. Ltd, 1905.

Malins, Edward, *Samuel Palmer's Italian Honeymoon*, London: Oxford University Press, 1968.

Marinelli, Peter V., *Pastoral*, London: Methuen, 1971.

Martin, Simon, Butlin, Martin and Meyrick, Robert, *Poets in the Landscape: The Romantic Spirit in British Art*, Chichester: Pallant House Gallery, 2007.

Massingham, H.J., 'The Wiltshire Flax-Mill, An Example of True Husbandry', *Geographical Magazine*, 1943-44, vol. 16.

Matless, David, *Landscape and Englishness*, London: Reaktion, 1998.

McCabe, John, *Alan Rawsthorne: Portrait of a Composer*, Oxford: Oxford University Press, 1999.

McCalman, Iain (ed.), *An Oxford Companion to the Romantic Age: British Culture 1776-1832*, Oxford: Oxford University Press, 1999.

Mclean, Ruari, *Joseph Cundall – A Victorian Publisher*, Pinner: Private Libraries Association, 1976.

McMaster, Juliet, *Woman Behind the Painter: The Diaries of Rosalie, Mrs James Clarke Hook*, Alberta: The University of Alberta Press, 2006.

Mee, Arthur, *Little Treasure Island: Her Story and her Glory*, London: Hodder and Stoughton, 1920.

Mellers, Wilfrid, *Vaughan Williams and the Vision of Albion*, London: Barrie and Jenkins, 1989.

Mellor, David, 'British Art in the 1930s', in Frank Gloversmith, *Class, Culture and Social Change: A New View of the 1930s*, Brighton: Harvester Press, 1980.

Michel, Walter and Fox, C.J. (eds), *Wyndham Lewis on Art*, London: Thames and Hudson, 1969.

Moore, Jerrold Northrop, *The Green Fuse: Pastoral Vision in English Art, 1820-2000*, Woodbridge: Antique Collectors' Club, 2007.

——, *F.L. Griggs (1876-1938): The Architecture of Dreams*, Oxford: Clarendon Press, 1999.

Morris, Richard, *John Dillwyn Llewelyn, 1810-1882: the First Photographer in Wales*, Cardiff: Welsh Arts Council, 1980.

Mundy, J., *Edward William Cooke 1811-1880: A Man of his Time*, Woodbridge: Antique Collectors' Club, 1996.

Murray, Peter, *Dulwich Picture Gallery. A Catalogue*, London: Sotheby Parke Bernet, 1980.

Nash, Paul, '"Going modern" and "being British"', *Week-End Review*, vol. 5, no. 109, 9 April 1932.

Ogg, David, 'The Etchings of Graham Sutherland and Paul Drury,' *Print Collector's Quarterly*, 16, January, 1929.

Olsen, Roberta J.M., 'A watercolour by Samuel Palmer of Donati's Comet', *Burlington Magazine*, November 1990.

Oxford Dictionary of National Biography, Oxford: Oxford University Press, 2004.

Palmer, A.H., *The Life and Letters of Samuel Palmer, Painter and Etcher*, London: Seeley, 1892.

——, 'James Clarke Hook, R.A.', *The Portfolio*, 1888.

——, *Samuel Palmer. A Memoir*, London: Fine Art Society, 1882.

Payne, Christiana, *Where the Sea Meets the Land: Artists on the Coast in Nineteenth-century Britain*, Bristol: Sansom and Company, 2007.

Pichot, Amédée, *Historical and Literary Tour of a Foreigner in England and Scotland*, London: Saunders and Otlay, 1825.

Postle, Martin, 'The Foundation of the Slade School of Fine Art: Fifty-nine Letters in the Record Office of University College London', *The Walpole Society*, 1995/96, vol. 58.

Prettejohn, Elizabeth, *The Art of the Pre-Raphaelites*, London: Tate Publishing, 2000.

Priestley, J.B., *English Journey: being a rambling but truthful account of what one man saw and heard and felt and thought during a journey through England during the autumn of the year 1933*, London: W. Heinemann, 1934.

Ray, Gordon N., *The Illustrator and the Book in England from 1790 to 1914*, New York and London: Pierpont Morgan Library and Oxford University Press, 1976.

Royal Academy of Arts, *The Great Age of British Watercolours. 1750-1880* London: Royal Academy 1993.

Sackville-West, Edward, *Graham Sutherland*, London: Penguin Books, 1943.

Sickert, Walter, 'The Future of Engraving', *Burlington Magazine*, vol. 27, no. 150, September 1915.

Sinclair, Iain, *London Orbital. A Walk Around the M25*, London: Granta Books, 2002.

Percy Bysshe Shelley, 'To a Skylark', in Sir Arthur Thomas Quiller-Couch, *The Oxford Book of English Verse*, Oxford: Clarendon, 1919 [c.1901]; (poem no. 608). [Online]. Available at: http://www.bartleby.com/101/608.html [accessed: 8 March 2010].

Smiles, Sam, 'Samuel Palmer and the Pastoral Inheritance,' *Landscape Research*, vol. 11, no. 3, Winter 1986.

Smith, Greg, *The Emergence of the Professional Watercolourist: Contentions and Alliances in the Artistic Domain 1760-1824*, Aldershot: Ashgate, 2002.

Smith, John Thomas, *Nollekens and his Times*, London: Henry Colburn, 1829.

Somerset House Gazette

Southey, Robert, *Specimens of the Later English Poets*, London: Longman, Hurst, Rees and Orme, 1807.

Spadafora, David, *The Idea of Progress in Eighteenth Century Britain*, New Haven and London: Yale University Press, 1990.

Tanner, Robin, *The More Angels Shall I Paint*, Monmouth: The Old Stile Press, 1991.

——, *The Etcher's Craft*, Ilkley: Scolar Press/Friends of Bristol Art Gallery, 1980.

Thornton, Robert John (ed.), *The Pastorals of Virgil: with a course of English reading adapted for schools: in which all the proper facilities are given, enabling youtm,* [sic] *to acquire the Latin language, in the shortest period of time*, 3rd edn, London: F.C. and J. Rivingtons, 1821

Tovey, Donald Francis, *Essays in Musical Analysis: Symphonies and other Orchestral Works*,[1935-39], London: Oxford University Press, 1981.

Trend, Michael, *The Music Makers: The English Musical Renaissance from Elgar to Britten*, London: Weidenfeld & Nicolson, 1985.

Vaughan Williams, Ralph, 'A School of English Music', *The Vocalist*, vol. 1, no. 1, April 1902.

Vaughan Williams, Ursula, *R.V.W. a Biography of Ralph Vaughan Williams*, London: Oxford University Press, 1964.

Vaughan, William and Barker, Elizabeth E., '"Mysterious wisdom won by toil": new light on Samuel Palmer's "Lonely tower"', *The Burlington Magazine*, CXLVII, September 2005.

Vaughan, William, Barker, Elizabeth E., Harrison, Colin et al., *Samuel Palmer, (1805-1881): Vision and Landscape*, London: British Museum Press, 2005.

Wakeman, Geoffrey, *Victorian Book Illustration – The Technical Revolution*, Newton Abbot: David and Charles, 1973.

Wark, Robert R. (ed.), *Sir Joshua Reynolds. Discourses on Art*, New Haven and London: Yale University Press, 1975.

White, Gleeson, *English Illustration 'The Sixties'*, Constable and Co. 1887; reprinted Bath: Kingsmead Reprints, 1970.

Whitney, Lois, 'English Primitivistic Theories of Epic Origins', *Modern Philology*, vol. 21, no. 4, May 1926.

Wilcox, Timothy, *Samuel Palmer*, London: Tate Publishing, 2005.

William Weston Gallery, *The English Vision*, London, 1973.

Wordsworth, William, 'Michael', in *English Poetry II: From Collins to Fitzgerald*, vol. 41. The Harvard Classics. New York: P.F. Collier & Son, 1909-14; (poem no. 372). [Online]. Available at: http://www.bartleby.com/41/372.html [accessed: 8 March 2010].

Wornum, Ralph N., *Lectures on Painting by the Royal Academicians. Barry, Opie and Fuseli*, London: H.G. Bohn, 1848.

Index